Judging Homosexuals

Sexuality Studies Series

This series focuses on original, provocative, scholarly research examining from a range of perspectives the complexity of human sexual practice, identity, community, and desire. Books in the series explore how sexuality interacts with other aspects of society, such as law, education, feminism, racial diversity, the family, policing, sport, government, religion, mass media, medicine, and employment. The series provides a broad public venue for nurturing debate, cultivating talent, and expanding knowledge of human sexual expression, past and present.

Other volumes in the series are:

Masculinities without Men? Female Masculinity in Twentieth-Century Fictions, by Jean Bobby Noble

Every Inch a Woman: Phallic Possession, Femininity, and the Text, by Carellin Brooks

Queer Youth in the Province of the "Severely Normal," by Gloria Filax

The Manly Modern: Masculinity in Postwar Canada, by Christopher Dummitt

Sexing the Teacher: School Sex Scandals and Queer Pedagogies, by Sheila L. Cavanagh

Undercurrents: Queer Culture and Postcolonial Hong Kong, by Helen Hok-Sze Leung

Sapphistries: A Global History of Love between Women, by Leila J. Rupp

The Canadian War on Queers: National Security as Sexual Regulation, by Gary Kinsman and Patrizia Gentile

Awfully Devoted Women: Lesbian Lives in Canada, 1900-65, by Cameron Duder

Judging Homosexuals

A History of Gay Persecution in Quebec and France

PATRICE CORRIVEAU

Translated by Käthe Roth

With a foreword by Barry Adam

UBCPress · Vancouver · Toronto

LIBRARY AND ARCHIVES CANADA CATALOGUING IN PUBLICATION

Corriveau, Patrice
Judging homosexuals : a history of gay persecution in Quebec and France /
Patrice Corriveau ; translated by Käthe Roth ; with a foreword by Barry Adam.

(Sexuality studies, ISSN 1706-9947)
Translation of: La répression des homosexuels au Québec et en France.
Includes bibliographical references and index.
ISBN 978-0-7748-1720-2 (bound)
ISBN 978-0-7748-1721-9 (pbk.)

1. Homosexuality – Social aspects – Québec (Province) – History.
2. Homosexuality – Social aspects – France – History. 3. Gays – Legal status, laws, etc. – Québec (Province) – History. 4. Gays – Legal status, laws, etc. – France – History.
I. Roth, Käthe II. Title. III. Series: Sexuality studies series

HQ76.3.C3C6713 2011   306.76'609714   C2010-905135-1

e-book ISBNs: 978-0-7748-1722-6 (pdf); 978-0-7748-5968-4 (epub)

Canada

UBC Press gratefully acknowledges the financial support for our publishing program of the Government of Canada (through the Canada Book Fund), the Canada Council for the Arts, and the British Columbia Arts Council.

This book has been published with the help of a grant from the Canadian Federation for the Humanities and Social Sciences, through the Aid to Scholarly Publications Programme, using funds provided by the Social Sciences and Humanities Research Council of Canada. The Canada Council for the Arts kindly provided a translation grant for this English-language edition.

Canada Council   Conseil des Arts
for the Arts   du Canada

UBC Press
The University of British Columbia
2029 West Mall, Vancouver, BC V6T 1Z2
www.ubcpress.ca

Contents

List of Figures and Tables / VI

Foreword / VII
Barry Adam

Preface / XI

Acknowledgments / XIII

Introduction / 1

1 Ancient Greece to the Seventeenth Century: From Pederasty
to Sodomy / 7

2 The Grande Ordonnance of 1670 to the British Conquest:
The Sodomist and the Stake / 29

3 The British Conquest to the Late Nineteenth Century: From the
Sodomist to the Invert, or From the Priest to the Physician / 51

4 The Late Nineteenth Century to the Sexual Revolution:
From Invert to Homosexual / 80

5 The 1970s to the Present: From Prison to City Hall / 117

Conclusion: From One Sexual Perversion to Another? / 163

Notes / 172

References / 189

Index / 205

Figures and Tables

Figures

5.1 Recognition of same-sex marriage in Canada by provinces and territories / 133

5.2 Chronology of legal recognition of gays in Quebec / 138

5.3 Chronology of legal recognition of gays in France / 160

Tables

4.1 Convictions for sodomy, Quebec, 1930-39 / 87

4.2 Number of convictions for sodomy, Quebec, 1946-59 / 97

5.1 Civil unions, opposite-sex and same-sex couples, Quebec, 2002-04 / 131

5.2 Marriages of same-sex couples, Quebec, 2004-08 / 137

Foreword

BARRY ADAM

This book takes on one of the most rapid and striking historical transformations of the twentieth century: the rehabilitation of homosexually interested people from the various abject statuses of the sinful, criminal, or mentally ill to that of people bearing the rights and responsibilities of citizens of liberal democratic countries. This transformation is all the more remarkable for having occurred in the space of a single generation. In 1968 in Canada gay men were subject to criminal penalties, and lesbians, although largely ignored by the law, were scarcely better off. Less than forty years later, they had acquired the right to marry. The reasons for this change are now the subject of a good deal of scholarly analysis; the explanations are often multilayered and, not surprisingly, influenced by the particular lenses of different disciplines. What Patrice Corriveau provides here is a close examination of changing official discourses, particularly legal texts, to reflect on the roots of this social change.

Judging Homosexuals takes on an even broader sweep of history, starting with the philosophical roots of Western civilization in ancient Greece. Starting there further heightens the profundity of the historical change. Whereas conventional intellectual histories of the West draw a (relatively) straight line from the Greeks to the Renaissance to the foundations of contemporary liberal democracies, this history looks more like an arc when viewed from the perspective of homoerotic practices among men. The Greeks regarded erotic and emotional connection between males not only as conceivable and tolerable but also as worthy of romance, nobility, and heroism. The heroic friendship between men is a staple of Greek mythology and a practice fit even for the gods. As Corriveau and others have noted, the Greeks did not characterize sexuality along a homosexual/ heterosexual divide. Rather, the meritorious relationship between men was one of mentor and acolyte, a relationship between inspirer and inspired, between the more experienced and the less. Alongside these relationships, marriage to women was expected and commonplace.

From this origin, male-male sexual and romantic bonding underwent 1,600 years of repression, censorship, and obliteration under the auspices of Judeo-Christian authority. Just why Judeo-Christianity has been so uniquely obsessed with active homophobia is only beginning to be explored. Corriveau points toward ways that homosexuality became caught up in a general prohibition against nonreproductive behaviour pressed forward by pro-natalist authorities of various forms in both church and state. Still, there is likely more scholarship to be done to explore this historical turn and to explain the ongoing ferocity of Judeo-Christian homophobia, which at least in its more fundamentalist forms continues to campaign for legal suppression, promoting referenda to abrogate the civil rights of lesbians and gay men across the United States and exporting its agenda by stimulating pogroms against lesbian, gay, bisexual, and transgendered (LGBT) people, particularly in Africa.

From this larger vantage point, the arc of history looks more like a recovery of lost origins than a movement toward something entirely new. Granted, as Corriveau points out, much of the fury directed against gay men in the twentieth century now seems to be displaced onto pedophilia. Just as the iconic "terrorist" arose as the nemesis of the West in the 1990s to replace the deflated "communist" – often using remarkably similar language and propounded by similar authoritarian sources regeared to identify new enemies – now the dreaded "pedophile" has replaced the newly domesticated "homosexual." Entrepreneurial politicians and police forces busy themselves with high-profile raids to "protect" Western civilization from "pedophile rings" and "luring by Internet." Many of the defendants swept up in these raids prove after years in court to be innocent, as these demons and witches of the twenty-first century infrequently turn out to match the terrifying status they are given in the media, but this incongruence seems not to slow down the need for moral panics.

Of course, the twenty-first-century homosexual is not the Greek mentor or acolyte. Now, homosexuals are always to have been adults; the Greek model of age-differentiated relationships skates too close to the pedophile idea to find a place in modern cultural systems. Mentorship has been strictly desexualized and policed. It is perhaps the case that the integration of lesbians and gay men into legal participation in liberal democracies signifies not so much a natural progression toward enlightenment as a remapping of the boundaries of the acceptable and the anathema.

In this book, Corriveau offers a unique lineage in tracing the course of Western legal and social discourses, travelling through France and Quebec, to understand the trajectory of Western constructions of sexuality. France proves to be an instructive example. Although the introduction of the Napoleonic legal code after the French Revolution marks one of the most significant changes in the state treatment of sexuality, which the code privatized and removed from direct regulation, Corriveau shows how vaguer legal precepts about moral order and decency nevertheless allowed legal authorities to exert a homophobic regime against men who would have sex with men. The Napoleonic Code, which became the legal founda- tion for much of western Europe and Latin America, has shown a similar dualism in other jurisdictions: homosexuality may be decriminalized, but legal provisions such as sanctions against "outrage to public morals" have given ample scope for repressive action by police and moral entrepreneurs.

Homosexuality so often finds itself buffeted by the winds of symbolic politics. Larger structural shifts in alliances and counteralliances, involving churches, political parties, popular movements, labour unions, and so on, have profoundly affected the fortunes of lesbian, gay, bisexual, and trans- gendered persons. Nevertheless, forged by centuries of repression in Western societies, LGBT desire and practices have coalesced into persons willing to take on and defend a right to their sexuality. The remarkable transformation toward citizenship is, at least in part, an accomplishment of people willing to take on LGBT identities and organize movements, and the endurance of this transformation cannot simply be presumed without their ongoing efforts.

Preface

This book is an adaptation of *La Répression des homosexuels au Québec et en France*, published by Les éditions du Septentrion in 2006. That work, in turn, was adapted from my doctoral dissertation on the sociology of law, completed in 2003 at Université Picardie Jules Verne, in France, and Université Laval, in Quebec. Since then, much research has been published addressing different facets of the subjects analyzed in this book. Therefore, this version has been updated with more than thirty new references. Moreover, my continuing work on homophobia and repression of homosexuality, which I began in 1998, has enabled me to clarify and refine my socio-historical reading of the evolution of criminal law in terms of its management of homosexuality.

It is important for readers to understand that this book is a sociological and criminological study of the judicial handling of homosexuality in Quebec and France over the past four hundred years, not a historical study of homosexuality per se. Indeed, it would be both risky and pretentious for me to claim to have painted an accurate and nuanced portrait of the many realities experienced by gays over such a long historical period. The contribution of my analysis is a better understanding of the legislative changes that have occurred in Quebec and France with regard to the social reaction to homosexuality – a contribution derived from my interpretation of both primary sources (for example, archives, jurisprudence, criminal statistics) and secondary sources (for example, theological research, medical treatises).

The primary objective of this research is thus to conduct a socio-historical analysis of the different dominant discourses (religious, medical, human rights) that have influenced how criminal law managed and controlled individuals with homoerotic behaviours, who were considered, in turn, criminal sinners, criminals with a disease, and citizens to be protected by criminal law. The main subject of this book is thus the evolution of the rationality of criminal law with regard to the "homoerotic issue."

But here, readers should be cautioned. As the criminologist Alvaro Pires (1998) emphasizes, criminal law should not be thought of as an empty shell serving other discursive systems that may transcend it (for example, religious, medical) in order to have their concept of "normalcy" and "appropriate" management of homoerotic lifestyles prevail. As readers will see in the pages that follow, sometimes criminal law refers to these discourses as a source of legitimization, but sometimes it distances itself in order to affirm its autonomy. In addition, we must pay attention to the specific affinities among these discourses and understand that although there is sometimes opposition between the law and religion, and between the law and "medicine," in their respective comprehensions of the "homosexual phenomenon," these comprehensions are not always mutually exclusive.

It is thus the interactions among these discursive systems that I delve into by analyzing the evolution of criminal practice and the legitimizing discourses that have supported criminal law in its management of homosexuality throughout history. In short, I set out to explain the complete reversal of criminal logic with regard to homosexuality, through which the "homosexual" went from pariah par excellence, his behaviour punishable by the death penalty, to citizen recognized by and protected under the law: from the stake to the town hall!

Acknowledgments

The publication of this book is a great source of pride for me, and I know that none of it would have been possible without the confidence of my editors at UBC Press, Darcy Cullen and Ann Macklem; the support of my colleague at the University of Ottawa, Manon Tremblay; and the excellent work of Käthe Roth, with whom it was a true pleasure to discuss the translation over a number of months. I extend my sincerest gratitude to all three. And I would also like to express my gratitude to the entire team at Les éditions du Septentrion, without whom this venture would never have started.

I would like to thank the Social Sciences and Humanities Research Council of Canada, which provided the support for the research that led to this work. I would also like to thank the anonymous reviewers, who gave me numerous suggestions for improving the text.

I cannot let the opportunity pass to mention the constant assistance of my colleagues and friends throughout the rewriting and translation of this new version of my research. My thanks go to Jean-François Cauchie, André Cellard, Jean-Philippe Côté, Michel Dorais, and Cathy Herbrand, as well as Olivier Clain and Denis Duclos, who guided my first steps into the strange world of scholarly research. My gratitude also goes to the research team Sexual and Gender Diversity: Vulnerability, Resilience, especially Line Chamberland, Danielle Julien, and Joseph Lévy, for having helped me to enhance this book.

And finally, I cannot forget Agnès, my companion and soul mate, for without her nothing would be the same or as beautiful ... especially life as a family of three.

Judging Homosexuals

Introduction

In June 1997, homophobia, the irrational hatred of homosexuals, struck me full force. Of course, I had long heard various people tell jokes about "queers," as funny stories are told to a group of friends, without thinking much about their significance. I also thought that I had glimpsed disgust in the eyes of certain people over the idea that two men might dare to kiss in public. However, before that Thursday night in June 1997, feeling that it didn't concern me, I had paid little attention to it. But on that warm summer evening of partying on the St. Lawrence River – a scene worthy of *The Love Boat* – I was confronted, in spite of myself, with all of the hate, incomprehension, and evil hidden within homophobia. Imagine: A young man is peacefully enjoying himself with friends. A gang of arrogant roughnecks, bursting with testosterone, decide to taunt him; they deem his attire too effeminate and conclude that he must be a "faggot," a "queer." With unbelievable violence, these brave souls shove the young man around as a crowd watches without reacting or intervening in any way, except for a couple of young women who try, in vain, to step in – claiming that he is heterosexual.

This concrete encounter with homophobia started me wondering about the origins of the social repression to which homosexuals are still subjected today. Had society evolved toward greater acceptance of sexual difference? No doubt! But where had this social resentment of homosexuals come from? Church discourse? The lingering stench of old psychiatric discourse that saw the homosexual as a sexual pervert – and one with a contagious disease? Was it a fear of difference transmitted from generation to generation? For there must have been some form of fear underlying this contempt for – or, worse, hate of – the homosexual. How could the nor-malization of same-sex marriages in the West, unthinkable twenty-five years ago, be explained? Because I wanted to understand the evolution of the repression of homoerotic lifestyles, was at a loss for more meaningful ideas, and was haunted by my inability to have put an end to the unfortu-nate incident in June 1997, being limited by my size and complete absence of pugilistic talent – in my defence, there were five of them – I decided to invest a few years of my life in doctoral studies on the subject.

My first readings quickly raised their share of questions with regard to legislative evolution. How can it be explained that in ancient Greece homo-eroticism was seen as a normal sexual behaviour and sexual relations between individuals of the same sex were part of a codified, generalized, and accepted reality, both socially and institutionally? What led societies to repress these lifestyles more and more in the Middle Ages? At first hap-hazardly as the Roman Empire came to an end in the twelfth century, then in a more generalized fashion between the thirteenth and eighteenth centuries, medieval societies formulated a litany of municipal, feudal, and royal rules against sodomists. Why were sodomists (they were not yet called homosexuals) so easily associated with heretics, infidels, and Muslims, and why was sodomy always defined as and linked to the Other, the foreigner – perceived as an Arab taste, an Italian penchant, or a French vice? How was it that during the Enlightenment the criminal sodomist, enemy of God, was transformed into the invert, a sexual pervert who might be treated? Why did society go from penal repression of a sexual behaviour deemed illicit to the idea of rehabilitation, control, and regulation of in-dividuals with homoerotic lifestyles? What conditions favoured the "cre-ation" of the homosexual as a distinct individuality? Finally, how is it today, throughout the West, that homosexuals are "coming out of the closet" and making their mark in society, the arts, and politics, that their sexual behaviours have been decriminalized, and that there is growing legal recognition of gay particularities? The "character" of those practising homoerotic behaviours, from the figure of the sodomist to that of the gay, via the invert, the pederast, and the homosexual, has been shaped and controlled by various institutions of power throughout history. Over the course of a few centuries, there was a complete reversal of legislative logic, from meting out the death penalty to such people to legally protecting them as individuals with distinct sexual behaviours. From capital punishment to legal protection, from the stake to the town hall – this is the complete societal turnaround with regard to penal control that I describe in this book on the evolution of legal repression of homoerotic lifestyles in France and Quebec from the seventeenth century to the present.

Because the two societies studied here have cultural roots in common but legal traditions that have diverged for almost two hundred years – inquisitorial system in France and adversarial system in French Canada – a comparative analysis is useful for revealing the underpinnings of the legislative evolution with regard to homoerotic behaviours. For each society, a number of aspects have been considered. In any given period, which social class held the centralizing power – the power to define and legislate on homoerotic lifestyles? Which discourse imposed its definition of the character of the homosexual and the legitimization of one type of intervention (clerical, penal, or medical) over another? What function has repression of homoerotic lifestyles fulfilled? To whose benefit? What role have the family, the clergy, medicine, and civil society played in the control of these behaviours? To answer these questions, I uncover the dominant discourses behind legislative changes in order to understand how certain social groups became influential enough in the eyes of the community to impose not only their representations of the deviant but also the forms of control that they deemed necessary to maintain social order.

I have divided this comparative analysis into four historical periods, corresponding to significant changes in the legal regulation of homoerotic lifestyles in France and Quebec from the seventeenth century to the present. However, before I look specifically at the repression that occurred in these two societal contexts, it is relevant to take a brief look at the earliest stages of the legal repression that burdened homosexuals for almost two thousand years. This history is the focus of an opening chapter on the regulation of homoerotic lifestyles from Antiquity to the Renaissance, which is more of a narrative than are succeeding chapters. On the one hand, the Ancients' distinction between sexual instinct and sexual object seems essential for an understanding of the repression that homosexuals would be subjected to in the periods that are examined in greater detail; on the other hand, this chapter sheds light on discourses on sexuality and shows how public interventions with regard to homoerotic lifestyles changed over time. Finally, this brief historical review highlights certain themes that recur in the evolution of social management of homosexuality, such as the influence of social crises on the repression of homosexuals, the role of homosexuals as scapegoats to discredit the enemy, and the fear that they inspired in terms of the family and children.

Chapters 2 to 5 deal expressly with the repression of homoerotic behaviours in France and Quebec. The first historical period studied covers from the Grande Ordonnance of 1670 to the British Conquest of 1760. During this period, the criminal justice system in New France reflected that of the parent country, France. Thus regulation of homoerotic behaviours in the two societies – it was in fact the repression of behaviours and not of a particular individuality – was likely to be similar in a number of ways. It therefore seems that in both societies, homoerotic lifestyles were punished according to a divine interpretation of sexuality under which the image of the sodomist was that of a sinner before God.

The second period extends from the British Conquest to the end of the nineteenth century. What emerge immediately are differences with regard to legitimization through criminal law between a rapidly evolving France and a French Canada still dominated by an omnipresent clergy. In France the revolution marked the victory of the bourgeoisie, the beginning of a wave of industrialization, and the modernization of society. In the name of liberty and universal reason, the law was laicized. The establishment of penalties was now based on egalitarian and rational principles. The French justice system also referred more and more to scientific and medical discourses in its management of deviancy and deviants; the invert was no exception. Conversely, in French Canada religious transcendence influenced and legitimized the institutions that controlled deviancy and criminality, notably with regard to lifestyles, and French Canadian society still adhered largely to the dominant ecclesiastical discourses. Whereas in France the label of sodomist gradually gave way to that of pederast (a legal term) and even invert (a medical term), in Lower Canada the sodomist, sinner before God, remained.

The third historical period extends from the end of the nineteenth century to the sexual revolution in the late 1960s. Given the evolution of medical knowledge within the justice systems in France and French Canada, it is possible to presume that the discourses that legitimized criminal law were similar: medical and psychiatric discourses were more and more prominent in the management of sexual deviancy. Furthermore, the character of the "homosexual" took shape. French Canada started down the path taken by France in the mid-nineteenth century – toward medicalization, correction, and rehabilitation of the homosexual. As this modification of criminal doctrine was taking place in Canada, France temporarily regressed in its regulation of homoerotic sexuality and lifestyles by returning to punishment of these behaviours, which were deemed a threat to the prosperity of the homeland.

Finally, I discuss the fourth historical period, comprising the legislative changes that have taken place from the early 1970s to the present. In this last period, criminal law was modified and homoerotic behaviours were gradually withdrawn from its field of intervention. The very rationality of formalist law was transformed from universal law deduced by reason to multiple legal logics that respond to individual particularities. Following this new judicial philosophy, gays – as homosexuals have chosen to self-identify – slowly gained legal protection and a number of civil rights. The law, which had once persecuted them, now protected them against discrimination based on sexual orientation. As persons possessing a particular individuality, they were recognized specifically in the name of human rights.

Given the scope of the task that I set myself, the old adage "Jack of all trades, master of none" comes to mind. Anyone who ventures into historical research on homosexuality must do so in terms of a global perspective, as the subject encompasses the history of morals, of medicine, of law, of the police, of religion, of politics, and of attitudes. If to this one adds a long historical period and a comparative analysis, one opens the door to the critiques that the repression of homosexuality cannot be reduced to specific historical changes, that histories of homosexuality are always inscribed within distinct socio-political contexts that vary by country and by region, and that these histories are quite relative and cannot be fit into simplified ideo-typical periods. To some degree, these critiques are legitimate, as the figures of homosexuality are necessarily multifaceted: attempting to reduce these multifaceted figures to ideo-typical categories cannot take full account of what is or was the complexity of social reality. I am aware that this approach leads to an emphasis on ruptures in judicial management of homoerotic lifestyles rather than on phases of continuity or simple reorganization: comparative sociology in fact forces us to "retrace the different successive steps in the development of societies," as Guy Rocher (1992, 186, our translation) puts it.

On the other hand, this method of analysis offers an opportunity to concentrate specifically on dominant discourses – the regulatory ideas that impose a conception of deviancy and a particular means of control. I consider the citizen-as-subject to be the product of a social system that shapes its subjects according to its own norms, rules, and laws. This is why, as an easily observable social fact, the law does not speak about conflict, fault, or contradiction within the group but presents solidarity against crime and conflict – in this case, the homosexual deviant. As sociology and critical criminology suggest, it is the rationality of criminal law and its method of coercion with regard to the homoerotic issue that have been modified over time. Émile Durkheim (1964, 81) was right to maintain, "We must not say that an action shocks the common conscience because it is criminal, but rather that it is criminal because it shocks the common conscience. We do not reprove it because it is a crime, but it is a crime because we reprove it." In other words, it is the law that creates the crime, and the history of judicial repression of homosexuality is a spectacular example of social deconstruction that presents the evolutionary and con-structed nature of what society has defined as "crime" and "criminal." Bringing to centre stage the institutional organs and discourses (repressive apparatuses, health apparatuses, family and religious apparatuses) that have defined and taken charge of social control of the individual with homoerotic behaviours is the objective of this book.

1

Ancient Greece to the Seventeenth Century

FROM PEDERASTY TO SODOMY

> I cannot imagine a greater happiness and advantage to one who is
> in the flower of youth than an amiable lover, or to a lover, than an
> amiable object of his love.
>
> – Phaedrus, in Plato's *The Banquet*

> If a man lies with a man as one lies with a woman, both of them
> have committed an abomination. They shall surely be put to
> death. Their blood shall be upon them.
>
> – Leviticus 20:13

In this chapter, I give an overview of the evolution of repression of homoerotic lifestyles in Europe before the seventeenth century and shed light
on changes in attitudes toward and perceptions of sexuality through the
ages. This chapter also offers a key to comprehension of the more systematic socio-historical analyses in successive chapters on repression of homoerotic lifestyles in France and Quebec from the seventeenth century to the
present. At the outset, the reader must be made aware of some facts that
are all too rarely discussed. First, this long period of history is far from
homogeneous but varies both from region to region in Europe and from
era to era. Second, because societies long tried to obscure this social reality, the data available are rather scarce and their validity is sometimes
questionable. Either the sources no longer exist – having been destroyed
by the authorities of the time, who did not want the population to be in-
formed about homoerotic behaviours, or by the homosexuals themselves,

who were scared (often with reason) to save letters or other objects that might have incriminated them as homosexuals – or they come almost exclusively from official sources – that is, the police, the judiciary, or the church; therefore, they cannot be analyzed fully. Sometimes, data have been falsified. For example, in a poem or essay, the love between Pierre and Paul might be transformed into a love between Pierrette and Paul! This complicates things for historians.[1] Some researchers have occasionally tried to interpret the available sources with a view to legitimizing them, notably with regard to the idea of a Greek paradise for homosexuals.[2] Finally, as Didier Éribon (2004, 6), correctly notes, we must be aware that "figures of 'homosexuality' are always specific to a given cultural situation." In this sense, the conclusions drawn here rely on what was probably conveyed by official sources in theology, the law, and the arts (poetry, painting, sculpture, theatre, and pamphlets).

Social Regulation of Homoerotic Lifestyles in Antiquity

In Antiquity – as in the Middle Ages – the homosexual personality as it is conceived of today did not exist: the "homosexual" individual appeared only in the late nineteenth century, when homosexuality was medicalized. The hostility under discussion here – and the resulting repression – has to do with homoerotic behaviour, not with homosexual subjectivity as such. Moreover, the contemporary notion of homosexuality does not adequately describe the sexual experience between individuals of the same sex in the pre-Christian era – in this case, Greek and Roman Antiquity (Adam 1985; Halperin 1990, 55). The Greeks and Romans did not make a clear distinction between the categories of "homosexual" and "heterosexual." They were bisexuals, and the object of pleasure was less important than how that pleasure was taken (Sartre 1998, 18; Veyne 1978, 50). What was frowned upon was an overly pronounced interest in sexuality, either homosexual or heterosexual. A revealing example is provided by the trial of Timarchus, who was accused of male prostitution. During his trial, in 346 BCE, Timarchus was never condemned for his homosexuality, as his accuser, Eschinus, openly declared that he, too, enjoyed the love of young men. Rather, Eschinus's accusation had to do with a question of illegitimacy. Timarchus was allegedly dishonouring his status as a citizen by prostituting himself. Male prostitution was legal and accepted by a large part of the population in Athens and Rome, as long as the prostitute was not a citizen; a festival of prostitution was celebrated on 25 April, during the Fasti de Praenesti (Veyne 1981, 77). The importance, visibility, and un-remarkable nature of prostitution would indicate that pederasty was also omnipresent and not problematic in itself (Halperin 1990, 94); in Timar-chus's trial, there was never an issue of unnatural practices or indecent assault. No penalty was provided by law specifically to punish homo-erotic behaviours (see Dover 1978, 23). Therefore, to define the issue of homoeroticism during this period, it is essential to step away, as much as possible, from modern sexual typologies, as pederasty in ancient Greece cannot be considered homosexuality in the modern sense of the term.

Ancient Greece: Statutory Sexuality

Although it is difficult to establish with certainty the origin of pederastic lifestyles in ancient Greece, Hellenists agree that homoerotic behaviours were openly practised, and even widespread, as of the sixth century BCE in Greece,[3] where homoerotic sexuality, as a codified and generalized sex-ual behaviour, was known to and accepted by all. It constituted "a normal fact of life in social relations" (Sartre 1991, 54, our translation); certain cities (such as Crete and Sparta) even raised homosexuality to the status of an institution. Furthermore, cohabitation by two men was not excep-tional. Although they were aware of different sexual preferences, the Greeks and Romans were not disturbed by the idea that an individual's desire, object of desire, and even sexual behaviour might oscillate between a man and a woman. In some circles, being with men even seems to have been more highly regarded than being with women (see Sartre 1998). Certainly, on the legislative level, homoerotic practices violated no laws. Violence in sexuality was not acceptable, however, and penalties were meted out ac-cording not to the victim's sex but to his social status.

It is important to understand the extent to which homoerotic lifestyles were hierarchical and codified. As Sartre (1991, 58, our translation) notes, "An attentive reading shows that these sexual customs invariably came under specific constraints: the choice of lovers dictated by their social rank, child abduction announced in advance and approved by the entour-age, gifts imposed by law (military equipment, an ox, and a cup), the duration of the stay in the countryside, the presence of friends, and so on." In Athens and Rome male culture was seen as the supreme power: penetration and phallic pleasure corresponded to social dominance not by a man over a woman but by a citizen over individuals of inferior social status (women, slaves, freedmen). The sexual relationship represented a power relationship between a dominant and a dominated person; *impudicitas* (passivity), associated with the feminine role, not homoerotic sexuality in itself, was suppressed. Therefore, it was unacceptable for the participants to invert the sexual role (active or passive) assigned to them by their social status. Although sodomizing someone (man or woman) was considered a virtuous act for citizens, being sodomized made a citizen despicable since his social status obliged him to be virile. An Athenian citizen who violated this rule of sexuality risked losing his status as a free man or being condemned to death (see Quignard 1994, 17-19). Conversely, for the slave, impudicitas was an absolute duty toward his master, and for the freedman it was an act of deference that he had the moral duty to show to his patron. In other words, homoeroticism could be, depending on the circumstances and social status of the participants, the "object of admiration and envy or, on the contrary, of profound disapproval" (Sartre 1991, 57, our translation).

Although it seems accurate to claim that homoerotic sexuality was unfettered – permitted by law, approved by public opinion, and supported institutionally – it remains that the homoerotic "practice of pleasures" was a source of concern among both the Greeks and the Romans. Both societies codified and regulated it. Among the Greeks, for example, initiatory pederasty between a lover *(eraste)* and a beloved *(eromenos)* was a functional ritual leading the young man *(gynaecea)* to fill his reproductive and citizenship roles. In this type of pederastic relationship, which was seen as preparation for married life and the role of citizen, the lover was necessarily active and older, and the beloved had to be young, beardless, and passive. Hirsuteness determined the boundary between the two sexual behaviours. Only beardless freedmen were expected to be passive. Once his beard began to grow, a young man was no longer considered a beloved. A "legitimate" pederastic relationship was possible between puberty and first growth of the beard; those who continued exclusive homoerotic practices after this interval were an unaccepted minority. In other words, this type of homoerotic sexuality remained acceptable as long as it followed various social ground rules, especially the teaching of the young eromenos by the older man. This is why pederasty was subjected to so many rules. Michel Foucault (1985, 196-97) defines the roles of the eraste and the eromenos as follows:

The first was in a position of initiative – he was the suitor – and this gave him rights and obligations; he was expected to show his ardour, and to restrain it; he had gifts to make, services to render; he had functions to exercise with regard to the *eromenos;* and all this entitled him to expect a just reward. The other partner, the one who was loved and courted, had to be careful not to yield too easily; he also had to keep from accepting too many tokens of love, and from granting his favours heedlessly and out of self-interest, without testing the worth of his partner; he must also show gratitude for what the lover had done for him. Now, this courtship practice alone shows very well that the sexual relation between man and boy did not "go without saying": it had to be accompanied by conventions, rules of conduct, ways of going about it, by a whole game of delays and obstacles designed to put off the moment of closure, and to integrate it into a series of subsidiary activities and relations. In other words, while this type of relation was fully accepted, it was not a matter of "indifference."

In theory, the passive partner was not allowed to show any sign of pleasure in the sex act and could not initiate a relationship with an eraste; he had to let himself be courted and coveted. The relationship between lover and beloved thus became one of rejection, evasion, and flight (Foucault 1985, 224).

Again, these conclusions must be viewed with caution since a number of experts, including Maurice Sartre (1998, 18) and John Boswell (1994, ch. 3), maintain that it is wrong to see the pederastic relationship in ancient Greece as limited to a rite of passage stripped of pleasure and desire. On the contrary, the dimension of pleasure was omnipresent in Greek life: men bonded in friendship with other men also visited female prostitutes and did not hesitate to have concubines. Boswell also rejects the idea that homoerotic relationships were mainly initiatory, short-term, and in a hierarchy between an older, active lover and a beloved who was always younger and passive. Referring to ancient Rome, he observes that many pairs of same-sex lovers had relationships that were for the most part permanent and exclusive. In his view, the sources as a whole suggest that homoerotic relationships "in the rest of ancient Europe were certainly far more varied and flexible than this, probably not very different from their heterosexual counterparts" (Boswell 1994, 71).

Yet an examination of Athenian comedy shows that such relationships between two adults of the same sex were almost always portrayed in a negative, pejorative fashion, particularly the (obligatory) passivity of one of the two participants. In comparison, pederasty – as well as love between two young men – was much less frequently portrayed in Athenian comedy and was rarely a source of mockery (see Henderson 1991, 208-9). The implication conveyed by Greek comedy is thus that Greek homoeroticism was regulated by moral rules in which the sexual role was dictated by the participants' social status, with passivity and lack of virility constituting laughable behaviours in a society whose culture was phallic, masculine, and dominating.

To these rules of good conduct were added that of temperance, in which "the primary dividing line laid down by moral judgment in the area of sexual behavior was not prescribed by the nature of the act, with its possible variations, but by the activity and its quantitative gradations" (Foucault 1985, 45). Athenians saw excess of any sort as a sign of weakness and lack of self-control. The matter of whether the sexual object was a woman, a boy, or a slave was not particularly problematic. On the other hand, a too-pronounced interest in sexual activity was a source of social disapproval. Symonds (1983) observes that the Greeks distinguished two forms of love: heroic (spiritual) and vulgar (carnal). For instance, the Dorians easily practised carnal love in wartime, but once war was over, such frolics were transformed into a form of vice: lust. This dichotomy must be viewed with prudence, however, John A. Symonds continues, since the Ancients largely tolerated carnal love of boys, with spiritual love being an ideal that was difficult to attain (see Éribon 2004, 162-65). It seems, in fact, quite surprising that homoerotic love would have been totally stripped of homoerotic desire.

Foucault (1985, 43-44) summarizes the management of customs in ancient Greece:

What seems in fact to have formed the object of moral reflection for the Greeks in matters of sexual conduct was not exactly the act itself (considered in its different modalities), or desire (viewed from the standpoint of its origin or its aim), or even pleasure (evaluated according to the different objects or practices that can cause it); it was more the dynamics that joined all three in a circular fashion (the desire that leads to the act, the act that is linked to pleasure, and the pleasure that occasions desire). The ethical question that was raised was not: Which desire? Which acts? Which pleasures? But rather: with what force is one transported "by the pleasures and desires?" ... What differentiates men from one another, for medicine and moral philosophy alike, is not so much the type of objects toward which they are oriented, nor the mode of sexual practice they prefer; above all, it is the intensity of that practice. The division is between lesser and greater: moderation or excess.

Pre-Christian Rome: Virile and Abundant Sexuality

As they were in ancient Greece, homoerotic lifestyles were widespread and tolerated in pre-Christian Rome. "Greek love" could just as legitimately be called "Roman love." According to Paul Veyne (1981, 77, our translation), it is a mistake to believe that homoerotic lifestyles in Rome were of Greek origin since, "like several Mediterranean societies today, Rome never compared love for women to love for boys: it compared being active to being passive. Being active was to be masculine, whatever the sex of the 'passive' partner." Rome did follow the example of Greece, however, with regard to the three main criteria for sexual morality: sexual freedom and exclusive matrimony, being active or passive, and the social status of the participants.

Was Roman sexual morality as rigid, strongly regulated, and statutory? Quignard (1994, 18-19, our translation) observes, "In Rome a man was said to be decent when he had not been sodomized (as long as he was active)." More than in Athens, masculine virility was the basis for sexuality in Rome. Although there was tolerance of the love of boys, there was strong repudiation of *mollitia,* effeminate lifestyles among freedmen. Roman puritanism thus did not concern sexuality in itself, but virility, since sexual relations still symbolized the power relationship between dominant and dominated. As Veyne (1998, 17, our translation) emphasizes, "Taking virile pleasure or servilely giving pleasure: this was the only distinction that was important in Rome, regardless of the sex of the partner."[4] On the other hand, on the legal front, the "guilty party" was never punished, as homoerotic practices were not a crime under Roman imperial law.

In spite of these similarities with ancient Greece, social regulation of sexuality and homoerotic practices differed somewhat among the Romans.

For the Greeks, the rule was temperance – that is, the capacity to attain self-control regarding one's desires – whereas for the Romans, sexuality had to be active and abundant; there was never too much. The Greeks saw the appearance of the beard as marking the end of passivity, but no Romans, whatever their age, were permitted to be passive. Because of this, some authors state that the pederastic tradition widespread in Greece was not philosophically accepted in Rome, as Roman morals did not accept passivity among freeborn young men (Lever 1985; Quignard 1994; Sergent 1986).[5] Veyne (1978, 51) invalidates this hypothesis, however, as he has found that pederastic relations were as common in Rome as in Athens.

In light of the above, it is unjust to claim that the Ancients were indifferent to homoerotic love. A "homosexual" nature was not seen as intrinsically bad, but the circumstances under which homoerotic love was experienced made it acceptable or not in the eyes of society. The Ancients were concerned less with the nature of sexual behaviours than with having such behaviours conform to the social status of those who practised them. They did not recognize two opposed desiring subjectivities. For them, desiring a man and a woman simultaneously or successively did not pose any moral problems; these were simply two different ways of obtaining pleasure. It was a sense of proportionality, framed by the partners' social status and sexual role, that came into play (Leroy-Forgeot 1997, 10). Certainly, sexuality in general – and homoerotic love in particular – was broadly supervised and regulated, but this control was exercised in a different fashion than it is today (Foucault 1985, 45). Under Christian Rome, control of sexuality and homoerotic lifestyles simply continued, although differently.

Very likely, management of homoerotic lifestyles among the Ancients was a matter mainly of regulating sexuality within certain limits, not a matter of sanctioning it or avenging an affront to the collective consciousness, since homoerotic sexuality was, in short, banal. The Ancients did not judge homosexuality in itself. It was considered no more or less a "normal" manifestation of sexual and loving desire than love of women, and it was totally acceptable socially. What made it criminal was violence perpetrated on the partner and a lack of temperance. It was not an offence against the gods or the natural order that was repressed, but violence against the citizen, as social control served first and foremost to maintain and regulate the established social hierarchy.

The Middle Ages: From Tolerance to Repression

The ancient form of sexuality described above ended in the first and second centuries CE, when it was replaced by a reproductive sexuality that mandated sharing and reciprocity of pleasure within the couple. Sexual morality was transformed into an affair of virtue that applied to everyone, independent of social status. The rule of proportionality was superseded by the rule of reciprocity. "From a morality of statutory acts to a morality of interiorized virtues: this was the great evolution between Caesar and Marcus Aurelius," observes Veyne (1978, 56, our translation). Whereas morality in ancient Rome suppressed passivity among citizens and forced it among slaves, starting with Marcus Aurelius morality universalized respect for the virtue of modesty. Thus sexual repression began to be increased during the century of Antonine law (96-192 CE), mainly with regard to abortion, masculine sexuality, and adultery (see Gauvard 1991, 824; Quignard 1994, 18; Veyne 1978, 56).

From Early Christianity to the Thirteenth Century: Mitigated Repression[6]

In 342 CE, capital punishment was introduced as a penalty for "passive homoerotic behaviours." This statute was amended twice: first, by Theodosius in 390, and a second time in 438 to include active homoerotic behaviours. However, no trace of people being found guilty has been discovered. Also, surprisingly, male prostitution continued to be tolerated and was taxed by Christian emperors during this period and up to when Justinian began to punish all homoerotic acts with castration and burning at the stake under divine law in 533. The increased repression of homoerotic lifestyles coincided with the rise of stoicism – that is, a desire to channel sexuality, confine it to its reproductive function, and anchor it to the institution of marriage – and with a terrible epidemic of bubonic plague that hit the empire in 542. Because of this catastrophe, Rome needed five children per woman to maintain its population, so all nonreproductive behaviours, not just homoerotic behaviours, came to be poorly viewed by the political powers. Paradoxically, during the same period, suicide – certainly not a reproductive behaviour! – was held in some esteem.

According to some researchers, the Scriptures simply did not have the influence with which they are sometimes credited, notably because the Bible was not at the time a single, standardized book with extended moral authority. Boswell (1980, 159, 92) goes so far as to state that the influence of the New Testament was nonexistent during this historical period, as the Roman Church did not officially establish the canon of the Bible until the Council of Trent in 1546. At least, he notes, it is wrong to believe that the Bible alone dictated the policy of states with regard to repression of homoerotic lifestyles. He gives the example of prostitution, which, despite being strongly condemned by the New Testament, was accepted as legal by states in the early Christian era, and remarks, "the Bible was not the only or even the principal source of early Christian ethics, and the biblical passages purportedly relating to homosexuality had little to do with early Christian misgivings on the subject" (Boswell 1980, 92). With regard to the role played by the Old Testament – mainly the story of Sodom – in the condemnation of homoerotic behaviours, it appears that this interpretation was made later than the time of early Christianity. Leviticus, which Boswell regards as the only text that explicitly forbids homoerotic relations, did not have a marked influence on the morality of the time. Boswell (1980, ch. 7) feels that Christianity should not be considered the source of repression of homoerotic lifestyles since, up to the thirteenth century, the few statutes that applied to these types of acts emanated from the civil authorities, which legislated without the church's advice or consent. Although these statutes were justified and written in terms of Christian morality, they remained purely civil. According to Boswell's research, there is no text that leads to the conclusion that Christian leaders supported, in any way, the promulgation of the first imperial statute repressing all forms of homoerotic behaviours in 533. Homoerotic lifestyles, although not ignored by the church, remained a minor sin. The influence of the Old Testament on the first laws written by the Christian emperors with regard to homoerotic behaviours was thus secondary (Demers 1984, 779).

On the other hand, the jurist and philosopher Flora Leroy-Forgeot (1997, 21-22) claims that Leviticus was the main theoretical basis for justifying repression of homoerotic behaviours as a crime against human dignity. Observing that the notion of "crime against nature" flows from a Judeo-Platonic interpretation of the order of the world that defines such crimes as an insult to God and man, she underlines the influence of St. Augustine (354-430), who advocated procreative sexuality within the institution of marriage. The place of sexuality in marriage remained problematic, however, since procreation, necessary to the survival of humankind, was inevitably accompanied by concupiscence. In addition, as the historian Michel Sot (1991, 193, our translation) rightly states with regard to the invention of Christian marriage in the medieval era, "It was not self-evident that marriage had to be monogamous, indissoluble, and based on the reciprocal consent of two individuals." Leroy-Forgeot (1997, 31) maintains, nevertheless, that there is evidence that the Augustinian concept of sexuality – and of unnatural sexuality – strongly influenced the authors who followed.

As Leroy-Forgeot (1997) notes, Athenagorus characterized participants in homoerotic acts as enemies of Christianity in 177. She posits that Christianity had a greater influence on the repression of homoerotic lifestyles than Boswell claims, and she buttresses her argument with the fact that the first Roman statutes incriminating homoerotic lifestyles came after the recognition of Christianity as a religion by the empire in 313; subsequently, in 342, marriages between men were banned – although, admittedly, male homosexual prostitution was still accepted, and homoerotic lifestyles were proscribed at the same level as adultery. Furthermore, she explains, with the fall of the Roman Empire and the Germanic invasions, homoerotic behaviours became common and were no longer considered a crime. In other words, before Christian rules influenced Germanic legal culture, the idea that homoerotic behaviours were criminal and sinful was not accepted because "the notion of homosexuality, as defined in a negative way by Christianity, was identified as originating outside of medieval Germanic law" (Leroy-Forgeot 1997, 29, our translation). From this, Leroy-Forgeot (1997, 29) concludes that Christianity greatly influenced the Roman legal tradition with regard to repression of "homosexuality." In light of the above, it is difficult to establish with certainty the point to which Christianity dictated the sexual morality of the High Middle Ages. The only thing that is certain, summarizes Le Goff (1998, 36), is that Christianity built the connection between flesh and sin.

Repression of Homoerotic Lifestyles: Urban versus Rural

In the tenth century, canon law – the body of rules of the Roman Catholic Church – began to mention the religious condemnation of homoerotic behaviours. A number of factors, including the transition from an urban to a rural way of life, the Germanic invasions, economic changes, religious puritanism, natural disasters, and the low birth rate of the upper classes, had a marked effect on the evolution of sexual morality. The hypothesis that there was a relationship between the mode of social organization (urban or rural) and the preponderance of moral issues and degree of sexual tolerance is interesting. According to this hypothesis, the transition from an "urban" to a "rural" society in the High Middle Ages had a decisive influence on the attitude toward behaviours between individuals of the same sex, an attitude that was increasingly characterized by an aversion to all forms of nonprocreative sexuality. Following this reasoning, the rural way of life favoured the creation of taboos and social rules to discourage forms of sexuality likely to upset the community's social organization. In contrast, in urban milieus, sexual morality stressed individual purity and conjugal fidelity more than regulation of the family and procreation. The anonymity found in cities would also have somewhat marginalized homoerotic lifestyles, making them more innocuous, less visible, and thus less disturbing to the rest of society. Homoerotic lifestyles, perceived as inoffensive to the community, would therefore have been more broadly tolerated.

Boswell (1980, 270) nuances this hypothesis by referring to twelfth- and thirteenth-century history. In fact, there is no proof that European populations in the twelfth century, a period considered to have been very tolerant of homoerotic behaviours, were more urban than were those in the thirteenth and fourteenth centuries, which were characterized by strong sexual repression. Although the transition from an urban to a more rural society may have influenced sexual morality, the transition from the social tolerance of the Romans to the generalized hostility of the Low Middle Ages is also based on other aspects of social organization, notably the rise of absolute power, both civil and ecclesiastical, which sought to standardize institutions and attitudes throughout the West. In response to this argument, Leroy-Forgeot (1997, 25) points out that the prohibition on homoerotic behaviours by the Scriptures is explained by an issue that went beyond simple respect for the norms of the Old Testament. The application of this ban had a political origin: the emancipation of the church, for which repression of sodomy encouraged the emergence of Christianity by enabling it to mark its break from pagan customs. In order to advance and consolidate its strength and power, the church needed an Other, foreign to the group, to fear; the "pagan homosexual" was the perfect figure!

This connection between sexual repression and political repression seems to be a constant throughout history. For a long time, "anti-homosexual laws [have] constitute[d] a choice weapon in the hands of skilful arbiters of power who intend, on moral pretexts, to dispose of burdensome adversaries or seize on coveted riches" (De Becker 1967, 99). Historical examples are numerous. Among others, Procopius of Caesarea – one of the most accomplished historians of his times – stated that Justinian and Empress Theodora used such laws as a way to discredit and punish their enemies and appropriate their riches.[7] Tendentious correlations were also created to influence the Christian conception of homoerotic love: the association between paganism and homoerotic behaviours, in which these acts contravened Christian asceticism by being oriented almost exclusively toward pleasure, and the close relationship between homoerotic behaviours and mistreatment of children. This latter conception, which appeared in the fourth century, was based on the fact that many unwanted children were abandoned and sold into slavery, a situation in which they often served as sexual objects. The connection between sexual exploitation of minors and homoerotic lifestyles – that is, a sexuality oriented toward pleasure – quickly spread. Christian penitentials were written about the need to protect the innocence of young people (see Poirier 1996, 32). And thus began a long association in the collective imagination between homosexuality and pedophilia.

Repression That Was Not Specifically Antihomosexual

Although it is difficult to determine exactly the factors that contributed to creating hostility toward homoerotic behaviours during the High Middle Ages, one fact remains: the social repression that condemned homoerotic practices was not directed specifically against this type of "abnormal" sexuality. On the contrary, the church's concern with homoerotic lifestyles paled in comparison to the shame that it heaped upon incest in the Low Middle Ages. Christian asceticism targeted all sexual practices that were not for procreative purposes (see Le Goff 1991, 180). The "Alexandrian rule," which was used by the early Christian theologians to repress homoerotic behaviours, also sanctioned all sexual relations not oriented toward procreation. As Bernd-Ulrich Hergemöller notes (2006, 57), "Humans were judged, following Classical views, according to their behaviour in relation to 'nature.'" The concept of "natural" (reduced to the notion of procreative sexuality) was then used to discredit homoerotic relations, as well as masturbation, fornication, bestiality, and incest.[8] Philippe Ariès (1982, 52-53) notes that society's aversion to effeminate men came from disdain not for a particular sexual practice – sodomy, for example – but for individuals who focused on the pleasures of the flesh and eroticism and who disregarded the sexual strictures that constituted one of the distinctive traits of early Christianity.

It was through the institution of marriage, set up mainly to contain sexuality within well-defined norms, that ecclesiastical power invaded the private life of its followers. Procreation became the single goal of sexuality, and abstinence became the ideal to attain. Marriage was accepted only as a makeshift solution – "it is better to marry than to burn" – said St. Paul, appealing to the faithful to remain virgins and chaste (see Le Goff 1991, 180). In fact, sexual pleasure was subjected to strong repression, even when it occurred in the context of a reproductive sexual activity; some penitentials associated too strong a love for one's own wife with adultery. In short, in the view of the professor of sixteenth-century French literature Guy Poirier (1996, 32) – referring to Jean Gerson, an author of famous penitentials (fifteenth and sixteenth centuries) – all of the church's commandments were intended mainly to repress behaviours that impeded procreation by pursuing sensual pleasures only.

In the High Middle Ages, the church thus was not really concerned with "homosexuality" – at least, not to the exclusion of other sins and forms of adultery.[9] For example, Reginon de Prüm's penitential required a three-year penitence for anal penetration, whether it was performed by two men or by a married couple. This infraction was no more severely punished than was fornication. Boswell (1980, 180) reported, on a lighter note, that Pope Gregory III's penitential set out a penitence of at least one year for homosexual relations and a penitence of three years for a priest found guilty of going hunting! In short, homoerotic behaviours were treated as one minor offence among others – that is, a form of fornication the goal of which was not procreation. They were part of a group of sexual behaviours designated as "crimes against nature," which were defined as "any sexual release of semen with a nun, a relative, the wife of a relative, a married woman, any woman in a way which precluded conception, an animal, or by oneself, whether through manipulation or any other means" (Boswell 1980, 203). Michael Goodich (1976a, 432) notes that, among the offences listed under the term "sodomy," the church – at least in the twelfth century – was interested less in homoerotic behaviours than in adultery, incest, and cohabitation. Although sodomy was seen as one of the most reprehensible sexual behaviours in the Middle Ages, this crime was not applied exclusively to a sin committed by two men but also included sexual acts perpetrated between a man and a woman.

In short, although the church did not overlook homoerotic behaviours, it did not treat them differently at first; rather, they fell into a group of sexual behaviours that were all equally reprehensible. Between the seventh and the early thirteenth centuries, there was even a period of great tolerance with regard to homoerotic lifestyles, particularly on the legal front, with national legislatures completely closing their eyes to the issue. Among the factors that encouraged Christian indifference to this type of sexual behaviour were the absence of a central power acting as a source of standardization of customs and the revival of certain Hellenistic values. The general attitude toward homoerotic behaviours must be seen as divided: whereas one group loudly advocated the reinforcement of the Chrysostome doctrine, characterized by hostility to sodomists, the official church showed a lack of concern, refusing to impose particular sanctions. Boswell (1980, 228) goes so far as to claim that the twelfth-century theologians who addressed questions involving sexuality had, consciously or not, completely decriminalized homosexual relations. This period also saw the rebirth of a homosexual subculture, and the tenth, eleventh, and even twelfth centuries may be viewed as centuries of tolerance and liberalism, in which sexual pleasure was recognized outside of procreative sexual relations within marriage. In addition, in high society, legitimate wives sometimes lived alongside concubines – in many cases, a large number (Sot 1991, 197).

The Low Middle Ages: The Spread of Repression

The climate of tolerance and liberalism at the end of the High Middle Ages quickly gave way to an attitude of generalized hostility toward minorities. The rise of certain absolute powers, notably ecclesiastical power, seems to have been one of the major factors in this change of attitude (Goodich 1976b, 295). A fascination with order and uniformity was one of the characteristics of the High Middle Ages (see Gauvard 1991), as exemplified by the Inquisition and the Crusades. Homoerotic lifestyles were repressed through criminalization throughout Europe from the thirteenth century to the late eighteenth century (Hergemöller 2006, 63). Far from restraining its discourses on sexuality, society strove to construct a "science of sexuality." Of course, such discourses sought to censure the morals of the time. Nevertheless, the absence of silence with regard to homoerotic sexuality demonstrated society's discomfort with this deviant form of sexuality. The church remained torn with regard to homoerotic love between its need to know – encouraging the sinner's confession – and the risk of what could result – suggesting new sins to the penitent. The use of Latin in French texts is an example of the church's attempt to control the dissemination of information and to avoid piquing sinners' interest (Poirier 1996, 43).

In the High Middle Ages, repression was still not directed exclusively against homosexuals. On the contrary, all minorities were targeted by rules for normalization in the West, and all forms of deviancy and nonconformity were subjected to increasing intolerance. The Council (Latran III) sanctioned moneylenders, heretics, Jews, and mercenaries as well as individuals guilty of homoerotic acts. Repression extended to all behaviours that went against Christian asceticism, which was characterized by rejection of pleasures of the flesh. The work of theologians thus consisted of legitimizing links among heresy, sins against nature, and foreigners (Muslims or Jews) (Chiffoleau 1990, 300; Goodich 1976b, 295).

Crimes against Nature and St. Thomas Aquinas

Christian influence was clearly present in the High Middle Ages: religious prescriptions, based mainly on theological notions of nature and crimes against nature, were the most powerful agents of repression. All of the criminal treaties that condemned acts against nature up to the late eighteenth century were based on Genesis. Strongly influenced by the Christian church, medieval society elaborated a litany of municipal, feudal, and royal laws against sodomists. St. Thomas Aquinas designated as crimes against nature all sexual practices that deviated from the function of procreation. This conception of sexual nature, far from being solely theological, had Aristotelian naturalist foundations. St. Thomas Aquinas felt that homoerotic behaviours had to be repressed along with masturbation, fellatio, and unconventional heterosexual relations (that is, in positions other than the missionary position). Following Thomist logic, homosexuality could not be considered the most serious crime in the hierarchy of sexual offences. In effect, masturbation and foreplay (preliminaries without penetration), which departed from both the reproductive goal and procreative symbolism, were classified above homoerotic behaviours because the latter, although they did not allow for procreation, at least symbolized the reproductive sexual exchange. On the other hand, unlike other forms of acts against nature, which were practised by a large share of the population, homoerotic behaviours could more easily be associated with foreigners, the perfect scapegoats for those in power.

The Sodomist: A Perfect Scapegoat

Historical evidence confirms that repression of homoerotic behaviours has been a preferred tool among political powers throughout history. On the one hand, those who were given to homoerotic behaviours served as scapegoats for scourges such as the plague, famine, floods, and earthquakes. "Famines, wars, plagues, mortalities, floods of water, treasons and losses of kingdoms, and much other mischief" were the blights that could be visited upon infidels, preached Jean Gerson in his penitentials (quoted in Poirier 1996, 33, our translation).[10] As in the times of Emperor Justinian, the association between sin and natural catastrophe was prominent in the public imagination; for example, the Black Plague of 1348-50 was perceived by a number of preachers as God's punishment for laxity of the flesh. Sodomy was thus exposed as a double threat to the repopulation of Europe (see Spencer 1995, 128; Tamagne 2001, 17).

Homoerotic lifestyles also became a pretext for repression of certain social groups. Easily likened to the crime of *lèse-majesté*, homoerotic lifestyles were highly stigmatized and allowed the enemy to be discredited, sentenced, and punished and his property to be seized with the relative support of the community. The medievalist historian Claude Gauvard (1991, 597, our translation) states that this was "a propaganda theme using well-known stereotypes against heretics." Like heretics, sodomists and Muslims were always described as coming from the East. The example of Muslims is revealing. With the failure of the Crusades, Muslims were accused of practising unbridled sodomy and presented as a threat to Europe. They were suspected of raping children, adolescents, old people, and even bishops (Chiffoleau 1990, 298-99).

Jacques Chiffoleau (1990, 302, our translation) observes, "The conjuncture of *nefandum crimen,* heresy, and *crimen majestatis* was accentuated during the thirteenth century. The word *'bougre'* then began to designate, in the West, in addition to 'Bulgarians' (Bulgarians were all, it goes without saying, Asian heretics), Western Manicheans and sodomists. In the 1230s and 1240s this comparison became a constant, at least in northern France." Repression of homosexuals was not, however, uniform throughout the kingdom. Whereas bestiality was a greater concern among judges in the north, sodomy was a primary concern in the south, as a result of the situation prevailing in Italy.[11] Claude Gauvard (1991, 597) notes that there were nevertheless few cases of homosexuality and bestiality in letters of remission; she estimates the proportion at less than 0.5 percent of all crimes. It may seem bizarre to the contemporary reader that the criminal law of the time freely associated sodomy and bestiality, which as crimes against nature were in fact considered equal with regard to sentence management. This should be remembered when some cases of bestiality are raised.

Because it could be used to discredit the Other, the foreigner, sodomy thus became an extra pretext for repressing infidels. The association between sodomists and heretics, which apparently dates back to 1114, reinforced the image of "homosexuals" as enemies of Christianity. This is why, as Chiffoleau (1990, 299, our translation) rightly observes, the category of *nefandum crimen* – unnameable crimes – inexorably became "the border between the fundamental theological and political space that was Christianity and the particular consistency of power relations that were deployed there." Poirier (1996, 103-4) mentions in this regard that Renaissance explorers almost always described non-Christian peoples as brutal people who practised sodomy and child abduction. The "sodomy-Other-foreigner-heretic" association made its way into the collective imagination: throughout this historical period, sodomy was associated with witchcraft, heresy, sacrilege, and sometimes incest. This is why Muslims and heretics, the two greatest threats to security presented to European public opinion, were characterized as men given to homoerotic lifestyles. Thus, it is obvious that alleged sodomists were effective scapegoats and tools for denigration of the frightening Other. Historians have uncovered a number of eloquent examples, including the Cathars and, especially, the Freemasons. In the early fourteenth century, Freemasonry was the wealthiest and most powerful religious order in Europe and the envy of various secular powers and ecclesiastical circles. In the late thirteenth century (1285), when Philip the Fair acceded to the throne of France – a country desperate for money and territory – he ordered the arrest of the order's members and the seizure of its assets. To justify his action – which was economic and political in nature, it goes without saying – he first launched a vast campaign of defamation in which the Freemasons were associated with heresy, sodomy, and Muslims; he was well aware that the accusation of sodomy – as a moral pretext – constituted a formidable weapon for casting his enemies in an odious light.

The combination of "heretic, Muslim, and sodomist" was to play an important role in a number of other defamatory campaigns against enemies of those in power. The fall of Edward II of England in the early fourteenth century (1312) shows how effectively sodomy could be used to discredit an enemy and, at the same time, legitimize his condemnation (Zeikowitz 2003, 113-18). King Henry III of France suffered a similar fate during his reign in the late sixteenth century (1574-89), when the Polish accused him of indulging in "French morals." This campaign of disparagement of the king's sexual penchants also had effects within France: his effeminacy and taste for sodomy were presented as symptoms of deterioration of the kingdom's social and economic condition.[12] The accusation of sodomy was thus used successfully throughout history by different powers to denigrate foreigners and enemies (De Becker 1967; Hergemöller 2006; Teasley 1987). Put forth first as an Arabian taste (eleventh century), then as a French vice (thirteenth century), and then as an Italian penchant (fourteenth and fifteenth centuries), sodomy allowed foreign cultures to be defamed. "In Asia and America," observes the historian of homosexualities Florence Tamagne (2001, 24, our translation), "the accusation of sodomy [was] a means of categorizing the indigene as inferior," foreign, or enemy. The example of the religious struggles between the Protestants and Catholics was relatively comical, as each party accused the other of tolerating, or even practising, sodomy. The repression of homoerotic lifestyles fits perfectly with what Foucault (1979) describes as political operators, in which repression has a privileged role in power dynamics.

It must be kept in mind, however, that this type of offence was viewed as minor compared with crimes such as Satanism, witchcraft, and heresy; witchcraft and theft were at the top of the hierarchy, far above homicide and rape (Bullough 1974a, 193; Gauvard 1991, ch. 18; Lagrange 1995, 64). In fact, there were few convictions for sodomy in France during this period

(Gauvard 1991, 597-98), and no sodomist was burned at the stake during the reign of Louis IX (1226-70)[13] or during the reigns of Philip IV (1285-1314) and Philip V (1316-22), except for Freemasons. These penal statistics must be viewed with caution, however, since it was customary to burn all documents relating to the arrest, trial, and judgment of the guilty party. Gauvard (1991, 792, our translation) also notes that the lists of crimes, even the most "outrageous," varied from charter to charter and that the charters were valid only for a precise locality. "The application of penalties, far from clarifying legal policy," she adds, "further increased the confusion. Disorder reigned over prevention. Although outrageous cases necessitated incarceration, since they threatened the security of society, the rule was not always strictly applied." The judge's discretionary power seems to have limited the formal imposition of penalties. One thing does seem certain: there was no "witch hunt" for sodomists.

The Renaissance: Philosophical Repression, Legal Tolerance[14]

During the Renaissance, a distinction began to be made between homoerotic acts (sodomy) and homosexual desire (virile love). The images of the bisexual and the libertine dominated the collective imagination until the seventeenth century. As a general rule, sodomists were seen as married bisexuals who were sexually attracted to both women and boys. Their masculinity – even virility – was not in question. The figure of the sodomist was gradually transformed into "an effeminate man who likes only young, virile men" (Hekma 1994, 182-83, our translation). This bisexuality, tolerated among the elite until the seventeenth century, was then "pointed out as a threat to the family unit, which was the new guarantor of social order, the only refuge of the love life" (Tamagne 2001, 54, our translation). Homoerotic behaviours – for these were still the behaviours in question – were subject to continued repression since they upset the hierarchy of sexes and genders and endangered the social order, which was based on male domination.

Thus, a generally repressive institutional discourse was built against homoerotic lifestyles, although it did not dwell on unmasking and punishing sodomists in particular. On the contrary, there was a certain form of renewal of "homosexual art and imagery." As Poirier (1996, 18, our translation) notes, it is difficult to assess the real influence of social discourses in the Renaissance era: "The idea of being able to summarize what was said in late-Renaissance French society about sodomy or unnatural acts is thus completely impossible." Such conclusions apply, "rather, to what was probably described and imagined at the time by theologians, jurists, pamphleteers, memorialists, and poets."

With regard to intervention by the justice system, the fifteenth, sixteenth, and seventeenth centuries were characterized by tolerance of homoerotic lifestyles. The repression was more symbolic than real; homoerotic lifestyles were repressed and proscribed in official discourse but downplayed in legal practice. "The reality fell far below the jurists' discourse, which might be termed incendiary" (Godard 2001, 201, our translation). Jean-Claude Guillebaud (1999, 22) observes that historians have listed only thirty-eight cases of capital punishment for homoerotic acts carried out between 1317 and 1789, most of them involving young people.[15] M. Guyot (1785, 337) lists only eight sentencings for sodomy in France between 1519 and 1783. Ludovico Hernandez (1920) reports ten more cases of sodomy, eight of which also involved a violent crime, and Alfred Soman (1984) lists 177 trials for sodomy and bestiality in the jail logs of the palace caretaker. As Michael D. Sibalis (2006a, 212) rightly points out, although these data are incomplete, they show that "harsh repression was the exception rather than the rule." In comparison, Chiffoleau (1990, 311, our translation) notes evidence of 10,000 accusations of sodomy in Florence in the fifteenth century, resulting in 2,000 convictions (many involving large fines), with respect to which the "night officers, in the sentencing notes, always mixed familiar themes: offences against the Crown, crimes against nature, safety, and the health of the city."

Therefore, in France sodomists were punished only when scandal became inevitable and the political order felt that it was under threat. Public and exemplary punishment was used only if these sexual acts were seen and recognized as such by the population. Poirier (1996, 58), referring to Pierre de L'Estoile, a seventeenth-century memorialist, observes that only the most serious cases, those that involved known personalities and foreigners or were perpetrated in conjunction with other, more serious crimes such as child abduction or murder, were brought to justice. Repression was directed only against those who did not belong to the community. Once again, history indicates that repression of homoerotic lifestyles was associated mainly with foreigners and child abusers, those figures of the frightening Other. As the feared common enemy and pariah, the figure of the sodomist strengthened the sense of belonging to the community. The perfect scapegoat, he thus drew attention away from problematic social conditions (see Godard 2001, 201; Mead 1918, 602).

2

The Grande Ordonnance of 1670 to the British Conquest

THE SODOMIST AND THE STAKE

In general fashion, repression dominates all law in lower societies.
It is because religion completely pervades judicial life, as it does,
indeed, all social life.

– Émile Durkheim, *The Division of Labor in Society*

There was not a single criminal law treaty, up to the late
eighteenth century, that did not refer in the preamble to the
story of Genesis to justify, if it could, the unprecedented force
of the law. More than one treaty of religious morals was based on
the thousand-times-repeated pronouncement of the biblical fable
of the Forbidden. Thus the son of Sodom was to cease to infest
the air that he breathed and rediscover his primal innocence in
the midst of the flames.

– Maurice Lever, *Les Bûchers de Sodome* (our translation)

In the second half of the Middle Ages, religious discourse began to strongly condemn homoerotic customs. Those in power repeatedly used sodomists as scapegoats for social ills or to discredit enemies. Nevertheless,
convictions in the courts remained a rare occurrence. Did this situation
continue to prevail in France and New France in the seventeenth and
eighteenth centuries? What discourses transcended these two societies and
imposed their visions of social control? What heritage did medieval
feudal justice pass on to seventeenth-century France? And were there
distinctions between the parent country and the colony in the control of

homoerotic lifestyles? If yes, what were they and how can they be explained? In this chapter, I attempt to answer these questions.[1]

France and Its Sodomists: The Paradox of an Unnameable Crime

An analysis of the repression of sodomy immediately reveals a paradox: how is it that this crime, "so disgusting, and so capable of alarming our Readers' decency" (Muyart de Vouglans 1780, our translation)[2] – even "the Church Priests found this crime so horrible that they did not want to give it a name" (Des Maisons 1667, our translation) – was sometimes put in the foreground of the legal ritual? Custom had it that trial transcripts were burned in order to commit this crime against nature to oblivion.[3] Thus, as the historian Pascal Bastien (2005, 45, our translation) notes, even though sodomy was considered by the legal system to be "one of the most horrible crimes on Earth" and was repressed by fire "as an example of the punishment that divine justice metes out," it proved to be more "stifled than vigorously condemned, as the magistrates preferred to quash a crime for which the exemplary nature of the sentence, they thought, might be inspiring as much as frightening." Thus the great majority of sodomists arrested by the police (constables or neighbourhood commissioners) did not become involved with the legal system. These "delinquents" were sent directly to one of the Parisian prisons (Bastille, Châtelet, For-L'Évêque, Hôtel de la Force), to medical institutions (Bicêtre for men, Salpetrière for women, Charenton for the insane), or to religious establishments such as Saint-Lazare (Merrick and Ragan Jr. 2001, 31).

Thus, "in practice, only homosexuals caught in the act or denounced to the magistrate were brought before the lieutenant general" (Lever 1985, 200, our translation). One example was the sentence of burning at the stake handed down to Jean Diot and Bruno Lenoir, who had been found "in the streets in the evening in flagrante delicto, pants down, for the purpose of buggery" (Barbier 1750, our translation). Given this aggravating circumstance, and probably because their crime had been committed in public, public repression (of a generally private and secret crime) was difficult to avoid, and these two men were burned.[4] However, noted the Parisian lawyer and chronicler Edmond-Jean-François Barbier in 1750 (our translation), "the judgment was not protested, apparently to spare the name and nature of the crime." This fact, as Pascal Bastien (2005, 48, our translation) justly notes, was a "no doubt fundamental detail that clearly conveys the magistrates' uneasiness with punishing a crime against morals that was difficult to control," for the police were concentrating more on the restraint of sexual activities that took place in public and on prevention of the corruption of minors than on eradication of sodomy. In the case of men discovered "in flagrante delicto," consummation of the act was not necessary; simply "making a move" on someone was enough to be brought in for questioning.

The police employed certain stratagems in order to "know about" and flush out these "undesirables." The use of snitches – commonly called *mouches*[5] – spies, and other informers was common. For example, Michel Rey (1989, 131) shows that in 1715, two Parisian police officers were assigned to stalking sodomists, and they hired, with the approval of the lieutenant general, provocateurs in order to obtain as much information as possible on these individuals: "For hours on end, police observers were on the lookout for those cruising for a sex partner" (Rey 1987, 179).[6] Policing of morals was instituted in the early eighteenth century – in Paris, at least.[7] Denunciation played an important role in the legal process, particularly in the search for information on potential suspects. The police and constabulary encouraged denunciations by occasionally rewarding informers and concealing, as a general rule, the identity of denouncers.[8] Police reports show that making a denunciation was the primary condition for being released, which also fostered an escalation in denunciations. As Michael D. Sibalis (2006a, 221) observes, "More ordinary men could win release by giving up the names of other sodomites or by getting family, friends, neighbours or employers to petition on their behalf." Denunciation became a preferred tool for defaming one's enemies and, in some cases, having them incarcerated,[9] thus opening sodomists to the threat of being blackmailed by their adversaries. Of course, all of these means of denunciation made it possible to compile a vast body of information on sodomists and other pariahs. In 1725, a "Master List" was created to keep track of sodomists and their relationships. Lieutenant General Lenoir estimated that there were twenty thousand sodomists in Paris. According to Maurice Lever (1985, 252), these databases were very useful to police officers; once the morals brigades were created in 1720, more than five thousand individuals of both sexes – pederasts, vagabonds, unemployed people, and prostitutes

– were brought in for questioning in less than eight days. The arrest of sodomists, pederasts, and muckrakers became an everyday occurrence,[10] although convictions in court were rare (Merrick and Ragan Jr. 2001, 31).

In other words, although the mental image of "homosexual crime" conveys the idea of rigorous repression, the reality of court cases reveals, instead, justice that was indulgent, unresponsive, or discreet and rarely spectacular (Bastien 2005, 46). As Michel Foucault (1979, 32) explains, there was a large gap between the arsenal of terror available to the justice system and the application of that arsenal. In comparison to its strongly repressive criminal doctrine, the Ancien Régime had a practice of leniency, with cases often settled out of court. Georges Vigarello (2001, 27-28) gives a good illustration of this when he shows that few cases of rape, in the absence of murder or serious physical injury, led to an exemplary sentence. The same was true for repression of homoeroticism, for which only seven sodomists were punished by burning at the stake during the eighteenth century.[11] On the other hand, the creation of the position of police lieutenant general in 1667 and the formation of teams of spies charged with finding and arresting pederasts in public meeting places testify to a real desire to control and suppress homoerotic acts. According to Rey (1989, 133), "In the second half of the century, a police inspector was specially charged with the surveillance of the known places where sodomites congregated." And although there were some arrests for sodomy in Paris – 44 in 1723, 146 in 1737-38, and 244 in 1749 – there were obvious exaggerations in the police reports of the time with regard to sodomists. This also conveys a societal anxiety, or at least uneasiness, with regard to this type of "deviant" sexual behaviour.

Three Scenarios: Settling out of Court, Banishment Order, Burning at the Stake

The historian Pascal Bastien and I found three scenarios in our examination of sentences and legal procedures for cases of sodomy. In the first, which was the most common, the sodomist was not sued and the affair was settled out of court (thus, as Vigarello notes [2001, 32], sodomy was both quietly ignored and loudly condemned). This procedure was the prerogative mainly of gentlemen, since justice assessed the seriousness of the crime according to the rank and social network of the accused.[12] According to Michel Delon (1987, 122-23), "Trial records show that aristocratic privilege was equivalent to immunity." In effect, starting in the sixteenth century, the formula of "punishment according to the quality of the person" predominated: the penalty incurred for a particular crime varied according to the accused person's social status. Whereas sodomy was tolerated among the nobility, it was more often punishable at the stake or in prison for the bourgeoisie and working class.[13]

Next was incarceration of "sodomists" by orders of banishment – that is, by direct royal justice that avoided triggering the legal process and kept the scandal quiet for the defendant and his family.[14] The individual's reputation was thus preserved, and this was essential, especially in working-class districts where people lived cheek by jowl (Rey 1989, 144). Here, families played a fundamental role in the fate reserved for the sodomist, for, following questioning, they were the ones who had the leisure of calling upon the lieutenant general to request incarceration or release. Justice acted as referee rather than as judge and executioner, observes Bastien (2005, 46). The lieutenant general of the police and his commissioners thus served as a filter between criminal justice and the resulting public opinion since the fate reserved for sodomists by royal justice was a direct result of their intervention. They were the ones who decided to bring suspects in, to interrogate them, and, finally, to send them to the magistrates for justice or not. In the name of the king, source of all justice, they held authority to stop "proceedings (letter of mercy), withdraw the case from the normally designated judges, and even organize a parallel repression (right of evocation)" (Tulkens and van de Kerchove 1993, 63, our translation).

The last possibility was sentencing the sodomist on appeal. In this case, three penalties were possible: (1) he was sent to the Bicêtre hospital for a prison sentence; (2) he enlisted in the king's army, promising not to repeat his offence(!);[15] or (3) he received an exemplary sentence: the guillotine or the gallows. Although the third option was rarely used, it was the one that captured the public's imagination. For example, Léonard Moreuil was hanged and burned on 16 July 1633 after being found guilty of rape and sodomy on victims aged thirteen and fourteen years, and Félix Simon was burned alive on 24 November 1650 for poisoning and raping his victim, as was Philippe Bouvet de La Contamine on 30 March 1677 for child abduction, rape, sodomy, blasphemy, and resisting justice. Maurice Violain was put to death on 28 November 1678 for the rape of a seventeen-year-old boy, and René du Tertre was condemned to burn at the stake on 19 January 1680 for sodomizing his young son. Interestingly, the guilty parties were never put to death expressly for the act of sodomy. Certainly, sodomy was an "aggravating circumstance," but it was not "responsible" for the death sentence.

In light of these convictions, one might easily believe that it was an assault on a youth that provoked the death sentence. Yet, the moral contamination associated with sodomy was so defamatory that the law generally condemned both the child seduced and the adult seducer. Both the agent and the victim became outlaws, since they had "made nature blush." Bastien (2005, 46, our translation) nuances this interpretation, noting that sodomists were put to death, whereas the victims of the rape (those who had been sodomized), often the ones who made the complaint, "were almost always released and compensated by the confiscation of the assets of those condemned." Nevertheless, the strength of the contagious degeneration produced by sodomy inevitably corrupted each actor. As a general rule, even when the boy was the victim of the "unnatural" violence (rape with sodomy), justice dwelled on the crime and the moral contamination, not on the violence suffered. "The child who 'yielded,' even to violence, was already 'corrupted,' lost to debauchery, conquered by evil, which explains the suspicion and the frequent absence of any investigation into his degree of responsibility," observes Vigarello (2001, 34). The exception was children under twelve years of age; their young age enabled them to escape the death penalty. Lever (1985, 220, our translation) further qualifies this observation by specifying that justice hesitated, in spite of everything, to deliver young people under sixteen years of age to the guillotine or the gallows. He cites the case of Isaac du Tremble, thirteen years old, who in 1667 was "accused and convicted of letting himself be known carnally and sodomistically by said Claude Fabre," but "the Court, in view of his youth and of the request and plea that he made to the Court to leave the Religion that claims to be Reformed that he had professed, orders that he be confined to a prison, with flogging, with bread and water, for two months. At the end of this time, he shall be freed." Du Tremble was considered to be both a victim, due to his young age, and an accomplice, or at least guilty, in the eyes of the law since he was now contaminated by the misdeed. In fact, medical science of the time attempted to provide treatment for such carnally corrupted youths. In this case, it appears that young

Isaac's promise of reconversion to Catholicism was the main factor in his avoiding the death penalty. Was this an example of the law serving the church? Perhaps, since the French Catholic Church held great sway over the morality of its flock due notably to the support of the royalty, which felt that the clergy provided the basis for social cohesion.

How can this uniformity in the treatment of sodomy cases during the last two centuries of the Ancien Régime be explained? Is it possible that in the seventeenth century the magistracy was quite indulgent with regard to sodomy but had strongly and spectacularly to repress sodomists occasionally in order to give its subjects the impression that it was controlling morals more rigorously than it was in fact?[16] For, of course, the Ancien Régime's justice system depended on its "arsenal of terror" – its capacity to conduct torture – to frighten and dissuade the population. Such exemplary and bloody rituals in no way reflected the daily workings of the justice system; on the contrary, episodes of violent torture often served to mask its relative paralysis. This sacrificial justice system served, rather, to weave the social fabric by imposing its representations of the social order, of good and evil. It had to induce the public to submit and consent to the established order.

This, no doubt, is why sodomy remained a crime for which, in general, notoriety through public execution was to be avoided, a crime that it was preferable to punish discreetly "because of the indecency of these sorts of examples, which teach young people what they do not know," according to Barbier (1750, our translation). Sodomy therefore appears to have been punished in two different ways that seem difficult to reconcile. On the one hand, sodomy alone led to discreet imprisonment (in Paris, at For-l'Évêque, Saint-Lazare, or Bicêtre). On the other hand, when sodomy was added to a violent crime, the punishment became exemplary, and the act of sodomy, rather than the blood crime, was placed in the foreground of the penal ritual. The famous Deschauffours sentence is a good example of this paradoxical practice. Although Benjamin Deschauffours was found guilty of poisoning and murder, he was publicly punished solely for "having committed the crime of Sodomy." Only the sentence for the crime of sodomy was printed and posted by the Parisian police, even though the original sentence also mentioned "other outrageous and detestable crimes" (Barbier 1750, our translation). In other words, the act of violence was subsumed within the crime against nature.

Sodomy: A Crime of Divine Lèse-Majesté

In short, up to the end of the eighteenth century, sodomists in France received the death penalty only when they were convicted of a violent crime or murder[17] that, alone, would suffice for the sentence. But why stage an execution for the crime of sodomy when this was not the crime that had provoked the event? Where is the logic of *nefandum crimen* in such a practice? Why avoid publicly sentencing sodomists while agreeing to make sodomy a horrible crime, very severely punished, when violence and murder, the true causes of the death sentence, would have had to be associated with the sexual act – at the very least – to justify the magistrates' decision?

The Durkheimian approach to the evolution of criminal law offers some ideas for interpretation. According to Émile Durkheim (1964), the rarer the type of crime, the more severely it will be punished. Violence was common and a part of daily life in French society under the Ancien Régime. Vigarello (2001, 9) notes this familiarity with physical violence; it was "a world where the shedding of blood did not always trigger legal proceedings, where sword-thrusts still had their financial compensation and deliberate murders their inevitability." Like Durkheim, Vigarello hypothesizes that the unremarkable nature of violent acts corresponded to the low rate of prosecution for them. In other words, rape, murder, and other forms of physical violence, because they were everyday occurrences, did not raise the ire of the public and the judges.

Again following Durkheim's logic, sodomy had to be heavily punished because it was a crime against morality, not a crime against the person – that is, an offence that contravened the sacred order due to its transgression of divine laws (crime against nature). Farge (1993, 179, emphasis added) explains that the sacrificial system of the Ancien Régime "can only owe its explanation to the individual and collective religious acts *taking place at the same time.*" In fact, treatises and jurisprudence regularly referred to Sodom and Gomorrah in their justification of severe and exemplary punishments for sodomy. Some texts defined sodomy as a challenge to God, a crime of divine lèse-majesté. In his *Traité des matières criminelles suivant l'ordonnance du mois d'août 1670*, Du Rousseau de la Combe (1756, 32, our translation) stipulates, "Of all the crimes of lust, it is the most serious and most detestable to divine and human law." Thus it was the religious character of the act of sodomy that legitimized strong and spectacular repression. Durkheim hypothesizes that sodomy, because it contravened divine law, became at the same time an offence against the community, given the omnipresence of religion in all spheres of society and its strong influence on individuals. Torture thus had the function of publicly and strongly avenging the common conscience, reaffirming divine power, and re-establishing the community certainties that had been undermined. To exact vengeance through punishment when the public conscience was upset by an unthinkable behaviour – this was the rule of the justice system. When it came to exemplary punishment, there was no hierarchy in acts committed since they were all irrational and contravened the law of God. As Farge (1993, 179, emphasis added) summarizes,

> The ritualization of the death penalty also required one to see no difference where differences did in fact exist. Given the arbitrary dispensation of the death penalty, it was essential that a domestic theft should not be deemed less culpable in the eyes of the public than a parricide or a rape for example. In that spacious wasteland created by the royal authority and the supreme punishment, *absolutely nothing had to interfere with the acts committed there, not even a hierarchy.*

Because physical violence (murder or rape) did not outrage the common conscience, it seemed appropriate for the justice system to punish sodomy, an odious crime against nature, a crime that offended the community as a whole. As had been the case in the Middle Ages, human life was worth little compared to crimes related to the sacred, observes Claude Gauvard (1991, 797). Furthermore, when the rapist was punished, he was always presented as a horrible monster of nature and associated with the contempt of God (Vigarello 2001, 15). Rape was thus no longer a crime against the person or an act of violence but was transformed into an offence against divine morality that provoked disgust and required public vengeance. This is why Durkheim (1900, 91, our translation) suggests that "while, in general, crime was conceived essentially as an offence directed against divinity, crimes committed by man against man were also designed on this model. I believe that they revolt us as well because they are forbidden by the gods and therefore outrage them." Similarly, for sodomy, "the bill of indictment mentioned only the crime that offended against morality and religion, omitting whatever might have injured the victim and his body" (Vigarello 2001, 34). Under the morality of the time, the law thus masked physical violence (murder or rape) and placed in the foreground moral fault – crimes against divine law and the community. Because violence was a common and everyday occurrence in society, justice was diverted to the act of profanation and impiety: sodomy.

Thus, repression was relatively gentle; after all, sodomists were rarely taken to court, as the justice system preferred to conceal the crime (even though it offended the common conscience) rather than expiate it as a society. In this regard, Foucault's (1979, 47-48) presentation of the political aspect that surrounded the power to punish is instructive. He rightly conceives of legal torture as a political ritual. To paraphrase him, one might hypothesize that it was not sensitivity to homoeroticism that changed but the policy regarding this type of crime. If ritualized torture was a political operator, this partially explains why the use of the death sentence was limited to pederasts who raped and murdered children.

The struggle with the same problem as the confessor faced with the penitent's sexuality – "how to uncover traces of sin without thereby teaching it to a perhaps still-pure soul" (Rey 1989, 138; see also Bechtel 1994; Delumeau 1992) – explains the use of official legal discourse. And although the stated purpose of this discourse was to punish a crime "the horror and abomination of which horrify nature itself," as Muyart de Vouglans (1780, our translation) asserted, it surfaced only when the criminal presented a direct threat to the public order through murder or assault. It was then, and only then, that the sexual act was brought forth. When the blood crime led to the gallows, it was the sodomist, enemy of God, who was presented to the crowd, not the murderer.[18] Sodomy, a dark, unnatural act, was thus deeply rooted in an imagination of horror – as the republications of François de Rosset's seventeenth-century *Histoires tragiques* show – in which public punishment paradoxically sits alongside the secret surrounding this unnameable crime. "There had long been no executions for this crime, and this provided some hope for those who were infatuated with this crime against nature," wrote Barbier (1750, our translation) on the putting to death of Deschauffours, adding that the public penalty might teach "many youths what they do not know." This curious opposition was conveyed by justice, was perceived by the public, and has often been retailed with confusion by historiographers.[19]

New France and Its "Despicable" Homosexuals

The justice system in New France was, in many ways, an extension of the French one: its legal structures, edicts, and ordinances followed the Custom of Paris.[20] Legal power was exerted via the Sovereign Council, created in 1663, most of whose officers of the court came from the parent country and referred to the criminal Grande Ordonnance of 1670. As was the case in France, denunciation (the triggering element for the legal system to come into play) and admission (the ultimate evidence) played a primordial role in the legal procedure of the time. Yet, due to the omnipresent violence in settlers' lives, the insufficiency of the police forces, and the fact that 80 percent of the population lived on remote farms – which reduced considerably the effectiveness of intervention by civil and religious administrations – denunciations and convictions in court were not common. The police force for the immense territory was woefully inadequate: in the eighteenth century, it comprised only some fifteen officers, sometimes assisted by a few soldiers (Lachance 1985, 9). The number of individuals brought before the courts thus represented only a tiny proportion of the real deviance, as the courts did not have the means to absorb all the cases.

As André Cellard (2000, 6) observes, in New France, as in France, "because criminals were rarely caught, it was believed that one had to make the most of punishment so that its severity and violence would make its mark on the imagination"; therefore, "expeditious and not very onerous, exemplary justice appeared all the more appropriate" for public authorities. In other words, the severity of the penalties was inversely proportional to the effectiveness of the legal system. Harsh public punishment of the few cases of serious crimes in order to make examples of them was the golden rule of the justice system. In this regard, the law was very clear: "'Vengeance,' someone wrote, is prohibited for men and it is only the King who can exercise it through his officers by virtue of the authority that he holds from God" (Cellard 2000, 2). Now, implementation of the penal system had to be interpreted not as a consequence of a normative rule but as a power play that enabled the one who held it to impose his vision of social order.

Crimes against Morals

In New France, the seventeenth and eighteenth centuries were marked by a strong doctrine of sexual repression due, at least in part, to the increased presence of the church in settlers' daily life. The state and the church worked together to regulate and purify morals in the colony. On the other hand, the application of the legal rules suggests the low priority that judges accorded to crimes against morals. André Lachance (1985, 15) has shown that 73 percent of offences processed in the lower court led to a light penalty or a discharge that closed the case.

From a quantitative point of view, there were fewer prosecutions for morals offences in the eighteenth century than in the seventeenth. "Morals cases" designated an amalgam of offences that included adultery, indecency, bigamy, bestiality, cohabitation, debauchery, fornication, incest, pimping, prostitution, child kidnapping for seduction, sodomy, vagrancy, and rape. Robert-Lionel Séguin (1972, 503-6) counted 105 court cases for moral offences during the seventeenth century, ranking this category in second place, after crimes against the person, with 21.1 percent of all crimes committed and recorded.[21] Lachance (1984, 53) found 55 people taken to court for these offences in the eighteenth century, representing only 5 percent of indictments brought before the royal courts of New France and making them, with the exception of crimes of divine lèse-majesté, the rarest type of offence. According to Lachance (1984, 54), these rates were similar to those for crimes against morals in France.

The drop in repression in the seventeenth and eighteenth centuries may be surprising given that social conditions (increases in both population and police) in the eighteenth century should have favoured a rise. The paucity of cases, the absence of accusations for a variety of crimes against morals, and the small number of defendants constitute, according to Lachance (1984, 54, our translation), "a series of corresponding indications that French Canadian society, like French society, was tolerant. As violations of sexual morality were less and less a source of indignation and scandal, they were less often brought to justice." More likely, however, these statistics are a clue to how difficult it was for the forces of order to apprehend people for these crimes given their low numbers and the extent of the territory. Although they were strongly repressed by criminal doctrine, crimes against morals were rarely brought to justice.

Homosexual Crimes: A Rare Occurrence[22]

Following the trend for crimes against morals, homoerotic acts were rarely criminalized in New France. Only three cases (five indictments) of unnatural acts were found under the French regime in Quebec before the British Conquest, all in the seventeenth century. The last of these was a case of bestiality; I discuss it here nevertheless because it was strongly associated in the public imagination with the repression of sodomists as criminals against nature. The first case of an unnatural act recorded among whites in New France dates from 1648. It involved the soldier René Huguet, known as Le Tambour (the drum of the French troops).[23] The Maisonneuve court sentenced him to capital punishment. The Jesuits were opposed to this penalty and demanded a second trial, in Quebec City. The accused used his right to appeal and had a second trial. This time, the death sentence was replaced by a prison sentence. This penalty was changed yet again due to unforeseen circumstances: since the colony no longer had an executioner, Huguet was offered a pardon if he agreed to fill this thankless role.

The second trial having to do with homoerotic acts took place in the summer of 1691. It began with a complaint submitted by the Sulpician Dollier de Casson, superior of the seminary of the Island of Montreal, to Chevalier Louis Hector de Callière, then governor of the Island of Montreal. According to the complainant, "Nicolas Daucy dit St-Michel, Lieutenant of a Company of the Navy detachment, Jean Forgeron dit la Roze, and Jean Filio dit Dubois, soldiers in Companies of said detachment, are accused of having committed the crime of Sodomy" (*Jugements du Conseil souverain*, vol. 3, 558, our translation). The accused parties were soon arrested and questioned on their private relationships. They refused to admit to their "crimes," and Saint-Michel refused to co-operate. He demanded to be judged by the Sovereign Council, not by the Montreal court. His request was heard on 12 November of that year. This time, Saint-Michel co-operated but was nevertheless found guilty "of having debauched a number of men, and having fallen into despicable and shameful acts to reach this bad end." His sentence was banishment from the colony for life and a fine of 200 pounds to be paid in alms.[24] Because they agreed to co-operate at the beginning of the trial, la Roze and Dubois were transferred from the prison in Montreal to the one in the town of Quebec, where their trial was held. The court found them guilty, sentenced them, respectively, to three and two years of prison, and forbade them to repeat the offence.[25] It reprimanded them for "having consented to shameful attachments and actions of said Saint-Michel for an amount of time during which they could have withdrawn or called for help" (*Jugements du Conseil souverain*, vol. 3, 558, our translation). As in France, both the criminal and his victim had to be punished for their offence, the act being so odious that it risked perverting the one who had suffered it.

The third and last trial for a crime against nature found in New France took place on 28 May 1697. The Sovereign Council heard a case of bestiality brought by the king's procurer.[26] The complaint had been made against François Judicth dit Rencontre. The court found him guilty of bestiality two months later and sentenced him to an exemplary penalty even though he refused to respond to the accusations. The guilty party was to be hanged then burned in a public square with all of his court transcripts.

> For reparation of which the Condemned to be taken and Removed from the Royal prisons of this city by the Executioner of High Justice Taken nude in a Shirt, a Torch in hand before the main door of the Parish Church in this city and ask the pardon of God the King and Justice for said Crime, then to be taken to the public square of the lower city and there be hanged and Strangled to a potency that the effect will be such that death Follows and Then his body burned with his transcripts all his goods acquired and confiscated to the king the Costs of Justice previously taken from Him. (*Jugements du Conseil souverain*, vol. 4, 111, our translation)

However, as custom had it, in the absence of an admission, the court proceeded to the question extraordinary: admission by torture. As torture did not garner results – the accused continued to proclaim his innocence – the court released him.[27]

In the eighteenth century, homoerotic acts disappeared completely from criminal statistics. No accusation of sodomy has been found from 1700 to 1759. This statistic might indicate that homoerotic lifestyles were so rare that the colony was really not concerned with them. Raymond Boyer (1966, 333, our translation) notes that "crimes of this nature were judged by lay courts, and here again the Sovereign Council showed a commendable tolerance toward the guilty parties." Surprisingly, Séguin (1972, 343, our translation) states that the almost total absence of homoerotic crimes is evidence that there were few pederasts in the colony since "all sorts of things transpired in a colony such as that of Saint-Laurent." He rejects the possibility, much more plausible, that such sexual practices may have taken place in private and away from the eyes of commentators of the time, given the immensity of the territory and the settlers' nomadic way of life. Séguin also posits that the harshness of the country created men brimming with masculinity! According to him, "This sort of effusiveness did not correspond to the type of man that the country forged. The Laurentian colony was a rough country, with a population to match. Soldiers, coureurs des bois, and settlers abounded with virility. The sweet and beautiful did not interest them."

In fact, the panoply of police ordinances and regulations covering homoerotic lifestyles would indicate that such lifestyles were common in the colony, even though the number of accusations and convictions was low. Certain edicts, notably those in the diocese of the town of Quebec, constantly warned the population against unnatural acts. In 1690, Monsignor de Saint-Vallier, the second bishop of Quebec, asked his confessors to be stricter with regard to absolution for the sin of sodomy.[28] In March 1694, the synod assembly of Ville-Marie proclaimed that absolution for the "detestable sins" of sodomy and bestiality was reserved for the bishop.[29] This request was upheld by the *Rituel du diocèse de Québec* in 1703.[30] The main objective of the reservation was to avoid public scandals, and this was no doubt one reason that there were so few publicly notorious cases of sodomy. The logic of *nefandum crimen* applied in the colony, as it did in France. All of the ecclesiastical prescriptions indicate that the issue of homosexuality was well established in public opinion, in spite of the absence of convictions in the courts in the eighteenth century. Although the crime, not the homosexual person, was repressed, sodomists were perceived as contemptible beings – sinners who must be punished or, at least, absolved of their sins by the church. However, it must not be forgotten that the Catholic Church's influence was relatively mitigated in the seventeenth and eighteenth centuries, as the identitary reference linked to Catholicism did not develop until after the British Conquest (Lemieux and Montminy 2000, 15ff).

Some Comparisons between France and New France

The above analysis of trials shows that repression of homoerotic acts remained a rather trivial fact in the justice system: only three trials in over one hundred years (1648-1759) have been found in New France; in France, only a minority of the trials of homosexuals led ultimately to the stake. There were only seven sentences of death by fire during the eighteenth century in France. Paul-François Sylvestre (1983) and Lachance (1984) explain the low rate of denunciation and indictment of sodomists in the colony as being due to greater social tolerance with regard to the sexual habits of the settlers.

In France, especially in Paris, the drop in the number of denunciations and sentences did not keep the public authorities from being concerned about homoerotic lifestyles. As Barbier wrote in his journal in 1726 (our translation), "The vice of buggery has reigned in this country for a long time, and in recent times it has become more fashionable than ever." The testimony gathered by the police and commentators of the time reveals a certain fear of pederasty, particularly among youths. Lever (1985, 224, our translation) has an interesting hypothesis about this: the authorities limited capital punishment for sodomy mainly in an attempt to avoid scandals and, especially, not to draw public attention to a vice the practice of which was feared to be contagious: "It is better not to make a spectacle of what one would prefer to bury in the obscurity of history."

A Need for *Nefandum Crimen?* Between Church Discourse and Judicial Power

In France, both the judiciary and the clergy were torn between the need to mete out harsh punishment for this type of "despicable" behaviour, in order to dissuade the population, and the need to hide it, in order to avoid educating this same population and run the risk of temptation.[31] It was the same in New France. In the first case reported, the accused, René Huguet, known as Le Tambour, avoided the death penalty by becoming the first executioner in the colony – for an unusual and extraordinary reason, it is true, but the result was the same: the absence of public punishment. In the second case, although both "victims," Jean Forgeron dit la Roze, and Jean Filio dit Dubois, were given sentences that were minor and not publicized (short-term imprisonment with the promise not to re-offend), the agent, Nicolas Daucy dit Saint-Michel, was sentenced to banishment. Although banishment was generally accompanied by public exposure or some physical mark, this form of public humiliation was not usually applied and did not catch the community's imagination. Finally, in the last case under consideration here, the accused, François Judicth dit Rencontre, was released after undergoing the question extraordinary. Thus none of the cases reported in New France was "brought to the street," and no capital punishment was carried out for homoerotic lifestyles.

Was it really a concern with *nefandum crimen* that explained the lack of denunciations of homoerotic lifestyles? It is difficult to give a definitive answer. Even if the main desire of the ecclesiastical authorities was to keep this type of offence quiet – as their requests to the colonial legal system to be lenient with sinners and limit exemplary penalties would indicate – how can the multiplication of edicts dealing with specifically this type of sexual behaviour be explained? The edicts allowed for social censure of sodomy and bestiality by the bishop alone. Nevertheless, the warning with regard to confessors – and therefore sinners – seemed to demonstrate the church's desire to understand and better control the morals of its flocks. It is possible that the church was simply concerned with handling this type of sinner itself and saw itself in a sort of competition with lay authorities. In any case, the legal system's tolerance with regard to sodomists in New France – just three cases recorded in almost one hundred years – was counterbalanced by greater intervention by the church, which wished to appropriate pederasts by defining them as sinners who needed to be absolved of their sins.

Although the crime was mainly a religious problem in New France since it was "a violation of natural, divine, and ecclesiastical law" (Boyer 1966, 44, our translation), in Paris it became mostly a legal affair under the authority of the police lieutenant general. Rey (1989, 145) notes that starting in 1738 "even the term sodomite disappeared," and "the police used the term 'pederast' more and more often, making a break from religious discourse."[32] The legal system now found its theoretical support in the writings of physicians and psychiatrists. From sodomy, a moral crime, there was a gradual shift toward inversion, a pathological offence, which inevitably led to a reduction in sanctions, counterbalanced by stronger censure of this type of "anomaly." The laicization of sodomy by the judicial authorities foretold a decrease in the influence of religion and a concomitant rise in that of psychiatric medicine in the spheres of deviance and sexuality. The historian Jean Delumeau observes the advent in the eighteenth century of a "drop in religious and moral conformisms," with philosophers and "scholars" of all stripes helping to create "a certain climate of general disrespect toward the clergy" (quoted in Garnot 1991, 137, our translation). In contrast to the increased secularization of the French justice system, in New France the clergy became a more and more prominent player in the control of deviance. The church's major role in colonization, evangelization, education, and hospital administration conferred on it a certain power and broad oversight respecting everything that affected social and legal regulation of the colony. As Cellard (1991, 59, our translation) notes with regard to the management of madness in New France, the physician was consulted "only after all human and divine remedies had been exhausted."

Whereas in New France the church sought to monopolize the sin of sodomy – probably with the idea of legitimizing, maintaining, and reinforcing a power that it was slowly losing in the parent country – in France it was mainly the justice system that dealt with these cases. According to Rey (1989, 140), "When the clergy did not play their role adequately, the police reacted." The French judiciary preferred to avoid public punishment for homoerotic offences, but in New France the church allowed itself to name, albeit under its breath, the unnameable. On the one hand, the colonial clergy encouraged admission during confession but sought to avoid exemplary legal penalties; on the other hand, the French justice system – in spite of relatively strong police intervention – tried to conceal this type of offence by limiting public executions to cases in which sodomy was associated with violence against a youth. Capital punishment "was no longer viewed as appropriate for the crime of sodomy" (Rey 1989, 141).

Sodomists: A Threat to Youth?

When one reads French trial transcripts, it is easy to see the predominance of cases in which the "victims" are young people and even children. The trials of Jacques Chausson and Jacques Paulmier, Philippe Bouvet de La Contamine, Félix Simon, Antoine Marouër, Claude Fabre, Maurice Violain and Lambert Trippodière, René du Tertre, Jean Baptiste Lebel, Deschauffours, and Jean-François Paschal all involved crimes against youths. In comparison, none of the trials of sodomists in New France mention rape or corruption of youths. How can this absence of "pedophile sodomists" in the colony be explained, when it was precisely this type of sodomist who was sent to the stake in France? Did the situation in France convey the Parisian authorities' fear – for it was mainly in Paris that this took place – that there would be an epidemic of such crimes perpetrated against children? It is difficult to imagine that this was so in the early eighteenth century since the concept of the "child as individual" was just coming into existence (see Ariès 1962). Needless to say, both the active party in and the victim (the child, for example) of the sodomy were severely punished by the law, as the criminal justice system considered sodomy an inevitably contagious evil. Vigarello (2001, 34, 38) stresses this "corruption caused by sexual violence, its power of contagious decay; the young victims were generally regarded as guilty, the moral offence taking precedence over the violent injury ... The participants were steeped in blasphemy, contaminated by the acts performed, immured in the categories of impurity."

If this was the case, it is not unlikely that Parisian justice was fearful of a contagious spread of these unnatural lifestyles in a city in which social control was becoming increasingly difficult to maintain. By punishing, severely and publicly, the "sodomist child rapist" – for it was almost exclusively crimes featuring children that were involved in exemplary punishment[33] – the French legal system may have been seeking mainly to demonize the image of the pederast with the hope of dissuading the population from being converted to this type of sexual behaviour and encouraging its denunciation. Meanwhile, strong social self-regulation was supposed to limit homoerotic assaults on young people in New France. So what was the situation in rural France, where 80 to 90 percent of the French population lived, according to Jean Carpentier and François Lebrun (2000, 159-60) – some 17.9 million rural dwellers estimated in 1675 by Benoît Garnot (1991, 7) (as opposed to approximately 500,000 urban dwellers living in Paris)?[34]

Self-Regulation by Rural Populations

One hypothesis for the low rate of morals denunciations (5 percent of all offences listed in the eighteenth century) in New France is that the colonial population exercised strong self-regulation; because of the rural way of life, the family unit was the primary source of social regulation, and reprehensible acts were less often brought to the attention of officials. In fact, New France was composed of a highly homogeneous population in which large extended families and tightly knit social circles were common. Since honour was often an individual's only asset, public punishment, which would permanently sully his own social reputation and his family's, had dissuasive power. Thus, it is highly possible that in the countryside social regulation was performed mainly by the family to avoid defamatory stigmatization. However, it is highly unlikely that rural dwellers were utterly beyond any control or supervision by urban social institutions since most lived within twenty kilometres of a town or city. Two thirds of the population lived within ten kilometres of the St. Lawrence River (Lemieux and Montminy 2000, 50). On the whole, settlers remained more or less under the oversight of the social institutions of the time despite the immensity of the territory.

This conclusion also applies to rural France. In the countryside, homoerotic lifestyles were less a subject of discussion "because the provinces had an extraordinary power of absorption, submersion, silence" (Lever 1985, 217, our translation). Yet, since homoerotic lifestyles were often associated with heresy and witchcraft, one might well wonder whether the situation differed with regard to sodomists. According to Lever (1985, 218, our translation), people living in the country "were more discreet," although there were some cases of sodomy recorded in the provinces, especially in the towns. The general observation remains more or less the same as in New France: in the countryside, people had to hold their tongues and avoid scandal, as social regulation was a more private matter.

It is therefore possible that the strong social self-regulation in the rural milieu gave rise, as a sort of perverse effect, to an intense sense of guilt among the victims that kept them from denouncing their assailants, through fear either of losing their honour or of not being believed. This may explain why few or no cases of sodomy or, as a corollary, of sodomy involving children were recorded in the countryside. As mentioned above, for there to be a conviction, in addition to a denunciation – rather unlikely when the accuser was a child because children had no social authority – an admission was essential. If there was no witness, which was often the case in the countryside, the chances of a conviction dropped. Thus, it is plausible that inhabitants of both provincial France and New France rarely denounced the "crime of sodomy" and did so only when the participants were caught in the act by a number of witnesses.

Physical Proximity: A Decisive Factor

This last observation concerns another factor that may explain the small number of sodomists recorded in the rural environment: that of physical proximity as a source for denunciations. Lever (1985, 223) notes that isolation – or, as he puts it, the poverty of the social environment in the French countryside – reduced the opportunity for encounters. The same conclusion can be drawn with regard to the situation in New France: the size of the territory and the small population inevitably facilitated discretion with regard to sexual behaviours, and the risk of being caught in flagrante delicto or being denounced dropped considerably. Thus, all of the cases of sodomy reported to the New France legal system came from the military, a milieu characterized by the physical proximity of the militiamen. Ironically, in France one of the penalties incurred for the crime of sodomy was the obligation to enlist in the royal army: "If he can't be made into a 'normal' citizen, we will make him into a soldier" (Lever 1985, 234, our translation).[35] The possible correlation between physical proximity and the rate of de- nunciation also applied to the "middle-class homosexual" in the city, since "the social structure of the neighbourhood encouraged denunciation and allowed for close observation of dubious people" (Lever 1985, 293, our translation). The urban milieu, defined by high housing density, afforded a physical proximity that allowed for constant mutual surveillance. "The police also used the family and the neighbourhood network as a means to monitor individual conduct more closely. It was undoubtedly the first time that a population was systematically supervised – through the reports in which earlier arrests were recorded and through the extensive lists of sod- omites periodically updated" (Rey 1989, 144-45).

Thus, one explanation for the low level of denunciation of sodomists in New France and rural France is the lack of physical contiguity offered by these two living environments, with the social and physical distance favouring the concealment of sins against nature. In the countryside, physical contiguity was still present in the home, as entire families often resided in a single room; however, it was obviously easier to find solitude there than in the city, particularly outside of houses. The daily lack of privacy probably eliminated all forms of modesty, as sexuality and naked bodies were in full sight of everyone. In this sense, the values transmitted by scenes of daily life differed from those transmitted by the religious authorities. It is very possible that "sex shows" became common and were less likely to be denounced to the justice system.

Finally, it is essential to understand that children had a different place in the traditional family than they do in today's family. Before they were "discovered" in the eighteenth century, children were not perceived as complete beings, as beings in themselves, although they were distinguished from adults. They were not yet a source of constant concern (training, education, and morals) to the family, a concern that constitutes the modern essence of the child as a complete being (see Ariès 1962; Flandrin 1991). "We know that little interest was taken in children," observes the sociologist Daniel Dagenais (2008, 57). High infant and child mortality rates were part of the daily landscape; more than one-quarter of all babies born died before reaching the age of one year, and another quarter died before reaching the age of six (see Garnot 1991, 12ff). In a context in which children were not treated as special, in which families saw them die every day, and in which they were relatively numerous, it is open to question whether it was truly sexual assault (sodomy) against minors that disturbed the community or, rather, the unnatural act, the sexual behaviour that defied the divine order. As noted in this chapter, most of the child victims of sodomy in France were also punished by the law or, at least, considered defiled for life by this incomprehensible act. Without totally discrediting the idea of a certain degree of societal indifference to the child, Gauvard (1991, 822, 827, our translation) maintains that "a study of these different crimes [against children], the rarity and specificity of their remission, goes against received ideas and shows the respect with which the child was surrounded in this society." On the other hand, she continues, although the child's life was already legally protected in the Middle Ages, the murder of children was severely punished because this crime was a transgression against the sacred.

3

The British Conquest to the Late Nineteenth Century

FROM THE SODOMIST TO THE INVERT,
OR FROM THE PRIEST TO THE PHYSICIAN

Reason has dispelled all the ghosts ... Henceforth, there will be no more saints, only doctors. It is man who has charge of man.

– Éric-Emmanuel Schmitt, *Le Visiteur* (our translation)

This vice, once called the beautiful vice because it affected only the great lords, intellectuals, and Adonises, has become so fashionable that it is today nothing more than a state of affairs, from the dukes to the lackeys and the common people who are infected with it.

– Mouffle d'Angerville, *Mémoires secrets pour servir à l'histoire de la République des lettres* (our translation)

I long hesitated to bring into this study the hideous portrait of pederasty.

– Dr. Ambroise Tardieu, *Enquête médico-légale des attentats aux mœurs* (our translation)

In the mid-eighteenth century, sodomy was primarily a religious problem in New France and a legal affair in France, particularly Paris. At the same time as the parent country was secularizing its criminal law, its colony was falling further into the grip of the clergy. With the conquest of the St. Lawrence Valley by the English in 1760 and the institution of a new legal doctrine, these differences between France and the part of Canada called New France not only remained but were accentuated.[1] That is the subject of this chapter.

France: Between Doctrine and Legal Practice

In pre-revolution France, sodomy was punishable by burning at the stake. Few received this sentence, however: pyres were built only when the crime was committed in public or in combination with other serious offences such as murder or child rape. From the sixteenth to the eighteenth century, 80 percent of convictions for sodomy also involved a conviction for violence or serious abuse of a minor (Demers 1984, 784). During the period that interests us here – 1760 to 1900 – only one public sentencing for the crime of sodomy was pronounced: that of Jean-François Paschal in 1783. Paschal was also found guilty of the rape and murder of a fourteen-year-old child.[2] Behind a legal doctrine that was very severe with regard to sodomists, tolerance remained the rule in application of the law. As Michael D. Sibalis (1996, 81) underlines, "The magistrates rarely bothered to prosecute arrested sodomites in the courts."

After the beginning of the French Revolution (1789), homoerotic offences were no longer charged in France, as the Declaration of the Rights of Man and the Citizen modified criminal procedure respecting the political and legal freedoms of offenders.[3] Although the notion of the homoerotic crime disappeared from the Criminal Code, the French justice system remained interested in pederasty, as the police considered pederasts a potential source of criminal activity (Peniston 2004, 3) and mobilized a vice squad to patrol the city. According to police reports, an epidemic of "infamy" was unfurling across Paris.[4] The criminal statistics kept by the chief of the Paris police vice squad, François Carlier (1981, 204, our translation), are eloquent: from 1860 to 1870, he listed 6,342 cases involving pederasts in the Paris region (2,049 concerning Parisians; 3,709, people from the provinces; and 547, foreigners). He noted, "From 1850 to 1870, the repression was so severe that there was a moment of real panic ... This repression was so heavy-handed that all foreign pederasts returned to their country, while a fairly large number of Frenchmen belonging to high society left France until the storm blew over." Moreover, between 1873 and 1879 the names of 939 men arrested for "offenses against public decency with other males or for solicitation for the purposes of prostitution" were recorded in the Paris police archives (Sibalis 1999, 20-21). William A. Peniston (2004, 3) remarks that, therefore, although France was the first country to abrogate its antihomosexual laws, it continued to have in place "a systematic practice of treating same-sex sexuality as crime."[5]

Although pederasty was a source of worry, it was not specifically homoerotic lifestyles that alarmed French society; rather, sexuality and moral order in general posed a problem. In particular, the proletariat, often associated with the criminal element, threatened the bourgeoisie with its unbridled sexuality, the source of disease. This fear was accentuated within the bourgeoisie in the early nineteenth century, when it was estimated that 14 to 15 percent of deaths were caused by syphilis and that the disease affected mainly people aged fourteen to twenty-one years (Hahn 1979, 61). The fear that depraved lifestyles among the young were going to send the bourgeoisie to perdition sent shivers through French society.

In this context, anxiety about the contagion of inversion – which was seen as a congenital perversion of the sexual instinct – among young people was raging. On the one hand, the justice system manifested a desire to protect children; on the other, medicine was concerned because heredity was involved. In other words, society was worried less about children being victims of pederasts than about the possible contagion of pederasty (Revenin 2005, 101). According to certain experts, it could be passed on to male children, whose character might be weakened or feminized if they contracted it. Such warnings raised the fear that youths might be seduced by perverts, and they had to be warned against this "disease," which was being transmitted to children at a younger and younger age. "Monitoring the child," notes Christian Bonello (2000, 79, our translation) "meant keeping inversion from taking pernicious forms, trying to rebuild [the child's] moral sense in order to prevent his behaving this way as an adult, trying to forestall his being the source of contagion through his example by diverting potential candidates for the vice of inversion." A crusade against onanism developed as a hunt for pederasts was undertaken. According to Carlier's (1981) statistics, between 1860 and 1870, 52 percent of convicted pederasts were under twenty-five years of age and 14 percent were between twelve and fifteen years of age. In Dr. Ambroise Tardieu's (1995, 167) study, out of the 212 cases examined, 82 were under twenty-five years of age, and sixteen of those were between twelve and twenty-five years of age (forty-six cases did not give their age).

As they had been in the Middle Ages, pederasts were used as scapegoats by a society disturbed by sexuality. The exploitation of the invert as a manifest cause of national decline, plagues, depopulation, and domestic crises was thus not a new phenomenon – for, as André Cellard (1991, 218-19, our translation) observes, "any economic crisis is also a social crisis," and thus the main steps in community empowerment "always take place in the wake of economic crises," when the authorities "protect their social privileges by trying to control and regulate the dangerous classes." Unfailingly, the French authorities maintained and held up the figure of the foreign pederast, the frightening Other, who personified all the vices of man. Violent acts against pederasts – blackmail, public acts of indecency, and murders – multiplied (Hahn 1979, 38).

Decriminalization in France

Adoption of the 1791 Penal Code marked a break with the Ancien Régime in terms of the French concept of public order. French law no longer regarded "crimes against nature" as criminal in terms of religious proscriptions.[6] Homoerotic acts such as sodomy, as well as consensual, nonviolent sexual acts, were no longer condemned in themselves in the Penal Code (a situation that lasted until 1942). These legislative changes resulted from the laicization of the public order, which put nonviolent sexual practices performed in private beyond the field of legal intervention. With the revolution, the distinction between public and private space was instituted as a universal principle.

The justice system proceeded to create an unprecedented hierarchy of offences. As it had been in the seventeenth century, judicial intervention was concentrated on the most visible crimes, generally those involving blood and meeting with strong public disapproval, such as offences against children. Following this penal philosophy, the 1810 code mentioned only indecent assaults perpetrated with violence or on a child below fifteen years of age; the penalty was a prison term with forced labour, with a life sentence if the guilty party had any sort of authority over the young person or was a domestic, functionary, or clergyman. The courts ignored sexual acts between adults and consenting minors (Lever 1985, 400). It was not until 1832 that nonviolent indecent assault and sexual relations with minors under eleven years of age were addressed; the courts then prosecuted all sexual acts performed or attempted with a child under eleven years of age – consenting or not – at the same level as a violent indecent assault. Two categories of criminals were created: those who assaulted adults and those who assaulted children; the latter were judged insane and incomprehensible. The effects of the statute were quickly felt. Georges Vigarello (2001, 151) has found that the number of assaults against children charged increased from 106 in 1830 to more than 800 in 1870. The age of consent for minors was increased to thirteen years of age in 1863.

Magistrates and Interpretation of the Law: Homoeroticism as Aggravating Factor

The invert was no longer persecuted in the French penal doctrine, although the absence of legal condemnation did not mean a lack of repression in penal practice. "The law did not provide any precise definition of the other offenses [public offences against decency, incitement to debauchery, corruption of young people, vagrancy], which left them to judicial interpretation" (Sibalis 1996, 83). Régis Revenin (2005, 167ff) presents a number of examples in which sections of the Penal Code were used against homosexuals between 1870 and 1918. He also lists from the police archives 216 guilty verdicts for the offence of public indecent exposure (article 330) and eighteen guilty verdicts for soliciting and public soliciting for unnatural purposes.[7]

In fact, although the new legislation protected pederasts against institutionalized violence to a certain extent, repression and social censure remained very common (see Peniston 2004). Foucault (1991, 336) confirms that police surveillance and interventions always constituted the most common forms of repression of homoerotic lifestyles. Although inverts were no longer burned at the stake, they were arrested by the hundreds in Luxembourg, Champs-Élysées, and Palais-Royal, especially in public urinals (see Sibalis 1999, 15-21).

Judges stopped using the old legal terminology ("sodomy," for example), but their interpretation nevertheless remained strongly influenced by religious morality. Jean Danet (1998, 98-99, our translation) comments,

> Although the homosexual nature of the act being judged was irrelevant
> to the nineteenth-century legislature, the magistrates were bent on calling
> attention to this detail using terms borrowed from moral and religious

vocabulary: "shameful passions," "immoral acts," "acts that revolt nature," and so on. It should be noted that these acts were not defined or specified in any other way. In all of these cases, one seeks in vain a definition of the "perversions" that the judges were out to stigmatize.

The homoerotic nature of the sexual act being charged generally served as an aggravating circumstance, especially when it was committed with a minor. Danet (1998, 99, our translation) observes that judges often tried to repress consensual homoerotic behaviours between an adult and a child of the same sex "by twisting their use of the notion of inciting a minor to debauchery." In fact, the Angers Court of Appeal legitimized the use of section 334 of the Penal Code – the section that forbade incitement of minors to debauchery – by authorizing the bringing of charges against individuals who "corrupted" youths, even though the objective of section 334 was to "affect procuring, not individuals who have corrupted a youth in the interest of their own pleasure" (Angers, 1 September 1851, *Dalloz*, 1854, 54, quoted in Danet 1998, 99, our translation). The argument made to justify this broadened use was that these sexual acts revolted nature and exposed youths to the most shameful depravity. On the one hand, this was misappropriation of a statute to condemn specifically homoerotic behaviours; on the other hand, it was differential treatment by magistrates in the judgment of sexual acts depending on whether they were perpetrated on boys or girls. "When the Penal Code closed its eyes to heterosexual relations between an adult and a minor, it was agreed ... not to disturb the sacrosanct nature of private life! But pederasts, beware! They were to be exposed to the full force of the law" (Hahn 1979, 31, our translation). Revenin (2005, 141, our translation) concurs: "Nineteenth-century society condemned male homosexuality more severely – morally and judicially – than it did violence committed against children."

How can this differentiation be explained? Why did magistrates feel the need to provide more legal protection from adult sexuality for boys than for girls? Did this situation express the fear that young boys would lose their "masculinity," or did it simply convey society's lack of interest in the female sex? The latter hypothesis is interesting. As Florence Tamagne (2001, 128) notes, in the nineteenth century both feminist women and effeminate men, judged incapable of reproducing, haunted the community.

Yet it was the image of the effeminate homosexual that spread rapidly within French society.[8] In a social context in which anxiety about a falling birth rate was widespread and pederasty was perceived as a contagious form of sexuality that might well lead to the degeneration and feminization of a man's nature – for a society formed of inverts inevitably threatened the nation's repopulation and survival – it was completely possible to envision that magistrates were eager to provide greater protection to young men with regard to their sexuality. It was feared that a homoerotic sexual experience would dictate the sexual future of the young man. As the physician Charles Féré (1904, 356) asserted, "If it is admitted that habit and example may by themselves alone develop inversion, mere contact with inverts is a social danger." Following this medical philosophy, heterosexual relations between an adult and a minor were deemed less problematic since, at least, they would not put at issue either procreative sexuality or the social roles still deeply anchored in the attitudes of the time.

This differential application of the law did not, however, make jurisprudence, as the Cour de cassation rejected the idea of a legal distinction between homosexual and heterosexual relations. The court maintained that section 334 of the Penal Code applied only when procuring was at issue. Tamagne (2000, 88, our translation) observes that when the magistrates "tried to condemn homosexuality by alternate means, these manoeuvres systematically failed." The legal battle between trial judges and the Cour de cassation endured, nevertheless, until 1937. It is thus not unlikely that magistrates used, even indirectly, certain sections of the Penal Code to repress sexual acts considered despicable and depraved. In addition to section 334, sections 330, on indecent exposure, and 331, on indecent assault, left the door open to interpretation by officers of the court in the questioning and indictment of homoerotic lifestyles since there was no clear and precise definition of indecent exposure or indecent assault. Section 330 stipulated simply, "All persons who commit indecent exposure will be punished by imprisonment of three months to one year, and a fine of 16 francs to 200 francs." Section 331 provided that "whoever commits the crime of rape or is found guilty of any other indecent assault, consummated or attempted, with violence, against individuals of one or the other sex shall be punished with imprisonment." Yet, as Vigarello (2001, 116) rightly notes, "It is culture, obviously, that defines the content of decency, and not the law; 'moral standards' remain 'conceptually elusive,' changing over time." Magistrates who took advantage of such latitude in interpretation of the law to associate the repression of pedophiles and prostitutes with that of pederasts also encouraged the creation in the public imagination of the homosexual who corrupted children.

The Emergence of Medical Authority: The Discovery of Sexual Perversion[9]

In addition to being stalked by the police and sentenced by the courts for assaults on morals, pederasts quickly came under the penetrating gaze of experts and were sent to insane asylums (Hahn 1979, 80). Until the 1880s, Dr. Tardieu "and his disciples dominated the medical discourse on pederasty ... and they also exerted their influence on the criminal justice system" (Peniston 2001, 181). As Revenin (2005, 155) notes, both the police and the courts turned to medical science, for repression was now inscribed within a broader context of moral order and public hygiene. The need for social control rapidly moved the criminal justice system toward psychiatric medicine, and the quest for normalization led to a remarkable breakthrough in the areas of penal law and control of deviance. From being a sinner or criminal, the sodomist was transformed into a particular subjectivity, an individual who was suffering from one or another perversion. That is, he became a sick person who had to be treated and from whom society had to protect itself.

In the West, the political, economic, and technical incentive to take sexuality in charge was instigated in the late eighteenth century, when societies sought objective and measurable knowledge about sexual practices in order to list and classify them. Now, the different perverse forms of sexuality had to be defined, controlled, and cured (Foucault 1990, 23-24). Among all of the perversions of human nature, inversion held a prominent place. A number of medical, psychiatric, and psychological theories were promulgated in an attempt to understand and treat the "homosexual patient." Medicine, and then psychiatry, began to develop "scientific" knowledge on individuals exhibiting homoerotic behaviours.

Even though theories about different sexual issues existed in Antiquity, it was not until the nineteenth century that sexual questions were examined intensively by scientists. Thomas Laqueur (1990, 62, 96) hypothesizes that from Antiquity to the Renaissance, reflections on sex were based on a single-gender model, in which the "standard of the human body and its representations is the male body," and there was a "propensity to see the female body as a version of the male." Laqueur posits that the precondition for anatomical and biological differentiation of the sexes was the appearance of the symbolic and social unification of the female and male genders. In other words, it was only when the ontological (and age-old) differentiation of genders was ended that it was possible to glimpse the difference between the sexes and, as a corollary, see the "creation" of the homosexual as a distinct individuality. Pierre Hahn (1979, 23) and Elizabeth Badinter and Lydia Davis (1995, 99n7) note, in fact, that in the eighteenth century the category of sodomist included lesbians, since the female sex was thought of in analogy to the male sex. The clitoris was, in a way, considered an imperfect penis (see Gowing 2006). Only in the nineteenth century, when the model of two opposed sexes became prominent, were females removed from this category.

From the dichotomy of the sexes developed a *scientia sexualis* that established the "solidification and implantation of an entire sexual mosaic" (Foucault 1990, 53) based not only on the sex act but also on the variety of individual desires and pleasures, which also had individuals as objects. Homosexuals, fetishists, sadists, pedophiles, and many other categories were created. As Michel Foucault (1990, 43) comments, "The sodomite had been a temporary aberration; the homosexual was now a species." Little by little, sex became the basis for the identity and intelligibility of the subject, and medicine proceeded to classify individuals according to whether or not they corresponded to a specific definition of normalcy. Thus, homosexuality was defined initially in relation to "normal" heterosexuality. As soon as nineteenth-century psychiatrists and specialists integrated the idea of a normal sexual instinct, by nature aimed at and focused on heterosexual copulation, they went on to categorize and stigmatize sexual problems. Homosexuality was one of these. The birth of the homosexual identity proved essential to the regulation of homoerotic lifestyles. Guy Hocquenghem (1993) is thus correct to conceive of homosexuality as a fabrication of psychologists and the police, with medicine taking the place held up to then by the church in the definition and control of sexual deviance.

Under the influence of emerging medical authority and knowledge, both the legal system and the figure of the criminal changed. As various sexual pathologies became medicalized, sodomists became inverts. The terminology used to describe them changed; the French police now preferred to use the laicized term, "pederast." The secularization initiated during the French Revolution transferred the power of healing from the priest to the physician (Goubert 1982, 6), so it is no surprise that many physicians played major roles in the laicization of French society. Paradoxically, it was upon request of the ecclesiastical power that medical authority was imposed to monitor public hygiene and to be the repository of scientific knowledge on sexuality.[10] For, in nineteenth-century France, which was struggling with the constant dread of depopulation and a falling birth rate, the church had joined with the state to promote the pro-birth values of the Republic. Guillebaud (1999, 353) summarizes the psychological trauma of a France faced with the "danger of depopulation" and "demographic fears" when he observes that medicine, history, morality, and the state were put to the task of urging the French to procreate. In this pro-natalist social climate, in which sexuality was a great source of anxiety, it is easy to understand how the fear of contagion of inversion was instituted and grew.

Inversion: A New Form of Contagion

Inverts were identified as a threat to the nation. They were perceived as the weak link in the community and capable of leading society to perdition. Because they could not reproduce, they were systematically stigmatized as a source of corruption, decadence, and menace to the family. Although homoerotic lifestyles were not punished under criminal law in France, they were considered a social blight, even a danger to society. To inverts were attached every possible vice and an image of physical and moral monstrosity (Hahn 1979, 77). The French bourgeoisie was particularly worried that pederasty was spreading in all levels of society, without respect for social or economic hierarchy. Identification of these "despicable people" was essential. Mouffle d'Angerville wrote in his *Mémoires secrets* (1784, 241-42, our translation), "This vice, once called the beautiful vice because it affected only the great lords, intellectuals, and Adonises, has become so fashionable that it is today nothing more than a state of affairs, from the dukes to the lackeys and the common people who are infected with it." The demise of the "beautiful vice" marked a major break from the Ancien Régime, under which everyone had looked for ways to camouflage this "mute sin," this vice against nature so abominable that it was better to keep sinners quiet than risk teaching them about it. Now, the quest for knowledge about sexuality advanced inexorably to uncover every detail about people who conducted such sexual activities in order to understand them. Moreover, "in the mid-nineteenth century, police officials and forensic scientists began to write about what they observed, and in books usually intended for the general public" (Sibalis 2001, 122). From saying nothing, they went to saying everything, maintains Foucault (2003). To prove that pederasts were committing crimes, police officers, following forensic physicians and psychiatrists, mobilized and undertook to reveal everything about the odious individuals whom they tore from the shadows in which they were concealed. Under the Ancien Régime, the less they were talked about, the better protected was the moral order. In the nineteenth century, after much debate, it was understood that the only way to limit the excesses of antiphysics (a nineteenth-century term for unnatural sexual acts) was to bring their night into the light of day (Hahn 1979, 73).

Medicine inherited the mandate of preventing the spread of the new form of contagious blight. Based on medical and legal observations and various police reports, a hunt for pederasts was launched in the 1850s (Hahn 1979, 41; Nye 1989; Sibalis 1999, 19-22). The goal was to recognize, monitor, and control inverts. In 1857 the famous French physician Ambroise Tardieu published his *Enquête médico-légale des attentats aux mœurs*. This "scientific" study of the pederastic personality was intended to enable more effective surveillance of emerging homosexual circles. As Tardieu (1995, 190-91, our translation) observes,

> The subject of this long, painstaking study, in which I recoiled from neither the image of moral degradation nor the most repugnant features of the physical deformations caused by pederasty, was solely to give the forensic physician the means to recognize pederasts definitively and thus to resolve, with more certainty and authoritativeness than previously, questions on which justice seeks his assistance to pursue and, if possible, extirpate this shameful vice.

Gradually, the French legal system became dependent on medicine in its intervention with inverts. By using medical expertise, criminal justice legitimized the isolation of the patient in the name of community interest, expressed through the new public-health doctrine.[11]

Physicians now served as medico-legal experts for the criminal justice system (Peniston 2004). They were responsible for examining the deviant personality according to criteria that were as objective as possible. The French Criminal Code, the Code d'instruction criminelle (section 44), and the Civil Code (section 81) gave medical experts an official role in the courts, authorizing them to detect traces of dementia and monomania and to confirm or invalidate signs of the act of sodomy.[12] Only the offending act was considered. The physicians gradually adopted terminology, created new symptoms, and suggested that these corresponded to the appropriate sections of the Penal Code. Through the specialty of alienist, medicine and psychiatry definitively took charge of the treatment of inverts. In France, the physician C.F. Michéa was the first to write about pedophilia and to take an interest not in the signs of sodomy as practised but in the brain anomalies that caused perversions. (Michéa designated male homosexuality as pedophilia and not, as etymology tends to describe it, as the love of young men.)[13] Inversion became a treatable pathology. Now, the deviant personality, rather than the sex act, came under the microscope. "The doctor was no longer solely the judge's ally in assessing the reality of the offence in order to punish it, but took on the mission of better understanding, better defining, even curing, and at least, protecting society from the scourge that threatened it" (Bonello 2000, 65, our translation). As an expert, the psychiatrist evaluated the deviant personality and, if possible, detected the criteria, significance, and objective evidence of deviance. In the late eighteenth century the sodomist was transformed into a pederast, now identified by his "antiphysic tastes" (Tamagne 2001, 61, our translation).

Guillaume (1990, 75) notes, however, that medical authority did not really develop in France until the 1850s. Before this time, power was held for the most part by a triumphant church, and the value of a moral, religious, and vocational education continued to rise.[14] Medicine held neither great knowledge nor great sway. But Christian faith did not keep the bourgeois moral order from being influenced by the sciences. Gradually, France entered a positivist and scientific era, in which the church was no longer the only guarantor of public morality. According to Pierre Hurteau (1991, 79-80, our translation), "A new normative discourse, this one of civil origin, articulated an ideology of public morality focused on the physical and mental hygiene of the population. The police and the civil courts replaced the confessional, and very quickly medicine came to their assistance to supply new ideological instruments that replaced Christian sexual morality."

In France – mainly in Paris and other urban areas – the role of medicine in social control grew constantly. The middle class increasingly relied on doctors and hygienists, now the holders of authority and knowledge previously conferred upon priests. On the other hand, medical authority did not extend uniformly throughout France; there was a close connection between medicalization and the urban milieu until the early-modern period. It was not so easy for medicine to gain a foothold in the countryside and among the urban working classes, mainly because physicians were seen as bourgeois university graduates (Ariès 1971, 397; Léonard 1992, 26-30). On the contrary, the Catholic Church maintained a firm grip on control of sexuality in rural France and among traditional families. This closely resembled the situation prevailing in French Canada, which was still mostly rural. As the Industrial Revolution gained strength, however, the dogma of progress and scientific advances developed and, as a corollary, trust in medical science rose. In the early nineteenth century, the influence of science and medicine on the justice system was negligible, but by the end of the century there was enough medical expertise to cover the vast sphere of criminal justice (Chauvaud 2000, 13).

French Canada: Repression of a Sin against Nature

In French Canada, the influence of medical discourse was limited; the legal system was still based largely on religious theses. As Cellard (1991, 198) notes, the clergy retained its role as the guardian of morals, becoming omnipresent in the care of the insane ("mad" people), an area of predilection also for medicine in the nineteenth century.

The Legal Framework under the English Regime [15]

With the conquest of the Province of Quebec by the English in 1760, the civil and criminal laws that governed life for the sixty thousand people living in the St. Lawrence Valley changed. In fact, the legal system as a whole was transformed. From the British Conquest until 1764, New France was subjected to a military system directed by General James Murray. Justice was administered by courts composed of militia officers; those found guilty could appeal to courts composed of military officers and, as a last resort, to the governor of the province. In 1764, through the Treaty of Paris, civil government was re-established and French Canadians were subjected to English law. In both Quebec City and Montreal, "courts identical to those in Great Britain were instituted: Court of the Commissioners of the Peace, Court of Common Pleas, Court of Assize" (Boyer 1966, 54, our translation).[16]

The British adversarial system was instituted for criminal proceedings. Unlike the French inquisitorial system, it allowed French Canadians to be judged by their peers and to appear before a jury in the selection of which they had participated. According to this new penal philosophy, the accused was presumed innocent and prosecution was incumbent upon the victim.[17] In addition, British law, like French law, proved to be strongly repressive. Both systems were based on the same punitive logic despite their numerous procedural distinctions. Lord John Russel and Sir Thomas Fowell Buxton list, respectively, 180 and 223 crimes subject to the death penalty in 1819 in the British Criminal Code (cited in Boyer 1966, 76), earning it the nickname "Bloody Code" among some historians.[18] In comparison, in France only six crimes were subject to capital punishment in 1822 (Boyer 1966, 76). Upon closer examination, however, French penal sanctions under the Ancien Régime were hardly less harsh. The French justice system functioned according to the postulates of vengeance and terror, and corporal punishment was propelled to the foreground in the legal setting. As late as 1780, Muyart de Vouglans, the last great commentator on criminal law in the Ancien Régime, listed the ten corporal punishments in force: use of the question (admission by torture), the galley, whipping, punching, tongue piercing, hanging, the gallows, quartering, shackles, and the pillory.

In 1774, the British Parliament adopted the Quebec Act to respond to growing discontent among the French Canadian population. It granted French Canada the re-establishment of French civil law, freedom of religion, and abolition of the Test Act.[19] In criminal matters, the 1777 ordinance was very similar to the 1764 ordinance. Only in 1794 was a new system adopted, involving three levels of criminal courts. The Court of King's Bench – one court each in Montreal and Quebec City – was the colony's court of last resort and the only one authorized to pronounce the death penalty. The sessions courts, which met every three months in each district, held trials for offences not eligible for the death penalty. These two judicial bodies

heard the great majority of criminal trials and respected traditional procedure (trial by jury, bills of indictment, and so on). Finally, in weekly
sessions courts, two judges practised summary justice concerning local
police matters.

At first glance, the British justice system seemed to be a "dense institutional web woven through the social fabric and cutting out a more or less
representative sample of deviant behaviours" (Fecteau 1985, 511, our translation). However, an analysis of real judicial practice clearly shows that use
of the criminal courts was exceptional. Jean-Marie Fecteau (1985, 503, our
translation) notes that institutional repression of criminality was marginal in feudal regimes because feudal justice was based not on institutional law but on local compromises that emanated from a normative
morality. The criminal justice system was seen as an instrument "of ultimate arbitration and sanction that was used only as a last resort." Although
the doctrine of English colonial justice remained strongly repressive,
judges sought various ways to avoid severe application of the law. English
statutes punished so many crimes with the death penalty that judges and
juries often used their discretionary power to avoid wielding the law's full
force, sometimes even hesitating to recognize a culpability that was strik-
ingly obvious. In addition, as Raymond Boyer (1966, 55) observes, the low
number of police officers in Lower Canada considerably limited legal
interventions; the police force in Montreal in 1818 comprised only one
chief, one assistant chief, and twenty-four constables. How were homoerotic behaviours – behaviours still considered so horrible that "they must
not be named by Christians" – treated under the British legal system?

English Law and Crimes against Nature

Researchers face a quantitative problem here, as French Canadian jurisprudence on homoerotic offences is very limited. Although Jacques
Crémazie (1842) and Boyer (1966) list no cases of sodomy up to 1842,
Hurteau (1991) has found ten arrests and appearance notices for the crime
of sodomy and one for attempted sodomy between 1864 and 1887 in Montreal as well as two trials at the Court of King's Bench between 1850 and
1889.[20] It was similar for religious repression. According to Lucien Lemieux
(1989), there were no cases of canonical censure or public penitence for
sodomy between 1760 and 1840, and public cases of sodomy were very rare.
Nevertheless, it is relevant to analyze the statutes in effect and the writings

by certain British legal commentators on sodomy and other crimes associated with homoerotic behaviours since the institutional discourses of the magistracy and the legislature must sketch out a definition of the image of the homosexual perceived and transmitted by the justice system. Alex K. Gigeroff's (1968) work on sexual deviations in Canadian criminal law and Hurteau's findings (1991) on the repression of homosexuality in Lower Canada prove very accurate. In the view of these researchers, interpretation of the Canadian legislation on sexual offences must be filtered through the analysis of the main commentators on English criminal statutes, who strongly influenced the criminal law in force in Canada.

Sir Edward Coke: A Description of Sexual Crimes

Edward Coke, with his *Institutes of the Laws of England* (1625), was one of the first legal commentators to take an interest in describing sexual crimes, including bestiality and sodomy. He grouped these crimes under a single heading, "Buggery." Although his commentaries were written long before the Conquest, they had a great influence on the work of his successors. Until adoption of Act 4-5 Victoria c. 27 in 1841, the law in Canada applicable to sodomy was British common law, particularly Statute 25 Henry VIII 1533. Both sodomy and bestiality were punishable by death under the premise of buggery:

> For asmoche as there is not yett sufficient and condigne punyshment appoynted and lymytted by the due course of the lawes of this Realme for the destectable and abhomynable vice of buggery comyttid with mankynde or beaste ... that the same offence be hensforth adjuged felonye ... and that the offenders ... shall suffer such peynes of dethe ... and that no pson offendyng in any such offance (shabbe) admyttid to clergie. (25H. VIII, c.6, MDCCCXVII, 441)

The vague wording, which seems to include both heterosexual and homosexual sodomy, displeased English jurists, including Coke. In fact, the jurisprudence shows that this legal definition left judges with a wide margin of interpretation. Coke redefined the crime of buggery, specifying that this offence against nature could be committed between two men, between a man and an animal, or between a woman and an animal.

Heterosexual sodomy was thus no longer legally proscribed. Based on the conception of Thomas Aquinas, Coke maintained that this form of sodomy should be defined as a mode of incongruous coitus. Defining the crime of sodomy as "a detestable and abominable sin, amongst Christians not to be named, committed by carnall knowledge against the ordinance of the Creator and order of nature," Coke (1979, 58), strangely, established a group of rules for interpretation that made accusations more difficult; further-more, proof of anal penetration was necessary, and the actors could no longer testify against each other. Hurteau (1991, 91) discusses two cases that confirm the need for anal penetration to be proved for a charge of sodomy to be made, implying that doctrine and jurisprudence followed Coke on this subject. On the other hand, as was the case in France in the seventeenth century, the justice system considered both participants guilty. No distinc-tion was made between the active party (the accused) and the passive party (the victim).

Finally, the high priority accorded to sodomy by Coke indicates that this subject was very important and a source of concern to the English legislature. Coke wrote more discourses on the crime of sodomy than on that of rape. This situation is reminiscent of the one described in the pre-vious chapter with regard to crimes against the person rather than against divine law. Rape, because it was above all an act of violence, provoked less disapproval from the community than did sodomy, a crime against God. Since British criminal law was still intertwined with biblical law, the sever-ity of the penalty incurred for this type of offence was seen as totally legitimate. Together, these indices show that homoerotic lifestyles remained a taboo subject, one that strongly offended a common conscience united by the divine conception of human nature.

Sir William Blackstone: Assault with Intent
British law, as established in the St. Lawrence Valley, thus had homo-erotic lifestyles in its sights. Around 1769, 150 years after Edward Coke, William Blackstone also took an interest in homoerotic offences. Unlike his predecessor, he tried to create some order in British law by classifying all offences in his book *Commentaries on the Laws of England*. In his cat-egorization of crimes against nature, Blackstone (1769, 205) included "such other crimes and misdemeanours, as more particularly affect the security

of his person, while living." Sodomy was found in this group alongside rape and kidnapping – all were considered crimes against human spirituality. In the physical sense, they were victimless crimes. On the other hand, because these behaviours were offensive to the respective spiritualities of the actors as human beings, the actors were judged responsible for each other and, at the same time, aggressors against each other. In other words, sodomy was no longer repressed because it might damage an individual's physical integrity but because it went against the spirituality of man – that is, the religious morality of the time. Unlike modern French laws, which repressed only sexual offences with violence, in Canada sodomy was still punished even in the absence of a victim.

Blackstone (1769, 205) legitimized British morals through religious discourse and through public morality, itself strongly influenced by religion. As a consequence, he refused to use the term "sodomy," feeling that this type of offence must be designated as what it was: a crime against nature. He used the example of the destruction of Sodom by fire to legitimize the death penalty for sodomists. His disgust for this sex crime was clearly conveyed in the words that he used to describe it: "the infamous crime against nature," "deeper malignity," "an offense of so dark nature," "miscreants," and "a crime not fit to be named" are examples of the expression of his repulsion. Thus, although he proposed to classify sodomy in the category of crimes against security of the person – and not in the category of crimes against religion – a religious influence remained perceptible in his interpretation. His conception of the human being also remained strongly imbued with religious discourse. Although sodomy was no longer under the jurisdiction of ecclesiastical courts, there was still a very clear impression that it was a crime against religion.

With a focus on generalized control of morals, Blackstone developed the concept of assault with intent – the intent, that is, to commit a crime against nature ("Assault with Intent to Commit Unnatural Crimes"). This new criminal category made it possible to broaden the penal net by offering the justice system an alternative for charging sodomists when it proved difficult to establish irrefutable proof of sodomy. Blackstone also described notions of "grossly scandalous and public indecency" in his category of "Offences against God and Religion." Later, individuals accused of committing homoerotic acts other than sodomy were charged with "acts of indecency." Thus, a group of rules was put in place – certainly less repressive with regard to the penalty incurred – with the goal of more easily monitoring and rounding up pederasts. It was no longer specifically the homoerotic act that was to be punished but, rather, the actor and his intention.

Jeremy Bentham: An Early Defender of Homosexuality [21]

Fifty years passed before a commentator challenged the religious foundations of crimes against nature. This honour went to Jeremy Bentham. His utilitarianist critique of criminal law led him to classify sexual crimes according to their degree of harm to the individual and society. In his view, consensual sexual relations were not to be subjected to criminal law but fell under, as Daniel Borrillo and Dominique Colas (2005, 223, our translation) put it, the "immunity of privacy." Following this interpretive logic, homoerotic behaviours should no longer be condemned in criminal law since they produced no evil whatsoever but, rather, a certain form of pleasure. By this light, it was difficult to find a legal justification for their criminalization. In relativizing all sexual conduct, Bentham attacked the principles of Blackstone and Voltaire, both of whom had interpreted homosexuality according to religious discourse. Bentham reproached Blackstone, in particular, for his use of pejorative adjectives to describe homosexuals, which were a source of cruelty and intolerance (see Crompton 1998, 46-47).

Bentham was thus one of the first defenders of homoerotic practices, as he refuted the hypothesis that homoerotic lifestyles might propagate in the absence of repression; he maintained that criminal law had very little influence on people's sexual behaviours. In fact, he stated, these lifestyles would never lead to generalized disinterest in the female sex or interfere with the reproduction of society. In spite of his many critiques of the administration of justice, his authority remained mitigated in England. His most important writings were published in France, and his influence was felt mainly in the writing of the Napoleonic Code, which he viewed as a "work of genius" (Crompton 1998, 19). Moreover, his *Essay on Paederasty* (1785) remained practically unknown until the twentieth century.

In any case, in England criminal repression for sodomists was still a fact of life, and they still faced the death penalty. As Polly Morris (1989, 392) observes, "Most sodomites were well aware of the dangers they ran in approaching other men – loss of reputation, death in the pillory, or hanging." A bill tabled in 1828 expanded the criminal net and facilitated charges of sodomy. Now, proof of anal penetration alone was enough to incriminate sodomists; proof of ejaculation was no longer necessary. In the view of Robert Demers (1984, 786), from 1533 to 1861 English society was relatively tolerant and not particularly obsessed with the homosexual issue; convictions for sodomy involved mainly crimes against children or were a pretext for political discrimination. Sibalis (2006b, 113) also notes, "Few trials took place before the 18th century." However, Randolph Trumbach (1989, 408) points out that in England "more men were put to death for sodomy between 1700 and 1850 than in the previous six hundred years." In fact, Morris (1989, 400) mentions an increase in prosecutions for sodomy and bestiality in Somerset County, and Sibalis (2006b, 119) has found that fifty-five men were hanged for sodomy between 1805 and 1835 in England and Wales. Thus, with the beginning of the Victorian era in the mid-nineteenth century, a sort of witch hunt was launched.

Sir James Fitzjames Stephen: The Maker of Canadian Law

James Fitzjames Stephen was the most influential figure in the writing of early Canadian criminal statutes and in the creation of the first Canadian Criminal Code. Stephen felt that religion and the law had to be brought together to buttress public morality. He therefore agreed with Coke and Blackstone that sodomy should be classified as a crime against morality. Unlike Coke and Blackstone, however, it was Stephen's opinion that neither sodomy nor bestiality deserved capital punishment. The death penalty for "the abominable crime of sodomy" was, in fact, officially abolished in England in 1861, twenty-five years after it was tacitly abandoned by the courts. The wording of the new statute was:

> The Offences against the Person Act: Whosoever shall be convicted of the abominable crime of buggery, committed either with mankind, or with any animal, shall be liable, at the discretion of the Court, to be kept in penal servitude for life or for any term not less than 10 years. (24 Vict., c. 100, s. 61, Unnatural Offences)

Sodomy was classified among crimes against the person, not crimes against morality, as Stephen wanted. Sodomy practised both by a man and a woman and by two individuals of the same sex was covered under this statute. At first glance, the statute seems to target a particular act (anal coitus) rather than a particular group of individuals (homosexuals). However, given what we know about the history of repression of homoerotic lifestyles, it is very likely that the great majority of charges based on this statute were made against individuals involved in a same-sex act, for it was possible to use the offence of intent to commit sodomy to indict various homoerotic acts. According to Edward E. Deacon (1831, 1238), "Where there is not complete proof of all the circumstances necessary to constitute the offence [sodomy], it is a better course to indict the offender for an assault with intent to commit the crime."

Adoption of this statute marked the beginning of a period of strong repression of homosexuals. It offered a legal alternative to police officers: from now on, they could arrest pederasts even when proof of anal penetration was not unequivocal. The situation for homosexuals worsened in 1885, when the British Parliament decided to punish all sexual acts committed between men. The Labouchère Amendment (Criminal Law Amendment Act 1885 (48 & 49 Vict. C.69)) allowed charges to be laid against

> any male person who, *in public or private, commits, or is a party to the*
> *commission of, or procures or attempts to procure* the commission by any
> male person of any act of gross indecency with another male person,
> shall be guilty of a misdemeanour, and being convicted thereof shall be
> liable at the discretion of the court to be imprisoned for any term not
> exceeding two years, with or without hard labour. (Emphasis added)

Although sentences incurred for homoerotic acts became lighter, the leeway possible in interpreting the statute facilitated the indictment of "despicable people." For the first time in the history of repression of homoerotic lifestyles, the criminal system no longer targeted a sexual practice but the sexual exchange between two men. As Jeffrey Weeks (1980, 119) observes, "Given the legal situation ... and the simultaneous refinement of hostile social norms, homosexual activity was potentially very dangerous for both partners and carried with it not only public disgrace but the possibility of a prison sentence." As a consequence, the number of court cases against pederasts increased. In 1898 the British Parliament passed the Vagrancy Act to extend its repression from lifestyles to soliciting for immoral purposes. This statute, states Tamagne (2004, vol. 2, 135), was applied only to homosexuals, and England repressed all sexual acts committed in private between two men until 1967.

The Canadian Legislation: The Influence of Church Doctrine

On 23 July 1840, the Imperial Parliament voted in the Union Act. Upper and Lower Canada were united in a single province represented by an elected assembly of forty-two representatives, which held the legislative power for the colony. England, however, maintained a right to veto bills tabled in the Assembly. The Catholic Church was also officially recognized, signalling the gradual return of triumphant clericalism and its Ultramontane ideology (Lemieux and Montminy 2000, 36-37). The church, a great defender of rural values, thus oversaw the faith, morals, and imagination of the French Canadian population. Through its influence, both social and political, it had a strong voice in the drafting of criminal laws.[22]

It was in this social context, with the church holding sway in the colony, that the first Canadian statute on sodomy was adopted in 1841. Under this statute, "the abominable crime of sodomy" was punishable by death, and guilt was established by evidence of penetration.[23] Parliament modified the statute in 1869, bringing it more or less in line with the 1861 English statute. A life sentence replaced the death penalty. In Canada the minimum prison term was two years, whereas it was ten years in the British statute. Like the British statute, the Canadian criminal legislation placed sodomy at the same level as attempted sodomy and indecent assault on a man. The wording of the law was:

> Whosoever attempts to commit the said abominable crime, or is guilty of any assault with intent to commit the same, or of any indecent assault upon any male person, is guilty of a misdemeanour, and shall be liable to be imprisoned in the Penitentiary for any term not exceeding ten years, and not less than two years, or to be imprisoned in any other gaol or place of confinement for any term less than two years, with or without hard labour. (S.C. 32-33 Vict. (1869), c. 20, s. 64)

There is no doubt that the offence of attempting to commit sodomy made it easier to cast a broad criminal net with regard to homoerotic lifestyles. Because this charge was applicable only to sodomy and not to other forms of sexual contact between two men, however, it offered relative protection to homosexuals. The jurisprudence also rejected attempted assaults when the acts charged were of a consensual nature. In *Her Majesty v. Laprise* (1880, Legal News, 139), for example, the lower court found the defendant guilty of indecent assault on a thirteen-year-old minor, but the Court of King's Bench reversed the ruling on appeal, as the defence succeeded in proving the consent of the minor. An analysis of the records for the Court of the Sessions of the Peace for the District of Montreal conducted by Hurteau (1991, 99-100) shows only one trial for attempted sodomy and two for indecent assault between 1850 and 1889. Nor did the number of indictments show a significant increase. Again according to the archives of the city of Montreal, seven men were charged with sodomy in 1869, two in 1872, one in 1876, and one more in 1881 (attempted). On the other hand, repression by the forces of order was well established, and the crime of indecent assault made it easy to take pederasts in for questioning (Hurteau 1991, 100). Although most of these charges did not lead to criminal court, the number of arrests shows that homoerotic lifestyles were a source of disgust and anxiety for local authorities.

When the statute was consolidated in 1886, the crime of sodomy was moved under the heading of "offences against public morals and public convenience," although the wording of the statute remained unchanged (R.S.C. 1886, c. 157, article 1). In 1890, however, the statute underwent a major modification. Now, all homoerotic behaviours committed by male adults were chargeable under the offence of gross indecency. Whether the charged parties were consenting or not, and whether the act was committed in public or private, did not matter. Guilty parties were liable for five years in prison with the possibility of flogging. This statute mirrored the English statute of 1885 and remained in force in Canada until the 1969 Omnibus Bill was adopted.

As a consequence, a shift occurred in French Canada with regard to criminal repression. Previously, a specific sexual behaviour (anal coitus) was to be punished. Now, the justice system was more focused on the choice of sexual object. It was no longer so much their acts that sodomists were charged with as it was their homoerotic desire, associated with a specific personality type. Little by little, the image of the pederast evolved in Canada:

> Sodomy was no longer an isolated gesture, a momentary departure from the path; it was the doing of effeminate-looking men with an exclusive sexual interest in other men, whom they sought to seduce. In fact, here one observes the same shift as already noted in the religious moral discourse, from the sexual act toward the sexual subject. (Hurteau 1991, 95-96, our translation)

This judicial and legislative evolution took place in a climate of social change that led to the marginalization and medicalization of deviants, notably sexual deviants. This occurred first in Europe and then in French Canada, where medical discourse began to grow in credibility despite the fact that religious discourse remained preponderant in the legitimization of criminal repression.

An Omnipresent Catholic Church

With regard to repression of homoerotic behaviours, it is essential to understand the church's role in social control of the population in the St. Lawrence Valley. From the Conquest to the attempted rebellion in 1837, the status of the Catholic Church was uncertain: the clerical elite, along with those who had gravitated to the French colonial power, returned to the parent country. Those who remained were settlers and an impoverished, uninfluential clergy – thanks to the religious freedom offered by the British regime. To defend its interests, the clergy had no choice but to present itself as the necessary intermediary between the British bureaucracy and the people. In fact, the new British colonial administration's desire to assimilate French Canadians was guided first and foremost by pragmatism, for social peace was a prerequisite to prosperity (Lemieux and Montminy 2000, 20ff). The Catholic Church appeared to be a natural ally for the colonial government. Thus, since the British government made sure that settlers were controlled domestically by the clergy, the church was able to tighten its grip over the population. Quickly, priests became leaders in the colony, as they alone saw to the formation of the French Canadian civil and social conscience.

In 1837, the Catholic Church began to gain ideological and social influence. It quickly became the only institution embodying the French Canadian collective identity, and it represented that identity to the British Empire. In charge of an education system, an imposing network of charitable institutions, and the entire health system, the church was omnipresent in the colony. Raymond Lemieux and Jean-Paul Montminy (2000, 31-33, our translation) note, however, that effective control of the population by ecclesiastical institutions remained mitigated by the immensity of the territory, which favoured both isolation and geographic mobility: "This is proved by the constant campaigns undertaken by the church to ensure and consolidate this control, which continued to elude it." Nevertheless, the church had exceptional power in the province, as it monitored and controlled the political and social spheres. Its resources, both human and financial, were greater than those of the entire state of Canada East (Lemieux 1989, 9).[24] By the mid-nineteenth century the clergy dominated French Canadian society.

French Canadians were thus distinct from the rest of Canada's population, most of whom were Protestant and English-speaking. Whereas priests, "experts in the soul, censors, directors of consciences, guardians of morals," tended to be the first recourse in Quebec parishes, "among anglophones, it was almost automatic to have a doctor intervene," observes criminologist and historian André Cellard (1991, 116, our translation). Using the example of insanity, he notes that only one francophone in eighteen appealed to a physician to attest to madness (sometimes, the priest replaced the doctor), compared to more than half of the people with English family names. At the time, Cellard continues, "anglophones held a sort of monopoly on scholarly medical culture, whereas francophones for the most part were cut off from the scientific relations that they might have had with French medicine."

Finally, it must be remembered that in French Canada homoerotic behaviours were at all times proscribed by law and a source of concern for the criminal justice system. Repression was legitimized almost exclusively by religious discourse, which influenced the community as a whole and shaped the common conscience. The terminology used by Canadian criminal law to describe homoerotic lifestyles was highly pejorative and included terms such as "against nature," "abominable," and "against public morality." Paradoxically, the law was applied relatively magnanimously: "[Judges] ended up performing unusual contortions to avoid applying the statute strictly" (Désaulniers 1977, 149, our translation). Changes in attitudes toward punishment in the nineteenth century certainly contributed to this lightening of penalties.

Between Medicine and Clergy: From France to French Canada

In France, medicine gradually took over from religion in the control of citizens' morals. Ecclesiastical power, however, remained a force in farming regions, where family tradition persisted. Medicine held authority initially only in the large cities, especially Paris. The marked influence of the church in French rural areas was similar to its influence in French Canada, although there were some distinctions between the two milieus. In French Canada, survival of the francophone nation seemed to be predicated on maintenance of the traditional Catholic peasant family. The family, which had been a modern and egalitarian social unit, was "retraditionalized." In effect, according to Daniel Dagenais (2008), before the Conquest and the ensuing generalized influence of the Catholic Church, the French Canadian family had a number of attributes of the modern family: nuclear, with fairly high mobility in the territory, and an egalitarian conjugal model. As Dagenais (2008, 129) observes, "there was too much individualism in the original spirit of the French-Canadian family, notably a very strong litigious spirit, for it to have been traditional." It was born modern.[25]

After the Conquest, the French Canadian family was "traditionalized" and transformed into the cornerstone of the Province of Quebec. Dagenais (2008, 129) posits that because the Conquest ended French Canadian governance of civil society – and was followed by the crushing of the Rebellions – the population was convinced, "so to speak, that society at large was not their sphere – hence the retreat to family sociability." As a corollary, the traditional family became the obligatory foundation for the social control exerted by the church. The Catholic religion now singled out French Canadians, and a "community identity" was built based on the traditional Catholic family, with the church and prominent figures in the countryside advocating a rural, agricultural Christianity and emphasizing humanist, community, and spiritual values (Hamelin and Gagnon 1984, 38, 43-48). The clergy also condemned industrialization, civil marriage, divorce, and freedom of opinion. Moreover, the church in French Canada did not completely recognize the legitimacy of the state with regard to citizens' moral conduct!

Wielding immense political power, the clergy in effect demanded that laws be based on religious doctrine. Even in the late nineteenth century, the state continued to come to the defence of religious marriage (see

Hamelin and Gagnon 1984, 43-48; Lemieux and Montminy 2000) by banning divorce in order to preserve the family institution and, thus, the nation's morality. Criminal legislation was also strengthened with regard to extramarital sex. The adoption of the 1892 Criminal Code clearly manifested the state's desire to control the male libido and confine it within the institution of marriage by severely punishing misconduct. This need to protect religious marriage and the traditional family at all costs provides an eloquent illustration of the church's influence in French Canada, and religious education was perceived as the most effective means of preventing criminality and ensuring social peace.

The situation was different in France. Except among traditional families – whose numbers and political influence were on the wane – the church was rapidly losing its hold on public morality. Medical public-hygiene discourse became embedded in the dominant ideology. Whereas in France urbanization and industrialization favoured the institution of a medical discourse that was detached from the traditional values of the church, in French Canada medicine was presented mainly as the defender of the church's traditional moral values through the definition of disease as a religious phenomenon rather than a biological problem. This, no doubt, is why alternative medicine remained popular among traditional families (see Bernier 1989, 96, 162). In France medicine and science played a dominant role in the laicization of society, whereas in French Canada science remained in the service of religion and went hand in hand with theology. Richard A. Jarrell (1987, 51, our translation) observes that "one unique aspect of nineteenth-century French Canada [was] that most of those who [worked] in science, at least as teachers, [were] clergymen."

Is it possible that this ideological gap between French Canada and France resulted from the absence of a dominant French Canadian middle class? This hypothesis is worth exploring since it was mainly through the middle-class family that medicine developed as a prevalent discourse in French society. In the St. Lawrence Valley, however, the Conquest put an end to the dominant French bourgeoisie. Later on, the failure of the Patriots' Rebellion considerably modified French Canadian ideology, returning to the church the power to exercise influence over the traditional family. Gilles Gagné (1996, 72-73, our translation) sums up the situation well when he remarks that the clergy formed "the administration of this civil society, a sort of welfare state without the title," in which the "French Canadian citizen [was] in a way the emissary of the family (and the church), an emissary with a freedom monitored in the sphere of the abstract identity of the state, to which he brought, as a duty to be paid, the vote of his tribe." Whereas in France republicanism, laicization, and the emancipating nationalism of the petite bourgeoisie gradually took over, in French Canada clericalism, Ultramontanism, the agricultural milieu, and the defensive nationalism of survival remained the main ideological themes. In addition, the conservative majority of the French Canadian middle class associated itself with the Catholic Church (Jarrell 1987, 62-63). The more liberal elements of the middle class, which might have favoured the emergence of a scientific movement similar to the one in Europe, lacked the economic power and political influence to prevail. Marcel Fournier and his colleagues (1987, 12) also observe, among the many factors that might explain the late development of science in French Canada, the lack of interest among the leading classes and the opposition of certain factions of the clergy.

For many years, the Catholic Church succeeded in distilling all of the features of French Canadian society and implementing its social organization and world outlook. "Religion had become a way of life," and that religion, Catholicism, "did not accept the world vision ensuing from the Reform and the French Revolution, centred on the liberty and historicity of man," summarize Jean Hamelin and Nicole Gagnon (1984, 49, 17, our translation).[26] The influence of Catholicism on French Canadian society was also reflected in the penal language used to define homoerotic behaviours. Whereas the Canadian legislature used terminology imbued with religious precepts, in France laicization of the public order sent homoerotic practices outside of the field of criminal law and confined them to private space. Furthermore, Canada, like Great Britain, was more severe with regard to penal doctrine than was France, which refused to incriminate homoerotic acts in themselves. Nevertheless, when it came to applying penal statutes, French magistrates tended to repress homoerotic acts by misappropriating the law. "The homosexual question could thus be tackled in the context of public indecency and indecent assaults, in particular on minors," observes Tamagne (2004, vol. 2, 177). In Canada it was a crime to attempt to commit sodomy, which enabled magistrates to find guilty even defendants for whom proof of anal penetration was difficult to establish.

In both France and French Canada jurisprudence remained limited. The legal system generally intervened only when the crime was committed in public. This corresponded to the situation in effect in the seventeenth and eighteenth centuries; only in the nineteenth century was there an explosion of medical interest in pederasts, particularly in France. The absence of jurisprudence must not be confused, however, with an abatement of repression. On the contrary, police repression was still going strong, especially in urban areas, where proximity favoured denunciations and tighter social control. In fact, the number of denunciations fluctuated enormously depending on population density and changes in sentiment about the violence and promiscuity that were a part of urban life. Most criminal trials took place in urban areas because "sensitivity became keener in cities and sexual crimes, those against children in particular, were increasingly denounced" (Vigarello 2001, 152). Since cases brought before the courts inevitably involved acts that took place before witnesses and in a public place, urban density became an explanatory factor in the increase in denunciations. Conversely, the rural style of life, still very common in Quebec – at the time there were only eleven towns with more than five thousand inhabitants[27] – surely facilitated "forbidden relations" and limited criminal indictments.

The following general conclusion may thus be drawn: in both France and French Canada repression and control of homoerotic behaviours remained mainly in the hands of the police and the justice system in urban areas and an issue of family and religious self-regulation in the countryside. Danet's (1998, 100, our translation) observations on the repression of homosexuality in France are very enlightening here:

> If the truth be told, if French criminal law and the judges intervened with regard to homosexuality only marginally throughout the nineteenth century, it was no doubt because in France social control of private life by the family and the village was particularly effective. The development in the cities of male prostitution in the last third of the century was, in this sense, another indication of the great secrecy of homosexual love. Criminal law was, fundamentally, at a minimum level of intervention because the society that it served might contain the very possibility of experiencing such passions.

4

The Late Nineteenth Century to the Sexual Revolution

FROM INVERT TO HOMOSEXUAL

Before any procedure, inverts in the genital sense must be examined by a physician. Only the physician has the competency to decide whether the defendant is an irresponsible insane person to be shut in an asylum, where we may try to cure him, or a vicious criminal, to be sent before the judges. For the vicious or corrupt person, I demand severity: the invert must be removed from society and be treated like the animal he is because he dishonours our species and has become dangerous. In effect, he cannot achieve his purpose without corrupting or perverting others.

> – Eugène Hubert, *L'Inversion génitale et la législation*
> (our translation)

The sodomite had been a temporary aberration; the homosexual was now a species.

> – Michel Foucault, *The History of Sexuality,* vol. 1

In the late nineteenth century, the criminal justice system in France did not explicitly punish homoerotic behaviours. Although no French statute mentioned homosexuality per se, however, certain forms of repression persisted. Pederasts were stalked by the police, examined under a microscope by medicine, and found guilty of various offences by the courts, although medical power/knowledge of human sexuality and homoerotic lifestyles was growing. In Canada the situation was different: criminal law, following English law and legitimized by religious doctrine, still incriminated homoerotic lifestyles. The broadening of penal categories presaged a shift in legal doctrine from punishment of the act to punishment of the choice of sexual object. In rural French Canada, the Catholic Church retained its influence over criminal matters, as the laws, in general, followed religious doctrine. Following the crises of the early and mid-twentieth century – two world wars, economic depression, the rise of communism, and so on – the situation of homosexuals in France and Quebec became more complex. Whereas the French legislative framework recriminalized some homoerotic behaviours, Canadian penal doctrine became less strict as the century went on.

Judicial Repression of Homoerotic Behaviours in Quebec

The judicial framework that governed sexuality and homoerotic lifestyles in Canada and Quebec in the late nineteenth century was based on British law. Either directly or indirectly, different sections of the Canadian Criminal Code applied to homoerotic behaviours. Marie-Andrée Bertrand (1988, 145, our translation) warns that any notion Canadians might have that the "means of criminal pursuit for homosexuality were less numerous and extensive than the Criminal Code in fact provided" is erroneous. A particular set of norms, although not specifically targeting homoerotic behaviours, seemed to apply more to homosexuals than to heterosexuals – the norms applied for the crimes of gross indecency, indecent assault, and sodomy.

Gross Indecency

The legislation on gross indecency emanated from the 1885 English Labouchère Amendment, which was intended to "correct" the absence in the common law of criminalization of male homoerotic acts such as fellatio and mutual masturbation. The amendment, responding to a sense of anxiety in nineteenth-century Europe regarding masculine morals, also covered homosexuality, male prostitution, and the corruption of boys. With a group of repressive measures, including the protection of girls and women, the suppression of bordellos, and a rise in the age of consent, the legislature hoped to stem excessive male sexuality. The amendment certainly was not designed specifically to repress homoerotic acts, but the consequences were disastrous for English homosexuals

(Weeks 1980, 117). Before it was adopted, homosexuals could be charged only with sodomy or attempted sodomy. Now, all homoerotic behaviours could be prosecuted.[1]

Emulating this English provision, the Canadian Criminal Code adopted the crime of gross indecency in 1892 (section 178). The most repressive legislation in Canada with regard to homoerotic behaviours committed in public or in private between consenting adults, it remained on the books until 1969. This new offence, which constituted "the reason most often cited for arrests of homosexuals" (Higgins 1999, 27, our translation), could be committed only by a "male person" who, "in public or private," committed "any act of gross indecency with another male person." The penalty was five years of imprisonment and the possibility of whipping – use of the whip being an extraordinary measure in Canadian law.[2]

A reading of the debates in the House of Commons shows that the statute was adopted as a preventive measure rather than out of concern with repressing a common type of sexual practice. According to Pierre Hurteau (1991, 155), Parliament was bowing to pressure from Anglo-Protestant crusades for social purity; the Catholic Church in Quebec did not get involved in this debate. The bill did not meet with unanimous Parliamentary approval; a number of members found it too confusing. Later, the statute was criticized by the courts for its lack of precision since, "without making the nature of the offence more specific, the legislature left it up to the courts to determine its content – the nature of the acts to be charged; nevertheless, the context of the debates surrounding the adoption of this section of the bill obviously referred to homosexual practices" (Hurteau 1991, 156, our translation).

It was not until 1953-54 that the statute was modified (section 149).[3] Parliament eliminated the wording "male person" and the penalty of whipping; it was now possible to charge lesbians and heterosexuals as well as homosexuals. The legal definition of gross indecency varied quite randomly from judge to judge. In 1968 the Manitoba Court of Appeal, however, declared that fellatio no longer constituted gross indecency (*R. v. P.,* [1968] 3 C.C.C. 129, 3 C.R.N.S. 302, 63 W.W.R. 222 (C.A. Man.)).

Indecent Assault

Like gross indecency, indecent assault is an offence that no longer exists in Canada; it was abrogated in 1983. Its judicial history is particularly interesting since it was an obvious source of discrimination against homoerotic lifestyles. As it was defined in the early twentieth century, indecent assault was covered in two separate provisions of the Canadian Criminal Code: one for assaults on women (section 259) and the other for assaults on men (section 260). An individual found guilty of indecent assault on a female person faced a maximum sentence of five years in prison, whereas the same act perpetrated against a male person was punishable by ten years in prison and whipping. The Criminal Code also provided that corroboration was necessary only if the victim was female. The legislature thus created discrimination based on the sex of the person assaulted. Section 260 was replaced by section 293 in 1906, by section 148 in the Criminal Code of 1953-54, and finally by section 156 in the 1972 Code, which eliminated the use of the whip.

Is it possible that this legislative distinction was linked to the fact that customarily a boy was less likely to resist an indecent assault than a girl would or should be? It is tempting to answer yes. In section 661 of the Criminal Code, covering sexual psychopaths and passed in 1948 – a law of extreme severity for Canada since those convicted faced a prison term of indeterminate length – only indecent assault on a male person (section 293) was initially included.[4] Gross indecency (section 149) and sodomy (section 147) were added in 1954. Thus, although in theory section 661 applied to both heterosexual and homosexual criminals – it was aimed primarily at protecting girls from assaults by men – the Royal Commission on the Criminal Law Relating to Criminal Sexual Psychopaths (Canada 1959, 27) stated, "With respect, we think there are profound problems raised by homosexuality."[5] The commission cited testimony by the chief constable of the Toronto Police Force, John Chisholm: "Homosexuality is a constant problem for the Police of large cities ... The saddest feature of all, however, is that homosexuals corrupt others and are constantly recruiting youths into their fraternity." As we shall see, this fear of the corruption of minors was also a key argument in the recriminalization of homosexuality in France in 1942.

Historically, those found guilty of offences committed against women have always received lighter sentences. For instance, in the eighteenth and nineteenth centuries, and even in the early twentieth century, defendants were found guilty of rape only if physical proof confirmed the woman's complaint. Women were, a priori, considered suspect, with the implication that they may have unknowingly seduced their attacker.[6] In other words, whereas an indecent assault on a woman presumed consent, implicit or not, by the victim, such an assault on a man could be the fruit only of an unforgivable subterfuge stemming from some sort of perversion, which had to be punished severely.

From the Crime of Sodomy to Anal Sexual Relations

Sodomy, as an illegal activity, was incorporated into the Canadian Criminal Code of 1892, in section 174, under the heading "Offences against Morality." The applicable punishment was imprisonment for life.[7] The section made no distinction between sodomy and bestiality: "Every one is guilty of an indictable offence ... who commits buggery, either with a human being or with any other living creature." The use of the term "indictable offence" in reference to sodomy, its classification under the heading "Offences against Morality," and the severity of the applicable penalty were admissions that the legislature of the time, and the society that it represented, had a strong prejudice against this type of sexual behaviour – a prejudice no doubt dictated by religious ideology. In comparison, incest was punishable by fourteen years in prison. The 1892 provision was not substantially modified when the Criminal Code was revised in 1954, although the maximum penalty for the offence of sodomy was reduced to fourteen years in prison.[8] In addition, although both sodomy and bestiality were punishable under section 147, they were differentiated in the French version of the statute, whereas in the English version they remained grouped under the term "buggery." It was not until 1988 that the term "sodomy" was replaced in the Criminal Code by the more laicized term "anal sexual relations."

The "Homosexual" Phenomenon and Judicial Practice

The above overview of the evolution of certain Canadian statutes with regard to homoerotic offences shows a certain softening of penal doctrine. Was it the same for judicial practice and police repression?

From the First Canadian Criminal Code to the End of the First World War: A Growing Crime?

Historically, statistical studies on indictments and convictions for homoerotic acts have not been very accurate: in *The Statistical Year Book of*

Canada (1901, 596-97), no distinction is made between sodomy, bestiality, and gross indecency. Robert Demers (1984) nevertheless feels that the statistics reveal some significant trends regarding repression of homoerotic lifestyles. He lists, in Canada between 1891 and 1900, sixty-nine men convicted of sodomy and bestiality, or an average of seven convictions per year. However, because these statistics are unreliable, Hurteau's (1993, 47) research of the minute books in the pre-archiving centre of the Quebec Department of Justice in Montreal is more instructive. His examination of the records of the Court of the Sessions of the Peace for the Montreal judicial district from 1891 to 1907 clearly reveals the effects of the statute respecting gross indecency on the repression of homoerotic behaviours, as a number of sexual practices other than sodomy or attempted sodomy could now be used to indict Montreal homosexuals. As he notes (our translation), "One is struck immediately by the impact of the amendment to the 1890 criminal statute." In the year of its adoption, nine men were charged with gross indecency. For the period 1891-1907, Hurteau (1991; 1993, 47) found sixty-seven charges of gross indecency for Montreal alone – an average of 3.9 charges per year. Although this average may seem relatively low, it is nevertheless a striking increase over the total of three cases listed for sodomy or attempted sodomy between 1872 and 1890.

Hurteau (1991, 157, our translation) also emphasizes judges' intention to hit hard once the new statute was adopted. This was manifested in the severity of the sentences handed down in 1891: "During that year, seven of the nine charged were sentenced to be whipped and six of them received more than two years" in prison. However, the severity of the sentences quickly declined. In 1906, ten of the fifteen convictions were settled with a simple fine. The judges' discretionary power was obvious: sentences ranged from a fine to five years in prison. As Hurteau (1993, 47, our translation) suggests, "The judges' personalities and moral ideas had some bearing." As examples, he cites the 1897 cases of Joseph Clément, who was sentenced to six months in prison for gross indecency with a fourteen-year-old teenager "four to five times a week for three months," and Victor Brunette, sentenced to five years in prison for touching an eleven-year-old boy.[9]

It is difficult to establish the exact number of charges involving minors, as the statistics do not give these details. Demers (1984, 793) claims, however, that most charges of gross indecency were for public indecency with a minor. Hurteau (1991, 158, our translation) – on the basis of the criminal archives – advances that between 1891 and 1907 about 50 percent of gross indecency offences involved minors, a proportion that is "quite high and no doubt signalled a turnaround in social tolerance, particularly within families, regarding the sexuality of adolescents." The new statute, combined with the emerging medical discourse on perversion, very likely drew families' attention to homoerotic acts that might occur between family members and children.

As they had been during previous centuries, homoerotic lifestyles were easily associated with corruption of minors. Society feared that homosexuality among young people would lead to general depravity and that nonreproductive sexuality would cause the nation to decline. "The myth of the homosexual as a corrupter of youth, a satyr or a criminal gained new life, however, in the wake of several sex scandals ... This all reinforced the caricatured image of the diabolical pervert and intensified the already severe psychosis about the dangers to young people" (Tamagne 2004, vol. 2, 46; see also Jenkins 1998). As Philip Jenkins (1998) and George Chauncey (1998, 100) observe, the image of the effeminate homosexual was gradually replaced by that of the dangerous psychopath, capable of committing the most horrible crimes against children, while the press spread the idea of the homosexual who was invisible and therefore impossible to detect. In other words, as long as the image of the homosexual remained that of effeminacy, which was easily identifiable, society had nothing to fear. With the masculinization of gay culture, homosexuals became difficult to distinguish; in fact, a good number of homosexuals sought to act virile in order to lose themselves in the crowd (Mosse 1997, 174). Their invisibility made them more frightening, especially for children. "In the 1920s," writes Chauncey (1998, 106, our translation), "'fags,' with their close identification with women, provoked more laughter and contempt than fear. In the 1950s, however, the sexual deviant, presented as a man situated outside the domestic and domesticating sphere of the heterosexual family, became a threat to children and women."

More generally, it was the sexuality of young people that was disquieting; the fear that masturbation would lead minors to homosexuality or madness, prevalent in the previous century, still hovered.[10] Starting in the 1930s, both moral and medical discourses demanded a return to family values. Paradoxically, in his examination of sentences for gross indecency,

Hurteau (1991, 157, our translation) finds no significant distinction between sentences meted out for two consenting adults and those for an adult and a minor, the whip being "reserved as much for consenting adults as for those sentenced for fellatio or masturbation with minors." Again, the particular act was being punished rather than a general act of assault.

The Interwar Period: The Effects of the Economic Crisis

During the 1930s police forces in the United States and Europe began to entrap homosexuals using a variety of strategies – with the exception of France, which did not officially recriminalize homosexuality until 1942.[11] In England, repression was in high gear and the number of arrests rose steeply. Police operations became so common that a climate of panic reigned among homosexuals. In 1931 the issue of homosexuality was pressing enough that a conference on homosexual crimes was organized in London (Tamagne 2004, vol. 2, 134-58). Apparently, the economic crisis and the rise of fascism were encouraging a return to more puritanical values. The more permissive "roaring twenties" were truly over.

In Quebec and Canada, from the 1930s to 1950, the crime for which homosexuals were most often found guilty was gross indecency in a public place (see Hurteau 1991, 152-56; Demers 1984, 794). The statistics in the *Annuaire du Québec* from 1930 to 1939 indicate a strong resurgence in indictments and convictions for sodomy and bestiality in Quebec. At the beginning of the century, there was an annual average of seven convictions in Canada; in the 1930s the annual average in Quebec alone was around forty convictions.

Table 4.1
Convictions for sodomy, Quebec, 1930-39

Year	Convictions	Year	Convictions	Year	Convictions
1930	29	1934	25	1937	56
1931	20	1935	25	1938	66
1932	31	1936	65	1939	34
1933	44				

Note: Before 1930, the *Annuaire du Québec* does not give details on the nature of the crimes committed. For the beginning of the century, I do not have Quebec-only statistics on the subject.
Source: Annuaire du Québec.

Demers (1984, 794) attributes the upsurge to both population growth and an increase in the number of cases brought under the statute on gross indecency conducted in private between consenting adults. He does not mention, however, whether the charges of sodomy were laid against pairs consisting of two men or of a man and a woman. Although these statistics do not seem very relevant for determining the true scope of repression of homosexuals, they are nonetheless indirectly useful since they show the increase in charges of sodomy, a sexual behaviour with a strong religious connotation that was generally associated with homoerotic lifestyles. It is not unlikely that all "unnatural" lifestyles were at risk of being legally sanctioned. The high conviction rate – that is, the ratio of the number sentenced to the number charged – for sodomy in Quebec in 1930, 1931, and 1932 is instructive. For these years, when the economic crisis was at its worst, the conviction rate was around 89 percent (80 sentenced out of 90 charged). In comparison, during the same period, the conviction rates for murder and rape were, respectively, 55 percent (17 sentenced out of 31 charged) and 65.5 percent (188 sentenced out of 287 charged), and the average conviction rate for all offences together was 79 percent. Surprisingly, it was easier to prove an act of sodomy than of murder or rape! In Canada as a whole, the conviction rate for sodomy was 82 percent, close to the rate for all crimes (83 percent). Given these differences between the Quebec and Canadian rates and the above discussion about the omnipresence of ecclesiastical discourse in Quebec society, compared to a Protestant Ontario that was more inclined toward medical discourse, it is plausible that Quebec judges were more inclined to deal harshly with sodomy than were their Anglo-Saxon counterparts.

Among the hypotheses proposed throughout history to explain the repression of homosexuality, one seems to be a constant: when socio-economic crises arise, the homosexual serves as a scapegoat to calm public opinion. In stormy periods – times of war, dropping birth rate, or economic crisis – repression of homosexuals (and other "deviants") increases. For example, when a nation suffers a dropping birth rate, the authorities act together to discriminate against nonreproductive behaviours that might impede reproduction and national prosperity. According to Paul-André Linteau and his colleagues (1991, 5), "The impact of the Depression [in Quebec and Canada] went beyond the economic sphere. The social and political instability it caused were evident throughout the decade." One effect was a dramatic drop in the birth rate, even though traditionalist ideology emphasized the duty to procreate; between 1931 and 1941, Quebec's population grew by 15.9 percent, less than the 21.8 percent during the previous decade. A period of upheaval ensued, with much dispute among governments, a resurgence of religious fervour, and the rise of extremist movements.

Church discourse regarding sexuality and the homosexual question remained very influential. The clergy, now acquiescing to a certain form of sex education, presented itself as the guarantor of this knowledge. The church still condemned homoerotic lifestyles and extramarital sex – a condemnation inscribed within a broader context of rejection of pleasure and idleness, which were said to put community morality, individual spirituality, and productivity at risk. With the expansion of capitalism, "pleasure was suspect more than ever," remark Georges Falconnet and Nicole Lefaucheur (1975, 137, our translation). Christian theory was fundamentally suspicious of pleasure; sexual pleasure within marriage was officially authorized by the church only in 1951 (see Bechtel 1994, 169, 247). In Quebec, Ultramontanism, based on work and conservatism, remained a core value in the first half of the twentieth century.

It is not unreasonable to think that in a social context of economic crisis, falling birth rate, and rejection of all forms of pleasure, criminal repression of homosexuals was accentuated – as it was for all minorities designated as scapegoats. According to Florence Tamagne (2004, vol. 2, 249), "In the 1930s, talk about a decline became commonplace. The disintegration of the political system, the fall in the birth rate, the penetration of society by foreign and Jewish influences were denounced as well as the liberalization of morals and homosexuality." For instance, 1932 and 1933, years in which the number of convictions for sodomy increased markedly (+55 percent in 1932 and +42 percent in 1933), were also years in which the unemployment rate reached an unprecedented peak of 27 percent in Canada. It had been 2.9 percent in 1929. The conviction rates for these years were also very high (89 percent). Another increase in the number of convictions began in 1936, the year following the election of Maurice Duplessis as premier of Quebec; his political mandate was characterized by a return to clericalism and the rejection of all deviances, including sexual. This trend continued as the Second World War began. Jean Caron notes, "Two hundred men [were] charged with corruption of boys between January 1942 and January 1944" (quoted in Hurteau 1993, 59, our translation).

Can we conclude from these statistics that socio-political changes led to increased repression of homoerotic lifestyles? Homosexuals were repressed almost universally; for example, in the United States the army described them as sexual psychopaths and set out to reveal and exclude them. The American government devised tests to screen for three types of homosexuals: those with identifying physical characteristics, those with effeminate clothing or behaviours, and those with a loose, relaxed rectum. Homosexuals had to be physically distinct from heterosexuals so that they could be discerned by the naked eye! At the end of the war, a panoply of new categories was created: "latent, self-confessed, well-adjusted, habitual, undetected or known, true, confirmed and male or female" (Spencer 1995, 350). At the same time, homosexuals began to recognize each other and realize that they were not alone. As had occurred in Europe after the First World War, a homosexual identity took shape in North America as urban density grew.

The Duplessis Years: Puritanism Makes a Comeback

After the suffering of the war, Quebec, and North America as a whole, saw a surge of social change, marked by signs of rebelliousness among young people and a general desire to enjoy life. Although homophobic stereotypes were still commonly conveyed by religious and public discourse, homosexuality became a fashionable subject, to be discussed and analyzed from every angle (Tamagne 2004, vol. 2, 73). This relative freedom, however, was short-lived; in the late 1940s and early 1950s the wind began to blow in the opposite direction, toward ideological puritanism and radicalism. The wave of repression triggered during the war returned in the 1950s, as conformism and traditional values were reasserted. In such a context, deviance, particularly of a sexual nature, was seen in a dim light. According to Jenkins (1998, 61), American homosexuals were seriously affected by the emergence of the campaign against psychopathology. Presented as a threat to the nation by the media and the political authorities, homosexuals took refuge in secrecy and shame. In both the United States and Europe, particularly Great Britain, a hunt for pederasts took shape. Quickly, homosexuals became associated with communism. In the United States, Senator Joe McCarthy's anticommunist campaign was used as a pretext for attacks against homosexuals. For example, candidates for employment in the United States public service not only had to profess their belief in God or to claim weekly church attendance but also had to inform their prospective employer of whether or not the statement "I am attracted to people of the same sex as me" (Bouchard and Franklin 1980, 50, quoted in Goreham 1984, 862, our translation) applied to them. A number of civil servants lost their job this way.

The postwar years in Quebec under Maurice Duplessis were characterized by an increased emphasis on a monolithic, traditional, clerical, and rural society, despite a constant and rapid rise in urbanization in the 1940s and 1950s (the urbanization rate grew from 61.2 percent in 1941 to 74.3 percent in 1961). A great defender of the established order, Duplessis stressed the maintenance of religious values and did not hesitate to use the judiciary, the police, and the legislature to combat the deviant minorities whom he considered dangerous and subversive. The church had considerable power; Linteau and colleagues (1991, 239) claim that its wealth and influence had never been so strong. According to Hurteau (1993, 42, our translation),

Church and state sometimes formed a common front to subordinate erotic life to marriage and to condemn or punish extramarital sex. They also made unprecedented efforts to promote domestic life based on dichotomous sexual roles. Medical discourse intensified this offensive by giving a scientific veneer and an appearance of objectivity to the dangers of venereal pleasures, the need to maintain public hygiene, and division of the sexes. Opinions issued on anything that was ambiguous or deviant were always severe.

Hurteau posits that the increased repression of sexuality responded to a political need to protect the Quebec family and the institution of marriage from depraved morals. Quebec society, he believes, judged homosexuality more severely than adultery because it both put the family at risk by being centred on a hedonistic and egotistical sexuality and transgressed the sacrosanct rigidity of gender roles.

Religious discourse endured at the core of Quebec's social regulation. Like the judiciary, the church escalated its rhetoric, trumpeting the threat that industrial capitalism posed to families and marriage and pressing for the *Kinsey Report* (see Kinsey, Pomeroy, and Martin 1948), which underlined the extent and frequency of homoerotic relations in the United States, to be banned in the province. This alarmism simply mirrored the anxieties of a society faced with the social changes brought by industrialization and urbanization (Hurteau 1993, 50-51). The rural exodus and the new separation between family and workplace led the clergy to mistrust the freedom enjoyed by urban young people, which might encourage the emergence of a homosexual subculture. The protection of children thus became one of the church's warhorses in its battle to preserve good morals, the institution of marriage, and the family (Lemieux and Montminy 2000). The clergy attempted to provide sex education for young people and to ensure that families were attentive to the sexuality of their children so that they could intervene rapidly if a scandal loomed. The increase in arrests for gross indecency in the 1930s and 1940s no doubt resulted from this increased vigilance – or, conversely, the increase in arrests incited parents to be vigilant. In either case, according to the penal statistics for Montreal, about 50 percent of arrests for gross indecency involved minors (for example, in 1937 10 arrests out of 20 involved minors, in 1946 19 out of 39, and in 1948 7 out of 15). This may have promulgated in the collective imagination the image of the homosexual as dangerous, particularly to adolescents. By the mid-twentieth century, the church, the police, medicine, and psychiatry were all condemning homosexuality. It was presented as a sin, a crime, and a disease. Given this, the courts turned increasingly to medical expertise.

The Rise of Medical Authority: A New Type of Pervert to Treat

In North America, including Quebec, judicial recourse to medical expertise fitted the current of scientific treatment within penal administration. Homophobic stereotypes were strengthened by the new medical discourses.[12] As had been the case at the beginning of the century, certain researchers maintained that heterosexuality was normal and that homosexuality could and had to be cured, notably American psychoanalysts such as Irving Bieber and Charles Socarides, who were convinced that homosexuality was reversible. In Bieber's (1987, 426) opinion,

> Humans are biologically programmed for heterosexuality, and all go through an early phase of heterosexual development and arousal capability before some veer off into a substitutive homosexual adaptation. Homosexuality develops only after early heterosexuality has been

dislocated by fears related to experiential factors such as a disturbed parent-child relationship, disturbed same-sex peer group relations, and other traumatic situations that inhibit heterosexuality.

Bieber claimed that 27 percent of the homosexuals whom he treated returned to exclusive heterosexuality. Other psychoanalysts, such as Wilhelm Stekel, saw homosexuality as stemming from an original bisexuality attributable to parents' impeding children's sublimation and suppressing their homosexual tendencies (see Lance 2000, 162-80). According to this view, it was essential to control and take charge of children's sex education. Socio-biological theories also became popular through media coverage. Advocates of these theories felt either that sexual behaviours were genetically programmed – that is, the genes of homosexual individuals differed from those of heterosexual individuals (Franz J. Kallmann) – or that homosexual genes, although not intrinsically different, had adaptive capacities that selected the individuals likely to reproduce them (Edward O. Wilson). Starting from these ideas, many researchers attempted to show the innate nature of homosexuality. Added to the mix were theories that posited that homosexuality was due to hormonal malfunction.[13] Although the results were contradictory, this research, most of it presenting homosexuals as sick individuals who might transmit their sexual disorder, influenced both public opinion and the justice system.

Medical procedures designed to treat homosexuals emerged in the prewar years. In 1937, Dr. Newdigate Owensby tried convulsive electroshock therapy with Metrazol, a chemical stimulant. Metrazol was quickly declared ineffective in curing homosexuals, although a number of physicians continued to use electroshock therapy (Spencer 1995, 351-53). Some scientists experimented with lobotomy to eliminate their patients' homoerotic impulses. Others hoped to treat homosexuality with castration; in Switzerland in the early twentieth century and in Denmark in the 1930s, more than two hundred castrations were performed on men accused of indecent assault and homosexual acts (Bonello 2000, 75).[14] In 1953, Karl M. Bowman and Bernice Eagle published an article in the *Journal of Social Hygiene* recommending therapeutic castration for homosexuals. In her excellent doctoral dissertation, the historian Isabelle Perreault (2009) also notes the use between 1948 and 1953 of psycho-surgical surgery (lobotomy) on homosexuals interned at Hôpital St-Jean de Dieu in Montreal, who were considered mentally ill by the psychiatrists of the time.[15] Furthermore, for the social worker Yvon Gauvin (1953, 55, our translation), who studied the effects of lobotomy on patients who masturbated or were homosexuals – the two often being linked – "out of a starting population of four homosexuals, only two were homosexuals following the operation, and they seemed to have conquered their bad tendencies after the operation."

In the late 1960s, the ideal of curing homosexuals was still widespread. A 1972 article in *France-Dimanche* stated that it was now possible to cure one-third of homosexuals using psychological treatment (see Hocquenghem 1993, 87). In 1952, homosexuality was classified as a sociopathic personality disorder by the American Psychiatric Association; in 1968, it was still considered a well-defined pathology in the *Diagnostic and Statistical Manual of Mental Diseases* (DSM-II). The term was withdrawn only in 1974 following a referendum among American specialists, in which 58 percent of the votes were in favour of depathologization of homosexuality.[16]

During the same period, other research raised questions about the pathological nature of homoerotic lifestyles. In 1948, the groundbreaking *Kinsey Report* showed that 37 percent of American men between ages sixteen and fifty-five had had at least one homoerotic encounter leading to orgasm, and about 50 percent had felt sexual attraction to another man. Paradoxically, although it tended to indicate a "normalization" of the homosexuality phenomenon, the *Kinsey Report* also served the interests of those determined to fight against this type of sexual behaviour. By stating loud and clear the scope of the homosexual phenomenon, the report ratcheted up the fear of an epidemic.

Influenced by the rise of medical discourse, the Canadian criminal justice system began to avail itself of therapeutic knowledge in the 1950s. Across the board, the courts turned to therapy as a way to control defendants' homoerotic impulses and, if possible, to direct them toward heterosexuality. In Montreal in 1949, the court ordered certain homosexuals to see social workers, and the Welfare Court sometimes sent young delinquents who claimed to be homosexual to foster homes for rehabilitation (Hurteau 1991, 171-72). Quebec became increasingly favourable to engaging the administration of criminal justice in the adventure of scientific treatment. The legislature modified or created statutes to make room for treatment in the penal system. The Royal Commission on the Criminal Law

Relating to Criminal Sexual Psychopaths (Canada 1958) emphasized the need to create institutions for the treatment of sexual deviants, whom it considered to be suffering from a personality disorder.[17] The commission concluded that the courts had to try to find ways to cure sexual deviants since they were a menace to public safety. Concerning the "homosexual problem" more specifically, the commission (Canada 1959, 28) emphasized that the Criminal Code's section 661, on sexual psychopaths (1948), "has been invoked against homosexuals ... only where the offences have involved juveniles," as though "'pathological' homosexuality were in some way linked to assaults on minors" (Corriveau 2007, 7, our translation). Hurteau (1991, 174-75) notes that the commission endorsed homophobic panic based on the stereotype of the homosexual who corrupted minors, even though there was no consensus in the scientific community on whether homosexuality should be included in the category of sexual psychopaths.

This image of the homosexual as an individual at risk and as pathological was conveyed in the Criminal Code in 1961 with the definition of the sexual psychopath, which aimed at "putting under lock and key anyone who cannot control his homosexual impulses, even if he presents no risk of violent aggression against potential victims" (Hurteau 1991, 167, our translation). The Supreme Court of Canada's ruling in the *Klippert* case (S.C.C. [1967], 823-36), which upheld the status of "dangerous sexual delinquent" for Everett George Klippert, an admitted homosexual, would lead one to believe that the legislature considered homoerotic behaviours in and of themselves to be a danger to the community. As Kinsman (2000, 143) observes, "In the 1950s and 1960s in Canada, state agencies and mass media reports defined gay men and, in a different but related way, lesbians as national, social, and sexual 'danger.'"

This definition resulted, among other things, in increased police surveillance of homosexuals. John Sawatsky (1980, 125-26) confirms that the Royal Canadian Mounted Police (RCMP) had a special investigation unit (A-3) specifically charged with unmasking homosexuals. Therefore, thousands of homosexuals were on the radar of the RCMP and the Canadian authorities during the Cold War years (Gentile and Kinsman 2008, 43; Kinsman 2000, 143; Ryan 2003, 61). The federal government funded research on how to detect them. A number of tests were developed and used in the Fruit Machine project, created by Professor Robert Wake of Carleton University, the medical researcher for the Royal Commission on the

Criminal Law Relating to Criminal Sexual Psychopaths (Gentile and Kinsman 2008, 48; see also Kinsman 1996, 177-81).[18]

Many experts claimed that they alone could identify psychopaths, who were able to cloak themselves in anonymity. Some asserted that homosexuals formed an organized secret order that spread through society by means of proselytization (Hurteau 1991, 175), an idea that may have emanated from the United States and the antihomosexual campaign led by Senator Joe McCarthy. The Canadian government included homosexuals on the list of undesirables under the Immigration Act.

The climate of social censorship built around the homosexual issue became a generalized taboo. The media were instructed to hush up the subject so that homosexuals would not have a chance to recognize each other. Such media censorship had existed since the late nineteenth century, when the church controlled the circulation of publications dealing with homosexuality – circulation usually linked to criminality. Ross Higgins (1999, 43, our translation) notes, "This moral and medical rhetoric exerted its power within society. All of the more reasoned voices were drowned out beneath the dominant heterosexist discourse, the only recognized social discourse, which did not admit the possibility of a homosexual life." Benoît Migneault (2001, 4), of the Government of Quebec's division of magazines, newspapers, and government publications, observes that publications for a homosexual readership remained subject to prosecution until the Omnibus Bill was adopted in 1969. When newspapers addressed the issue of homosexuality, the slant was invariably negative. Homosexuals were often described as monsters, child rapists, or transvestites. From the 1940s to the 1960s the mainstream press, tabloids, and bestselling novels reinforced homosexual stereotypes, notably "those of the pedophile homosexual and the lesbian who seduces poor innocent women" (Demczuk and Remiggi 1998, 18, our translation; see also Jenkins 1998).

Thus the print press fed on, and fed in its turn, the social panic over homosexuality. The media often associated homosexuals with violent crime and alcoholism and reiterated the association between homosexuals and pedophiles (Higgins and Chamberland 1992). Higgins (1999, 58, our translation) gives the example of a headline in a 1965 tabloid: "Homosexuality Advancing: A Threat to Our Children." According to Migneault (2001, 5), out of 157 articles on homosexuality between 1952 and 1970, 25 percent

Table 4.2
Number of convictions for sodomy, Quebec, 1946-59

Year	Convictions	Year	Convictions	Year	Convictions
1946	113	1951	87	1956	135
1947	70	1952	73	1957	117
1948	n/a	1953	97	1958	68
1949	55	1954	212	1959	104
1950	68	1955	173		

Source: *Annuaire du Québec.*

dealt with criminal matters, 41 percent with morality, and 34 percent with an analysis of this reality – these last resulting from the new interest in the subject raised by adoption of the 1969 Omnibus Bill. He notes that the media used science predominantly to strengthen the image of the sexually perverse homosexual and rarely to justify or legitimize homoerotic lifestyles.

Despite the climate of persecution and censure that endured until the mid-1960s, the postwar wave of industrialization favoured the marketing of all types of sexual desire, including homosexual desire. Gay bars, saunas, and meeting places sprang up. At the same time, there was an increase in police and judicial repression. Once again, the use of penal statistics poses a problem. The number of convictions for indecent assault on a man – the only exclusively homoerotic crime – is available only for 1956, when there was one charge, and for 1957, when there were seventy-one. This is explained by the fact that the statistics of the *Annuaire du Québec* do not include convictions by summary proceeding, which was likely the most frequently used procedure for charges involving homoerotic lifestyles since it enabled both the severe penalties and the visibility associated with a trial to be avoided. This hypothesis seems plausible since, at the time, both defendants and the courts were trying to hush up this type of offence. Simply as a rough guide, Table 4.2 shows the *Annuaire du Québec*'s penal statistics on convictions for sodomy, the offence most strongly linked to homoerotic lifestyles.

From 1946 to 1959, a total of 1,162 people were found guilty of sodomy or bestiality, for an annual average of ninety convicted, with a spike in numbers in 1954 and for several years after.[19] This may be explained by changes to the Criminal Code in 1954 that reduced the penalties for sodomy and added sexual psychopaths to the definition of dangerous criminals. Two hypotheses come to mind: either judges found more defendants guilty because the sentences were less severe, or the change to the Code led to a renewed interest in this type of crime. The second hypothesis seems more plausible, as 1954 was a time of strong police repression in Montreal. Since 34 percent of the population of Quebec lived in Montreal in 1951 and 40 percent in 1961, it is very likely that what happened there heavily influenced the province's penal statistics as a whole.

The case of Montreal in the 1950s is instructive. According to Luther A. Allen (1998, 92) and Higgins (1999), the increase in police repression in the mid-1950s was a reaction to demand by public opinion and the leading class, which expressed a desire to see stronger action taken against sexual deviants. It was in this climate of general moral indignation that Jean Drapeau was elected mayor of Montreal, in 1954, promising to fight the social scourge of homosexuality. After he took office, the number of arrests and raids rose to a draconian level. Gross indecency arrests thus varied more as a function of the degree of police repression than as a real increase in criminality. For example, whereas there were 65 charges of gross indecency in Montreal in 1953 and 75 in 1955, there were 311 in 1954. Montreal's chief prosecutor, Jacques Fournier, admitted that the "necessary measures" were taken to purge Mount Royal Park of homosexuals. The Montreal police came up with strategies to preserve the moral and social order; among these, as Allen (1998, 91-92), notes, was the use of provocateurs to ensnare homosexuals, reminiscent of the use of *mouches* in France in the seventeenth and eighteenth centuries.

A number of arrests were made for indecent action (section 158a). Unlike gross indecency, which was limited to sex acts committed between two consenting people of the same sex, this offence did not require that proof of complicity between the individuals be established. Because the penalties were relatively light, the majority of those charged were encouraged to plead guilty in order to avoid the publicity of a trial (see Saunders 1967-68, 26).

The Quiet Revolution: Homosexual as Corruptor of Minors?[20]
Police repression continued throughout the 1950s and 1960s. From 1959 to 1966 – the period called the Quiet Revolution in Quebec – the annual

average number of convictions for sodomy was 128.5, with a peak of 212 in 1964; this fell to 55 in 1968, the year in which began the debates on the Omnibus Bill, which would decriminalize all sexual behaviours conducted by consenting adults in private. Although these figures give some indication of the changes in public opinion regarding sodomy and deviant lifestyles, they do not give a precise number of convictions of homosexuals. A look at the situation prevailing in Toronto during the same period is therefore instructive. Alex K. Gigeroff's (1968, 173) analysis gives a good overview of the trend in charges of gross indecency, an offence often used to repress homosexuals, in the early 1960s. Out of the sixty people convicted for gross indecency in 1961 (sixty-eight charges), forty were consenting adult males. Only four of those charged, or 6.6 percent, were heterosexuals. Interestingly, nine adult men were accused of sixteen offences perpetrated against young people between fourteen and twenty-one years of age (one of them, however, was convicted on seven counts). In five of these cases, the young person was also found guilty (three of these trials involved young people between nineteen and twenty-one years of age, and the other two were sixteen and seventeen years old). Finally, eleven of these crimes took place in a private place – a residence or hotel room – and charges against children under fourteen years of age constituted only 5 percent of the sample (four individuals).

Two observations can be made. First, the offence of gross indecency was used mainly to charge homosexuals. Second, the image of the homosexual as corruptor of minors was exaggerated in public opinion: in fact, only 5 percent of cases were linked to young people under fourteen years of age, and out of the nine cases in which adults were found guilty of gross indecency with youths between fourteen and twenty-one years of age, five young people were also found guilty. According to Gigeroff (1968, 179, our translation), these data are representative of the judicial reality concerning use of the statute on gross indecency. He concludes, "Offences committed under the statutes controlling homosexual, exhibitionistic, and pedophilic acts form only a small proportion of crimes, but *these offences represent the major sexual deviancy offences and the great majority of all sexual offences in the community*" (emphasis added). Keeping Gigeroff's observation in mind, I compared the Quebec statistics on repression of sodomy in the 1960s with those in the 1930s. First, there was a clear increase in criminal convictions. From an annual average of 39.5 convictions for sodomy and bestiality in Quebec in the 1930s, the average rose to around 129 in the 1960s, an increase of almost 225 percent. One might presume that this is explained by the growth in urbanization (about 78 percent in 1966), which corresponded to a rise in numbers of homosexual bars and meeting places. This concentration of the homosexual phenomenon, I believe, favoured and encouraged police interventions. Might this hypothesis apply to pedophilia today? Could it be that the global reach of the Internet has increased the visibility and mutual recognition of pedophiles, previously socially isolated, and at the same time favoured an increase in repression?

Larger police forces no doubt had something to do with increased interrogation of homosexuals in the 1960s; in Montreal, the number of police officers grew by 80 percent between 1950 and 1965.[21] Interviews conducted by Higgins (1999, 31, our translation) give a picture of police interventions regarding homosexuals: "Men who lived in the gay milieu in the 1960s state that police conducted their raids with lies, violence, and hate and that they aimed to meet arrest quotas through roundups, as well as by luring potential offenders through the procedure called entrapment."

Surprisingly, judicial repression of homosexuality increased as Quebec's economic situation improved (between 1962 and 1967) and as the church's influence over the population and government decisions was on the decline. With the deconsecration of institutions and secularization of social life in the early 1960s, the church's power as a maker of dominant discourse and a central institution in the community gave way to a more materialistic and rationalistic social philosophy.

Two conclusions may be drawn. First, homosexuality tends to be repressed in periods of depopulation or low birth rate. This seems to have been the case in Quebec, which saw its birth rate fall and its influence within Canada fade in the 1960s. Second, as homosexuality is more often than not associated with corruption of minors, the more attentive a society is to its young people, the greater the repression of threats to their well-being is likely to be. It is thus not impossible that Quebec society continued to repress homoerotic lifestyles with the aim of protecting its "most valuable asset." Linteau and colleagues (1991, 322) observe, in fact, that the 1960s were characterized by what they call the youth phenomenon. The state took charge of managing youth-protection services and recognized the primacy of the child's interests. In Ottawa, a number of members of Parliament and senators argued in parliamentary debates that decriminalizing homoerotic practices would put the protection of minors at risk. Nevertheless, Jenkins (1998, 101-6) maintains that from 1958 to 1976, paradoxically, pedophilia and incest were generally perceived by society with some indifference.

Turning Backward in France[22]

At the time of the French Revolution, criminal law in France was laicized, and the private and public domains became separate spheres. Following this legal rationale, sexual behaviours, homoerotic or not, practised in private between two consenting adults were not chargeable. This did not mean that homosexuality was tolerated but simply that the law did not pay particular, strictly defined attention to it. In 1942 France changed legislative directions.

Judicial Practice Regarding the "Homosexual" Phenomenon before 1942: A Unique Case of Nonrepression

From the revolution to 1942, France was unique in Europe for its lack of repression of homoerotic lifestyles. However, "behind this theoretical impunity, a practice of monitoring homosexuals developed that was based on a certain homophobia in the legal and police sectors" (Tamagne 2004, vol. 2, 175).[23] On the one hand, police forces exerted indirect repression by actively monitoring "homosexual" milieus; on the other hand, the magistracy seemed to consider homosexuality an aggravating factor in criminal trials, notably for the offences of indecent assault and molestation of a minor.[24] As had been the case in the nineteenth century, French judges used certain neutral laws that were not biased against homosexuals, although "such manoeuvres systematically failed on appeal," observes Tamagne (2000, 88, our translation). Nevertheless, according to Tamagne (2004, vol. 2, 178), "It is important to note that the finer details of the law were applied only reluctantly; and it would be a mistake to think that the system of justice in France was completely indifferent to homosexuality." Homoerotic behaviours, in effect, were often considered an indecent assault, as well as a threat to the public order and national security.[25] Numerous homosexual scandals captured the public imagination in the late nineteenth century, provoking a return to a puritanical ideology. In England, the trial of Oscar Wilde sent shock waves through nascent homosexual communities. His conviction marked the victory of British puritanism and also fixed the image of the homosexual who corrupted minors, a source of danger and depravity in the social imagination. The sensational proceedings were followed in Europe by a conspiracy of silence about homosexuality in order to safeguard family morals.

A vast campaign of censorship and surveillance was instituted in France – especially in port cities, where the military feared that homosexuality would lead to treason. Surveillance of relations between sailors and civilians was increased. Tamagne's (2000, 88, our translation) research at the Archives nationales uncovered a file containing lists of meeting places and names of homosexuals: "The police listed all the sexual proclivities of suspects, and some officers devised what amounted to psychological essays on homosexuality. The most serious cases, titled 'homosexual sailors and communists,' betrayed phantasmic anxieties and suspected links between homosexuality and treason. For example, sailors were suspected of revealing state secrets during 'pillow talk' and of spreading communist propaganda."

All likely sites for homosexual encounters were placed under police surveillance. As Régis Revenin (2005, 165, our translation) notes, "The Paris police surveyed, opened files on, and arrested numerous homosexuals, at a time when the law did not punish homosexuality." It was important to know about homosexuals' living habits; thus the police legitimized their surveillance through the need to provide scientific descriptions of homosexuality. By subscribing to the proliferating medical discourse, the police sought to play a significant role in the fight against perversion. Homosexuals also used medical descriptions to define themselves and sometimes to excuse their behaviour – for instance, "I am a homosexual since birth and there is nothing I can do against this vice which is incurable for me, as it is for so many other individuals" (report of 7 August 1930 [Toulon], quoted in Tamagne 2004, vol. 2, 191). The passive or active nature of the sex act was of enormous interest. Tamagne (2004, vol. 2, 192) notes that the discourse of the French police was very different from that of the British police in that it went "beyond a discussion of criminal investigation to become a tool in the regulation of social life." She mentions the existence of certain special files, in which the homosexual character of an offender

– whether or not the offence had to do with morals – was described in detail in the police report; in many of these cases, it was considered an aggravating factor.

Given the medical stigmatization and the strict police surveillance, the homosexual became an ideal "instrument" for attaining certain political objectives. For example, when Hitler disbanded the S.A. (Sturmabteilung, or Storm Battalion) and had its leader, Ernst Julius Röhm, killed, he used the pretext of homosexuality to legitimize his action. Röhm was presented as a traitor and a homosexual – his homosexuality making him vulnerable to corruption. Tamagne (2004, vol. 2, 271) emphasizes that "for those who were promoting the theory of decadence, the lead-up to the war needed to include the elimination of the weak, the degenerate, the parasites. Homosexuals were first in line." Throughout the Second World War, homosexuals were regarded with suspicion. They were suspected of being traitors, communists, fascists – in short, the enemy within, who, vulnerable to blackmail, might put the nation's security in peril.

In addition to being associated with treason and fascism (Mosse 1988, 14), homosexuality raised fears of the worst for French youth.[26] According to some police chiefs, it was up to the public authorities to protect young people by limiting the spread of homosexuality, which threatened to weaken every social class in France. This fear of national degeneration and perversion of minors corresponded well to the tenor of the times. Since the late nineteenth century, France had been bogged down in a sort of national psychosis with regard to its birth rate: "Everything – literally *everything* – worked together to accentuate a procreative and puritanical moralism in sexual matters" (Guillebaud 1999, 241, emphasis in original). Furthermore, with the huge losses of French troops during the First World War, the situation was getting worse. Demographic deficiency, which was associated with immorality, became "the scapegoat onto which the French unconscious piled defeats, the loss of global – then continental – dominance, [soon] the loss of an empire, and the inexorable decline of its power and influence" (Poursin 1992, quoted in Guillebaud 1999, 243).

Discourses by public authorities such as the legislature, the civil service, and the magistracy were, as a rule, unfavourable to homosexuality because it challenged the hierarchy of social classes and was becoming more and more visible. As had been the case with the downfall of the "beautiful vice," the fear of a homosexual epidemic propagating throughout society haunted public opinion, so homosexuality was condemned in the name of morality and the survival of the nation. The authorities considered the visibility of homosexuality in the public sphere to be a direct threat to the public order and sexual morals. New regulations were promulgated in order to censor public representations of homosexuality in plays, movies, and cabarets (see Chauncey 1998, 99-100). It should be noted that in the early 1920s the press, radio, and cinema mushroomed in size and popularity, and they had an undeniable influence on public opinion.

Interestingly, the homosexual issue was treated differently by the mass media from country to country. Whereas the French press mentioned homosexuality only rarely in legal columns and editorials on youth, in England it was almost constantly discussed in legal columns. Tamagne (2004, vol. 2, 17) summarizes the situation: "In Germany, the problem was publicly discussed and the terms 'homosexuality,' 'inversion' and variations thereon were acceptable usage, for they now bore the imprimatur of science. In England, the press followed the prevailing code of silence and did nothing to acquaint the public with homosexuality. In France, the press was more loquacious, but remained extremely prudent."

Magazines and other publications that spread subversive ideas such as homosexuality, sexual liberation, divorce, and contraception – in short, everything that went counter to an overall strengthening of good morals and reproduction – were censored in France. The protection of good morals by legal censorship had existed in France since before the 1880s. Although the 1881 statute eliminated the offence of indecent exposure, it still included indecent assault. This provision was modified to include homosexual writings in 1920, 1939, 1949, and 1956. The homosexual magazine *Inversions,* sued for indecent assault, although there was no justification for banning it, was an example of the fear inspired by homosexuality. In its ruling, the court stated

> that almost every page of this publication constitutes a cynical apology for pederasty, a systematic appeal to homosexual passions and a ceaseless provocation of the unhealthiest curiosities; that also, in spite of the studious care to avoid any improper language, such articles constitute not only an attack on morals and a propaganda liable to compromise the future of the race through its neo-Malthusian tendencies, and also

ventures into obscenity, if not by words, at least by the indecency of some of the topics covered and by the general tenor of the publication. (Quoted in Tamagne 2004, vol. 2, 181)

Provisions of the Penal Code were also invoked to sanction pro-homosexual propaganda and thought. Section 14, added in 1949 and modified in 1958 by section 42, banned the display of magazines of a homosexual nature. Sections 263 to 290, on indecent assault, also applied to publishers and editors of these magazines. In the Civil Code, sections 6, 375, 900, 1133, 1172, and 1726 emphasized the obligation not to depart from "good morals" (Girard 1981, 20, our translation). As Tamagne (2004, vol. 2, 196) points out, "Once again we see that the civil authorities compensated, when they could, for the lack of legislation on homosexuality by eliminating wholesale those homosexuals who were most vulnerable. The foreign homosexual was considered most dangerous, as he might be a spy." Many foreign homosexuals were arrested and illegally expelled from France. Popular discourse freely associated homosexuals with foreigners, as it had numerous times throughout history; in the sixteenth and seventeenth centuries, for example, the majority of sodomy charges were made against foreigners, many of them Italians (see Godard 2001, 201). Later, homosexuality was identified with Germans in France and as a French disease in Germany. Overall, homosexuals were always seen as intruders into society. They might be anywhere, and their presence might undermine public morality.

Penal Doctrine under the Vichy Regime: Homosexuality, the New Social Scourge

On 6 August 1942 French law once again began to specifically repress homosexuality, marking a return to "a traditionalist and backward-looking concept of the state and society" (Romi 1988, 30, our translation). The legislation involved a complete reversal of the penal philosophy that had emerged from the French Revolution, under which the lack of legal repression of homoerotic lifestyles was inscribed within the rejection of religious ideology. A wind of puritanism was blowing through France, as it was through various countries in Europe after the Second World War. Citizens' morals had to be controlled and traditional values restored so that the nation could be re-established. "The factors responsible [for the defeat and the occupation] were identified: joy, democracy, foreigners, intellectuals who corrupted youth. 'Pleasure debases ... pleasure weakens,' declared Marshal Philippe Pétain as he announced the institution of 'moral order'" (Suyeux 1983, 64, our translation). Based on notions of Christian civilization, the Vichy regime resuscitated the old bans of the Ancien Régime.

Section 334 of the Penal Code (Act 742) read as follows:

> We, Marshal of France, Chief of the French state, the cabinet of ministers included, decree: Anyone who, either to satisfy the passions of another who is excited, encourages or facilitates debauchery or corruption of a youth of either sex, below the age of twenty-one years, or, to satisfy his own passions, commits one or more *indecent or unnatural acts with a minor of his own sex aged less than twenty-one years of age*, whether he is consenting or not, shall be punished by imprisonment of six months to three years and a fine. (Our translation, emphasis added)

Before enactment of the new Penal Code, there had been no distinction in the doctrine between heterosexual and homosexual corruption of a minor. Now, sexual majority was set at thirteen years of age for heterosexual acts and twenty-one years for homoerotic behaviours.[27] The imprecise definition of indecent and unnatural acts allowed for a broad interpretation of the statute, under which all acts with a sexual connotation could be repressed. As Boninchi (2005, 159, our translation) notes, the offence of homosexuality "directly penalized the performers of sexual acts [under twenty-one years of age] by forbidding them to 'satisfy their own passions,'" and couples both of whom were under twenty-one years of age could also be found guilty under section 334 of the Penal Code. Interpretation by magistrates and the police varied enormously. Homoerotic acts committed *in private* by two people over twenty-one years of age were not forbidden under the law. However, the rationale for not enacting "penalization of all 'deviant' sexual behaviours" was "neither tolerance nor respect for individual freedoms" but that doing so proved to be "ineffective or counterproductive" (Boninchi 2005, 158, our translation). Other common-law statutes were also occasionally used to control homoerotic behaviours between two adults over the age of twenty-one via section 330, on indecent exposure.[28]

These statutes were simply a manifestation of pro-birth and national-ist policies that had existed since the 1930s, along with an elevation of the family to cult status and a puritanical attitude toward sexuality. In fact, "after the rout of 1940, Philippe Pétain's French State, with its slogan, 'Labor, Family, Fatherland,' by no means went against the grain in France. On this matter at least, it coincided with a general climate that predated him" (Guillebaud 1999, 245; see also Boninchi 2005, 149). The Vichy regime simply brought these policies to bear directly on the control of morals: the statutes of 29 July 1939, on the family, and 25 January 1940, on procuring, venereal disease, and anti-birth propaganda, are perfect reflections of the fight against degradation of the nation's morals, which was blamed for France's military defeats and economic difficulties (Lascoumes 1998, 113). In the view of Michael Sibalis (2002, 304), "The origins of the new law, which predated the regime by more than a decade, lay in the expressed concerns of the Parisian police and the French naval authorities."[29] In his excellent book *Vichy et l'ordre moral,* Marc Boninchi (2005, 150, our trans-lation) explains that the new statute initially aimed to provide better protection of French minors against acts of corruption or debauchery.[30] He quotes a letter by the chief of the first Bureau au Garde des Sceaux that reveals the desire to "place the homosexual question on the legislative terrain" in order to fight the development of "homosexual practices likely to corrupt youth," as such corruption might create "particularly serious disorder."

In England, homosexuals were seen as potentially dangerous to the maintenance of national values and the prosperity of the state. This image was purveyed by the press and supported by repressive policies (mass ar-rests and charges). According to Colin Spencer (1995, 415), the number of prosecutions for homosexual behaviour rose from 800 to more than 2,500 per year between 1945 and 1955, and more than 1,000 convictions led to prison sentences.

Rather curiously, Pétain's ordinance was retained almost unaltered by Charles de Gaulle after the Liberation. Adopted on 27 July 1945, paragraph 3 of section 331, on indecent assault, repeated, almost verbatim, the word-ing in the 1942 ordinance: "Without prejudice to more severe penalties set out by the above paragraphs and articles 332 and 333 of the present Code, anyone who commits an indecent or unnatural act with another individ-ual of his sex under twenty-one years of age shall be punished with a fine

... and imprisonment of from six months to three years." Legal discrimination against homoerotic behaviours was maintained: whereas heterosexual acts were allowed between two minors, homoerotic behaviours were forbidden. An ordinance of the prefect of Paris dated 1 February 1949 also banned men from dancing together (Pierrat 1996, 149). Homosexuality was described by the authors of the penal doctrine as a disgusting passion that soiled and perverted minors. A surveillance group systematically gathered information on recognized homosexuals. "France remained one of the freest countries for homosexuals to live in," notes Sibalis (2002, 314), "and Paris was still the capital of European homosexuality in the 1950s and 1960s, but the government, the medical establishment, and the media preached the values of social conformity and family life, which many homosexuals themselves internalized."

In a 1959 article titled "Homosexuality and Its Influence on Delinquency," the director of the judiciary police, Mr. Fernet, confirmed "the interest that the police have in knowing this milieu well and making every effort to identify its members ... It is above all a secret, closed world, from which evidence, rarely given, is in any case guarded, and clues and denunciations are almost nonexistent" (quoted in Girard 1981, 21, our translation). All of this repression met with relative consensus in a Europe that was advocating a return to family values. The population question so disquieted France that in 1945 de Gaulle created the Institut national d'études démographiques (INED) in order to preserve the demographic equilibrium. With the support of numerous demographers, de Gaulle preserved the 1920 statute that banned anti-conception propaganda. He even received majority support from the population when he advocated a France with 100 million inhabitants in the 1950s and early 1960s (Guillebaud 1999, 246-47).

The strict morality and judicial segregation instigated during the Second World War continued into the 1960s. The statute on indecent exposure adopted on 25 November 1960 distinguished between homosexual and heterosexual indecent exposure, with the homoerotic act becoming an aggravating circumstance that was more severely punished. Under section 330, paragraph 2, "When the indecent exposure consists of an unnatural act with an individual of the same sex, the punishment shall be imprisonment of from six months to three years and a fine of 1,000 to 15,000 francs."

In comparison, heterosexual indecent exposure was liable for a fine of only between 500 and 4,500 francs or imprisonment for between three months and two years. The use of the term "unnatural" in the statute's wording is eloquent. From 1960 to 1982 homoerotic acts were also considered aggravating circumstances for indecent and unnatural acts (section 331-2). Guy Hocquenghem (1993, 65), a famous gay activist, states that to this obsession with discriminatory persecution must be added the fact that it was possible to prosecute

> two minors of between eighteen and twenty-one for practising homo-sexuality and to put the *case under the same heading as reciprocal assault and battery.* It is the height of paranoia that in cases concerning minors, *indirect proof or the examining magistrate's personal conviction is sufficient* (there is no need for a complaint to be lodged by the family); that in cases of indecent exposure, action may be taken against someone who does not repel an indecent caress quickly enough; that one simply needs to stay too long in a street urinal to be convicted of indecent exposure; that policemen may go as far as incitement (in Turkish baths, for instance) in order to provoke the offence. (Emphasis added)

The age of sexual majority for homoerotic acts was lowered to eighteen years in 1974.

To the recriminalization of homoeroticism under certain circumstances was added the inclusion of homosexuality on the list of social blights. On 18 July 1960 a member of the Assemblée nationale, Paul Mirguet, stated to the legislature, "You are all aware of the seriousness of the scourge that is homosexuality, a scourge against which we have the duty to protect our children" (Assemblée nationale, 18 July 1960, our translation).[31] Legitimized by psychiatric medicine, which left no shadow of a doubt about an epidemic of sexually transmitted diseases and contagious homosexuality, an amendment tabled by Mirguet was passed in the Assemblée nationale by a vote of 290 to 163 (68 abstained). Jacques Girard (1981, our translation) gives examples of doctors warning parents against the "homosexual peril." The new legislation placed homosexuality on a par with alcoholism, tuberculosis, and prostitution. Lawmakers had two objectives: first, to repress certain specific homoerotic behaviours; second, to control prophylaxis –

that is, "to prevent the development of a blighted sexuality or disease by keeping it from reaching minors" (Danet 1998, 101, our translation). Borrowing from the medical discourse of the time, the legislature saw it as a moral duty to impede propagation of homosexuality, even if medical theories had not totally demonstrated or concurred on the pathological or transmissible nature of this disease. If there was any doubt, it seemed better to prevent than to cure! "Sick people had to be kept from contaminating others; similarly, those with the misfortune of being homosexuals had to avoid transmitting their misfortune," observes Jean Danet (1998, 103, our translation).

By declaring homosexuality a social scourge, the French legislature could legitimately distinguish between and increase the penalties incurred for homoerotic acts without prejudice to sections 331, 332, and 333 of the Penal Code. Act 60-773, on social scourges, authorized the French government to take extraordinary measures to wage an effective battle against the behaviours defined in the statute. Buttressed by the press, which made connections among homosexuality, prostitution, and corruption of minors, the amendment was aimed more at repression of homosexuals themselves than at repression of their homoerotic behaviours. Girard (1981, 17) observes that the number of convictions grew until 1968 as the police used tried-and-true stratagems: informers and provocateurs. He notes that the fact that homosexuals were living more and more openly had an impact on the number of convictions. The government also wanted to stem displays such as those in the magazines *Futur, Arcadie,* and *Juventus,* created in the 1950s for a homosexual readership. For example, Olivier Jablonski (2001, 236, 239-40) reports that the courts found that "*Futur* constitutes a danger to public morality and an offense against morals" and *Arcadie* "a danger to youth." "The French authorities," Jablonski (2001, 240) continues, "obviously did not want a homosexual press to exist in France." Danet (1998, 102, our translation) points out that repression was not conducted systematically: "Statistics on the number of convictions as a quantum of penalty were convincing ... Works on penal law do not reveal a doctrine very passionate about the subject. In fact, the commentary on these rulings received minimum attention."

As the zeal for public health took hold, the potential for the spread of venereal disease played a prominent role in stoking paranoia about homosexuality. Anti-homosexual measures were justified in press campaigns that sounded the alarm about the resurgence, no doubt connected, of syphilis and homosexuality.[32] "The basis of syphilis is the phantasy fear of contamination, of a secret parallel advance both by the virus and by the libido's unconscious forces; the homosexual transmits syphilis as he transmits homosexuality," notes Hocquenghem (1993, 70). Echoing the situation that prevailed in the late nineteenth century, when societal anxiety regarding procreation was high, one of the great fears that haunted French society in the 1960s was that the nation would disintegrate due to a sudden downturn in population growth. In this context, it was necessary to contain the homosexual "epidemic." (This discourse resurfaced in the 1980s when the AIDS epidemic expanded.) Danet (1998, 101-2) claims that these statutes were aimed specifically at repressing certain homosexual acts – and the preventive treatments associated with them – and at averting the propagation of homosexuality among minors. It is interesting to note that the wave of repression that lasted from the 1960s to 1982 corresponded to a stagnation in population growth in France and throughout Europe caused by factors such as a drop in fertility and birth rates, women remaining single for a longer time, a dramatic increase in the divorce rate, and a decrease in the number of children per family.

Some Comparisons: The Place of the Individual in the Public Conscience

Most surprising in the history of judicial repression of homoerotic lifestyles in France and Quebec during this period is that, in the mid-twentieth century, France returned to a certain form of judicial repression after 150 years. In Quebec and Canada a new era of urbanization and industrialization engendered far-reaching changes in gender and family relations, and in sexuality in general, including the process of decriminalizing homoerotic behaviours with the adoption of the Omnibus Bill in 1969 (discussed in the next chapter). To the laicization and liberalization of society corresponded a relative softening of penal doctrine concerning sexual behaviours seen as deviant. In the mid-twentieth century, Quebec society (and Canadian society in general) was moving toward relative acceptance of, and social and judicial tolerance toward, homosexuality, in spite of very real repression by the police and the courts. In fact, as Quebec began to free itself from the grip of religion on all spheres of social life, Canada laicized the part of its penal law that dealt with morals by changing the meaning of "homosexual crime." In Quebec more particularly, with the emergence of individuality in the modern liberation movement that was swept in with the Quiet Revolution, the sex act in itself was no longer seen as disturbing, whereas violence and socially risky behaviours (especially with regard to children) associated with it grew in importance. In 1977 this tolerance reached its ultimate expression, as Quebec's legislature became the first in the world to adopt a law that protected homosexuals against discrimination.

In France, meanwhile, after the defeat suffered in the Second World War, politicians seemed to be stepping back down the path travelled since the French Revolution with regard to protection of private life, including sexuality, as indicated by a return to more traditional values, the strengthening of nationalist and birth-rate-oriented policies, and legal repression of all behaviours deemed harmful to the French state. Thus, homosexuality reappeared on the list of social scourges. As the country was suffering greatly in terms of both population growth and morale as a result of participation in two major wars, it was not surprising to see more conservative discourses re-emerge, particularly on sexual morality. France so feared for its demographic health that citizens were alerted to the importance of procreative activities, and homoerotic lifestyles and other behaviours that might be harmful to the nation's well-being were recriminalized. For example, advertising of condoms was not allowed in France until 27 January 1987.

Thus, homosexuality was repressed no longer for being an unnatural behaviour but for the risks posed by homosexuals (physical or moral injury). Since individuals were now at the core of the common conscience, it was no longer sodomy in itself that was disquieting but its effects on the individual. Whereas previously sodomy had been punished because it upset the divine order of the world, homosexuals now had to be expiated because they created a danger to the health and equilibrium of society by attacking its members. With regard to the specific fear of depravation of youth, it is possible that societal shame was displaced from the homosexual to the pedophile.

The Medicalization of Homosexuality: Toward a New Penal Rationale

Before I end this chapter, it is important to take a brief look at the widespread idea that the emergence of medical authority had a positive effect on the perception of homosexuality. Of course, modern medicine played a decisive role in the decriminalization of homosexuality. Although homosexuals remained discredited as individuals – they were still seen as outsiders who might impede the development of society – how they were labelled and treated changed. Whereas sodomists had been punished for their unnatural sexual behaviour, homosexuals, defined as inverts, were shut away because of the disease that afflicted them and the risk that they posed to the community. In other words, sodomists, transformed into homosexuals, became an object of study. In the late nineteenth century, all of the great psychiatrists were interested in various forms of perversion; now, perverts found themselves scrutinized no longer solely by judges but also by physicians and psychiatrists.

Graham Robb (2004, 41) notes, "As the medical profession gained in confidence and prestige, medical views of homosexuality became increasingly specialized and ingenious. Homosexuality was one of the undiscovered continents on which doctors could stake a claim to originality and build a career." Law and psychiatry competed to have their respective concept and treatment of sexual perverts prevail. Rather than being substitutes for penal repression of homosexuals, psychiatrization and medicalization were simply a complement and, in fact, provided legitimization for it. In the late nineteenth century, the sodomist, a "criminal before God," guilty of a despicable act that merited exemplary punishment, gave way to the invert, whose crime was antisocial. He was considered both sick and degenerate, and he belonged as much in the doctor's office as in the courtroom (Tamagne 2001, 92). In the early twentieth century, the use of experts in the justice system became systematic as the desire for categorization took hold.

In the quest for classification of sexual perversions in the late nineteenth century, scientists tried to define individuals with homoerotic behaviours according to their desires, sexual practices, and distinct physiological signs. A series of labels was created in an attempt to define the subject's sexual reality: uranist (Heinrich Ulrichs, 1864), intermediary sex (Magnus Hirschfeld, 1936), sexual invert (Havelock Ellis, Jean-Martin Charcot, and Victor Magnan 1822), and finally homosexual (Richard Krafft-Ebing 1892).[33] Different medical theories saw sexual identity as an instinct, a fate, and a destiny. In spite of sometimes contradictory definitions and an interpretation of causality that oscillated between the innate and the acquired, one fact remained: the focus was no longer solely on homoerotic acts but also on a particular individuality. From the sodomist, the judicial subject responsible for his acts, medicine fashioned the homosexual, an individual defined by his impulses, orientation, or sexual tastes, deemed irresponsible due to his disease. Michel Foucault (1990, 43) writes famously in *The History of Sexuality* about the medical invention of new "psychiatric species" and the new ways that they were controlled:

> As defined by the ancient civil or canonical codes, sodomy was a category of forbidden acts; their perpetrator was nothing more than the juridical subject of them. The nineteenth-century homosexual became a personage, a past, a case history, and a childhood, in addition to being a type of life, a life form, and a morphology, with an indiscreet anatomy and possibly a mysterious physiology. Nothing that went into his total composition was unaffected by his sexuality. It was everywhere present in him: at the root of all his actions because it was their insidious and indefinitely active principle; written immodestly on his face and body because it was a secret that always gave itself away. It was consubstantial with him, less as a habitual sin than the psychological, psychiatric, medical category of homosexuality was constituted from the moment it was characterized – [Carl] Westphal's famous article of 1870 on "contrary sexual sensations" can stand as its date of birth – less by a type of sexual relations than by a certain quality of sexual sensibility, a certain way of inverting the masculine and the feminine in oneself. Homosexuality appeared as one of the forms of sexuality when it was transposed from practice of sodomy onto a kind of interior androgyny, a hermaphrodism of the soul. The sodomite had been a temporary aberration; the homosexual was now a species.

With the medicalization of his sexual deviance, the homosexual became a subject. Because the notion of disease invalidated the subject's judicial capacity by creating the category of unfree and irresponsible, his rights and obligations were taken away due to his disease and for the protection of society. At the same time, the dictates of therapy excluded him from the category of subjects. The criminal sanction was thus replaced by a diagnosis of irresponsibility that forced him to undergo treatment, willingly or not, if he wished to be free again one day. Among these treatments were castration, therapies of all types (from hypnosis to operant conditioning), and medication. In the name of freedom, security, and well-being for all, the judicial domain was invaded by the medical world and its ideal of healing. Although homosexual deviants were punished less severely, the legal system now gave itself the right to remove them from society and lock them away, often for an indeterminate time, in its pursuit of the ideal of rehabilitation for all.

The main purpose of the penalty was displaced toward nonrecidivism – a desire to punish in order to prevent more effectively.[34] To address this new threat – the Other – a new vision of penalty was generated, pushing to "extremes the principle of collective defence which has been the aim of the law since the end of the eighteenth century, no longer condemning only the social gravity of the crime but a more intangible gravity, the dangerousness of the criminal himself, the offences he might commit and the harm he might do in the future" (Vigarello 2001, 237). There was now unprecedented confusion between penalty and treatment for various forms of deviance, but particularly sexual deviance. According to Denis Duclos (1997), director of research at the Centre national de la recherche scientifique, the melding of disease and criminality is understandable from the point of view of a desire to assign psychiatrists the role of policing morals, as they had policed sexual pathologies in the early twentieth century. For, asks Duclos (1997, 24-25, our translation), "Is it not obvious how regressive it is to treat as a patient a criminal who is certainly not a criminal due to the orientation of his desire or choice of object but because he chooses to perpetrate acts that are determined by society to be reprehensible?" He suggests that the technical, judicial, and medical mobilization around this form of sexual deviance testifies to a desire for "sex to return to the logic of people monitoring each other" and a "general pedagogization of behaviour." In fact, the French statute on recidivism debated in October 2004 went in this direction.

To the modern mind, *forcing someone to be under control,* psychically, surgically, or biochemically, was seen no longer as vengeance and punishment but as opening the possibility for the patient-criminal to return to a "normal" social life. Physical, electrical, or biochemical castration, however, was reminiscent of practices linked to repressive law. There was no reason to doubt that a new form of demonization was created by the collective conscience, as a defence mechanism against its own liberalness, to legitimize a fundamental historical shift to a new type of penalty that was thought of as preventive. The criminal was punished, of course, but he was also subjected to treatment that was supposed to cure him of the disease that he had contracted. The sanction referred no longer to accountability but to bio-psychological causality outside of the individual. Antoine Garapon and Denis Salas (1996, 89-90, our translation) rightly note that "only an indeterminate sentence, involving periodic examination, was now relevant" in penal intervention, which was crystallized around the flexible notion of dangerousness – a concept "that falls under impulsive, random, unpredictable risk."

In other words, although punishment was ideologically restorative and therapeutic, it remained strongly repressive in application. The shift from law to medicine, from punishment to political management and the use of behavioural technologies, is still current today. As Foucault (1991, 374, our translation) observes, whereas "legal thought distinguishes the licit from the illicit, medical thought distinguishes the normal from the abnormal; it appropriates and seeks means of correction that are not exactly means of punishment but means of transformation of the individual, an entire technology of behaviour of the human being." What I call *preventive law* penalized the deviant by modifying his body and personality technically and scientifically in order to restore him to a "normal" social life and prevent recidivism.[35] This new model of judicial management envisaged a criminal justice system whose goal was not specifically repression. It was intended to be a sort of hybrid of treatment and penalty that offered alternative sanctions more comparable to social responses than to penalties in the strict sense. This should not, however, make us lose sight of the fact that these sanctions also involved a superimposition of an old repressive form (punishment) that sometimes led to a reduction in the legal guarantees offered to individuals and "a qualitative and quantitative expansion of control and sanction" (Cartuyvels et al. 1997, 241, our translation).

5

The 1970s to the Present

FROM PRISON TO CITY HALL

[There are] those who say "you" to homosexuals then reproach them for not wanting to say "we"!

– Jacques Girard, *Le Mouvement homosexuel
en France, 1945-1980*

The law is no longer nowhere, it is everywhere, its significance undervalued, its power overvalued.

– Irène Théry, *Le Démariage, justice et vie privée*

The one charm of marriage is that it makes a life of deception absolutely necessary for both parties.

– Oscar Wilde, *The Picture of Dorian Gray*

Homosexuals Come out of the Closet: Affirmation, Repression, and Protection[1]

In the late 1960s, judicial repression of homoerotic lifestyles was still very common. In France, it reached a peak with the inclusion of homosexuality on the list of social evils. However, a revolutionary and libertarian wave was seeping through industrialized societies: the sexual revolution. In this roiling social environment, homosexuals began quietly to come out of the closet, advocate for their right to equality, and demand legal protection against all forms of discrimination.

The 1970s: The Birth of Gay Liberation Movements

On the evening of 27 June 1969, an unprecedented event in New York changed history for homosexuals; a group of gay men chose to resist a routine police raid on a bar called the Stonewall Inn. Three days of rioting ensued. This event marked the birth of the gay and lesbian liberation movement. In a number of countries every year since, Gay Pride Week has commemorated this first step toward coming out of the closet. Encouraged by the Stonewall incident and by feminist challenges to traditional sexual identities and roles, a number of homosexuals dared to drop their secrecy. First, they appropriated the language that identified and stigmatized them. Instead of the term "homosexual," associated with a type of perversion by the medical community, they chose "gay" to designate their specific, positive culture.[2] Then they formed liberation movements and became more and more visible on the political, artistic, and cultural scenes. In short, gays put themselves on display. Having won the right to individual and collective visibility, a number of gays and lesbians formed political organizations that sought to improve the legal and social status of homosexuals and lobbied for legislative change.

The revolutionary and libertarian current of the early 1970s was not without some contrary effects. A homophobic campaign took shape in the United States under the banner of religion, morality, and protection of children just as homosexuals were beginning to organize politically. Philip Jenkins (1998, 125) observes that the rhetoric linking homosexuality and pedophilia returned to prominence in the mid-1980s. As one slogan promulgated in the United States put it, "Homosexuals can't reproduce, so they have to recruit" (quoted in Jenkins 1998, 124). On the other hand, the American Psychiatric Association demedicalized homosexuality in a 1973 referendum, although 37 percent of its members were against this change. Pierre Thuiller (1989, 1131) notes that a study conducted in 1977 by the journal *Medical Aspects of Human Sexuality* found that 70 percent of American psychiatrists continued to see homosexuality as being the result of personal problems rather than as a construct derived from social stigmatization![3] Even in 1980 the third edition of the *Diagnostic and Statistical Manual of Mental Disorders* (DSM-III) defined "dystonic" homosexuality as an anomaly in development or a degeneration of an anatomical structure. The World Health Organization did not strike homosexuality from its list of diseases until 1993. Meanwhile, countless medical research projects in the 1980s and 1990s attempted to uncover the nature of homosexuality. Like Irving Bieber (1987, 432), many psychiatrists continued to see homosexuality "not [as] a normal sexual variant but [as] a manifestation of psychopathology."[4]

The 1980s: The AIDS Crisis

When the AIDS crisis hit homosexual communities in the 1980s, the image of the homosexual was tarnished once again. The epidemic reinforced prejudices and was used as a political pretext for advocating a return to the moral values that had prevailed before the sexual revolution. Some media outlets exploited the panic surrounding AIDS to revive the old stereotypes that homosexuality was contagious and a threat to the family. In France the Front national orchestrated its propaganda around fear of people with AIDS. A 1984 Sofres-*Le Nouvel Observateur* poll found that French tolerance of homosexuals had lost five points in the three previous years, due mainly to the AIDS epidemic. Ross Higgins (1998, 122-24, our translation) has appropriately dubbed the homosexuals of the years 1980-85 "the AIDS generation." In his view, the media and the government almost systematically defined AIDS as a disease that attacked mainly homosexuals and other minorities. From the beginning of the epidemic, the members of these at-risk groups were "treated as a separate category because they risked death through the sex act" and were increasingly isolated. Even though they had come out of the closet, gays were still not universally accepted by the late 1980s, and the AIDS crisis proved to be one of the main reasons – although since 1981 the European Court had rejected penal repression of homoerotic acts between consenting adults under the right to privacy (*Dudgeon* case, 22 Oct. 1981, A. n. 45).[5]

The 1990s: A Renewal of Freedom and Recognition

Although the AIDS crisis haunted gay and lesbian milieus throughout the 1980s, judicial and institutional recognition made progress. Based on the Roth Report, on equal rights for homosexuals and lesbians in the European Community (see http://www.france.qrd.org/texts/RapportRoth1994/affichage.html), in 1994 the European Parliament adopted a resolution aimed at eliminating inequalities based on sexual orientation. It proposed to abolish the ban on same-sex marriage so that homosexuals could benefit from legal provisions similar to those for heterosexuals. It also suggested the elimination of all restrictions on homosexuals' rights to be parents (or adopt children) and of discrimination with regard to age of consent for homoerotic behaviours. Although the resolutions did not have the force of law, judicial recognition of homosexuals was gradually instituted. Among the most famous provisions is protection against discrimination based on sexual orientation under the European Convention on the Rights of Man, recognized by the European Council (forty member states) and by the European Union (fifteen member states). As Catherine-Anne Meyer (1998, 153, our translation) observes,

> The European Convention on the Rights of Man did not explicitly make mention of sexuality or sexual orientation, [but] it recognized that "all persons" under the jurisdiction of signatory states had "fundamental rights and freedoms." Thus homosexuals were likely to receive more or less satisfactory protection from attacks on their physical and moral integrity (by prosecution) and some recognition of rights proper to their sexual identity.

This judicial protection was provided under two rules of law: section 8-1, concerning the right to privacy, and section 14, protecting against discrimination in the "enjoyment of recognized rights and freedoms." These sections confirm that penal repression of homoerotic acts performed in private between two consenting adults constitutes an assault on privacy in democratic societies. Furthermore, section 13 of the Treaty of Amsterdam, adopted on 2 October 1997, states, "Without prejudice to the other provisions of this Treaty and within the limits of the powers conferred by it upon the Community, the Council, acting unanimously on a proposal from the Commission and after consulting the European Parliament, may take appropriate action to combat discrimination based on sex, racial or ethnic origin, religion or belief, disability, age or sexual orientation."

On the other hand, the convention did not recognize the right of gays and lesbians to have the family life guaranteed in section 8. Under section 14, it allowed nations to use their immigration legislation to favour heterosexual couples over homosexual ones, married or not, who lived as a family. The European Commission felt that such discrimination was legitimate in the name of protection of the family. However, since 7 December 2000 the European Union's Charter of Fundamental Rights has stipulated that all forms of discrimination based on sexual orientation are forbidden.

Jurists Caroline Mécary and Flora Leroy-Forgeot (2001, 15, our translation) downplay the real effect of these laws. Although they "have the merit of inscribing within the social and judicial order the issue of sexual orientation and the need to treat it without differentiation," their implementation may be problematic since votes on each proposed new statute must be unanimous. For a subject as taboo and sensitive as homosexuality, unanimity is no doubt difficult to obtain. For example, in the *Fretté* case (*Fretté v. France*, no. 36515/97, s. 32, ECHR 2002-I), "the European Court ruled that in the absence of consensus among member states of the Council of Europe, the refusal of France to authorize adoption by homosexuals was not contrary to section 15 combined with section 8" of the European Convention on the Rights of Man (Cohen-Jonathan 2002, 109-10, our translation). Nevertheless, in Meyer's (1998, 179) view, jurisprudence under the European Convention on the Rights of Man favours decriminalization of homoerotic acts and the protection of homosexuals under the rights to privacy and freedom of expression. Olivier de Schutter (1993, 137) concludes that discrimination against homosexuals was essentially not tolerated in Europe and that decriminalization of homoerotic behaviours practised in private was complete.

The anticipated effects of sexual liberation and of homosexuals coming out of the closet were not immediate, as decriminalization and legal protection occurred only in the late 1970s in Quebec and in the early 1980s in France. Here, I shall simply give an overview of the different statutes, as brilliant analyses have already been performed by a number of authors.[6]

The Legal Situation of Homosexuals in Quebec: Extraordinary Judicial Recognition

With the Quiet Revolution, Quebec shook off traditional values, and religious discourse lost its position as the hegemonic ideology. As the state was secularized, the Catholic Church saw its control over the social institutions governing education, health, recreation, agriculture, and even unionism, which it had directed for more than a century, instantaneously withdrawn. With the advent of broadcast media such as television and new communications technologies, the cultural field to which Quebecers were exposed changed greatly: "Up to then saturated with religious images and symbols, the popular culture of Quebecers was soon imprinted with other representations testifying to a world very different from those of their communities of origin" (Lemieux and Montminy 2000, 54-55, our translation). These new social avenues introduced ways and models of life enormously different from those that had been conveyed by religious discourse – a discourse that was gradually replaced by a litany of different discourses. And thus the church lost its capacity to control Quebecers' attitudes, behaviours, and thoughts.

Quebec evolved from a "community of believers," as Raymond Lemieux and Jean-Paul Montminy (2000, 59, our translation) put it, into a "community of citizens," making a definitive cultural break with the church's social supervision. The debate surrounding Quebec's entry into modernity remains very complex. Whereas some authors perceive a discrepancy between the culture (still traditional) and the society (relatively modern), others see this discrepancy as being between political and social institutions. Some view these distinctions through the prism of the urban-rural model, whereas others explain it via social classes. Andrée Fortin (1996, 26, our translation) rightly notes, "The analysis of modernity and its advent may change entirely [from author to author]; one may think of it as early or late or else locate it primarily in social practices, the economy, or the world of ideas." For my analysis, I hold the view that Quebec reached modernity rapidly during the 1960s – that is, it freed itself from the overarching discourse of the Catholic Church, notably in the field of social regulation, and also proceeded to secularize sexuality.[7] It now distinguished between moral rights in public life and private life. The intervention of medicine in the area of sexuality played an important role, for it enabled individuals to dissociate somewhat their sexuality from the religious discourse. "The contemporary climate is therapeutic, not religious," notes Christopher Lasch (1979, 33). This meant that sexual practices, including homoerotic ones, became a fact of life. With the "universalization of identity" that characterized modernity, in which "the modern individual was an undefined person without a social a priori" (Dagenais 2008, 4), homosexuals had to be understood and tolerated as long as they did not assault others or cause offence to public morality.

The Criminal Code of Canada: Decriminalization Well Underway
In 1968, caught up in the liberal current of the sexual revolution, the Canadian government tabled the Omnibus Bill (Bill C-150), which began to

decriminalize sexual lifestyles practised in private. As Pierre E. Trudeau, then minister of justice, stated in 1967, "The state has no place in the bedrooms of the nation." The House of Commons passed the bill on 27 June 1969. It came into effect four days later, on 1 July. Through section 158 of Bill C-150, the Canadian legislature created an exceptions regime that limited the application of sections 155 (sodomy) and 157 (gross indecency) of the Criminal Code.[8] Interestingly, Pierre Hurteau's (1991, 208) archival research on parliamentary debates reveals that this statute predates gay liberation movements in Canada. It probably emanated from Canadian society's greater tolerance, not from political demands by homosexuals, and fell within a vast societal movement to develop different techniques for regulating social and sexual life.[9] In this movement, medicine's new power-knowledge, manifested in sexology and psychology, gradually took over from judicial discourse on normalization and control of private sexuality.[10]

The role played by medicine in legitimizing the passage of Bill C-150 is a good example. An analysis of parliamentary debates shows that both opponents and proponents of decriminalization developed their arguments based on medical discourse. Whereas the former presented the model of innate, irreversible homosexuality, the latter emphasized that no medical study had proved that this sexual orientation was a threat to the health of the state or the family or that it promoted corruption of minors.[11] The judiciary, however, came down on the opponents' side: the Supreme Court of Canada's 1967 ruling in *Everett George Klippert v. Her Majesty* declared that all repeated homosexual acts could be classified under the notion of sexual psychopathology. Hurteau (1991, 209-19) notes that some of the old prejudices regarding homosexuality persisted, including one associating it with youth decadence. Some members of Parliament claimed that increased tolerance of homosexuality would inevitably encourage young people to experiment with it – a situation that bespoke the deterioration of Western civilization. This, of course, was nothing new: throughout history, societies have freely associated homosexuality with degeneration of the nation or the corruption of minors.

Adoption of the Omnibus Bill authorized sodomy between a husband and wife, as well as between two individuals at least twenty-one years of age if there was consent and if such acts took place in private rather than in a public place or in the presence of a third party. The statute thus instituted a defence of consent that had not existed previously for this type of offence. The act was considered illegal in itself, but, with the addition of the exceptions regime, sodomy and gross indecency became punishable only when "the consent is extorted by force, threats, or fear of bodily harm or is obtained by false and fraudulent misrepresentations respecting the nature and quality of the act, or if the court is satisfied beyond a reasonable doubt that the person could not have consented to the act by reason of mental disability" (R.S.C. [1985], c. C-46, article 159[3]).

Now, sodomy could no longer be considered an illegal act in the great majority of cases. On the other hand, doctrinally, the exceptions regime simply reversed the burden of proof. As Diane Labrèche (1977, 371, our translation) explains, both the Criminal Code and jurisprudence stated that the exceptions regime forced the person charged to prove to the court that an exception was applicable, at the same time relieving the Crown of the burden of proving that "these facts would not be essential to constitution of the offence." The Quebec Court of Appeal also saw it as a means of defence for which the defendant totally assumed the burden of proof. Marie-Andrée Bertrand (1988, 148-49) observes that the definition of privacy is restrictive on this point: because the definition of public places has a tendency to get broader, few statutes are able to comply with it. She concludes that the addition made with regard to sex crimes by the Omnibus Bill did nothing substantive to change the law. Far from decriminalizing homoerotic acts, it simply limited the scope of sections that defined sodomy and gross indecency. In the case of acts of gross indecency, the jurisprudence showed that in 1975 "it [was] not essential to allege in the charges that the offence being charged was committed in a public place" and that "masturbation between two persons of the same sex [was] still an act of gross indecency."[12] It was up to the courts to decide what was to be judged indecent, and this definition varied from judge to judge and province to province. For example, in 1994 the Nova Scotia Court of Appeal opined that "an act of gross indecency is the performing of something flagrant, shameful and offensive to common propriety, a very marked departure from the decent conduct expected of the average Canadian in the circumstances."[13] Hurteau (1991, 223, our translation) observes that although the statute on gross indecency applied, in theory, to both heterosexual and homosexual practices, "in fact, few cases were brought before the courts for heterosexual acts of gross indecency ... in public places."

In addition, the 1968 modification applied neither to indecent actions, the charge "usually invoked to bring homosexuals before the court," nor to indecent assault by a man on another man, "the only openly homosexual crime" (Bertrand 1988, 147, 149, our translation). Bertrand (1988, 149) notes that the "desexualization" of prostitution in the Omnibus Bill had the perverse effect of making it more likely that homosexuals would be charged. For instance, solicitation for the purpose of prostitution became, with indecent actions, the main source of charges against homosexuals, as the extension to the statute left the door open to charges against men and women who solicited individuals of their own sex or communicated with them for the purpose of prostitution. In other words, various sections of the statute made homosexuals subject to arrest. The statute on indecent assault was abrogated in 1983 – even though the Committee on Sexual Offences against Children and Youth (Canada 1984, 57) had recommended that it be kept on the books in order to provide legal protection for minors from depravation of morals. That the committee's recommendations were legitimized mainly through medical expertise buttresses the hypothesis that legal discourse, once strongly influenced by religious discourse, was now based on other discourses, such as those of medicine and psychiatry (Corriveau 2007).

The crime of sodomy was replaced in the Criminal Code of Canada by a new offence: anal sexual relations. This change seems significant with respect to legitimization of criminal law: a term with a strong religious connotation ("sodomy") was replaced by a generic and laicized term (reminiscent of nineteenth-century France, where the courts and the police started to substitute the laicized term "pederast" for that of "sodomist"). Unlike vaginal sexual relations, anal sexual relations were still regulated specifically by the Criminal Code. It was possible to proceed with summary judgment for this new offence. Similarly, the offence of sexual assault replaced the offence of indecent assault. Since this new provision eliminated the distinction with regard to the sex of the victim, the offence of sexual assault was "neutral."

It would be interesting to compare the judicial treatment of homosexual assaults and heterosexual assaults in Canada to see whether the justice system differentiates in its intervention. According to a study by Anthony Walsh (1994, 339) on sexual assaults on children in the United States, "It was found that homosexual molesters were 6.79 times more likely to be imprisoned than were heterosexual molesters after adjusting for the combined effects of the crime's seriousness, prior record, and acceptance/denial of full responsibility for their actions." It might also be relevant to examine whether the old "homosexual offences" were truly eliminated from Canadian criminal law or simply transferred to another section of the Criminal Code. Gross indecency is one example: it is possible that this crime is now punishable under section 173, which states, "Every one who wilfully does an indecent act ... is guilty of an offence punishable on summary conviction." As "indecent act" is not defined in the Criminal Code, acts once considered to be gross indecency might now fall under this section.

Anal Sexual Relations: A Crime Not Like Others

A closer examination of section 159 of the Criminal Code, which deals with "anal intercourse," reveals certain prejudicial aspects. The statute contains an exception concerning the age of legal consent for sexual relations, which is set at fourteen years for sexual practices as a whole but at eighteen years for anal intercourse. The legislature deemed that adolescents between the ages of fourteen and eighteen could not consent to anal intercourse, although they could consent to all other forms of sexual relations. The statute also banned anal sexual relations between people who were not married but not between a husband and wife, even if they were under eighteen years of age. According to the Quebec Court of Appeal, this law discriminated against young homosexuals, who did not have the right to marry. The court declared section 159 unconstitutional and void because it

> clearly establishes a prohibition and a distinction based on age with regard to minors, whereas two adults may practice these activities unimpeded. This distinction is discriminatory because it imposes a heavier burden on adolescents from fourteen to eighteen years of age, which does not exist for adults and is absent from other sexual offences ... There is no question that *section 159 Cr.C. produces discrimination on the basis of sexual orientation. Due to its effect on homosexual persons, it impedes minor homosexuals from engaging in usual, consensual sexual activities in private* before the age of eighteen years. (Roy c. La Reine (C.A.) [1998] R.J.Q. 1044, our translation, emphasis added)

To buttress their ruling, the three justices on the Quebec Court of Appeal analyzed the legislature's objectives in writing the section in question. Following an examination of the parliamentary debates, the court concluded that the legislature had three objectives when it reformed section 159 in 1988: first, to strengthen moral precepts; second, to keep young homosexuals from recognizing their sexual orientation and engaging in unusual sexual practices; and third, to protect minors from the physical and psychological risks associated with anal intercourse. Because the statute was meant to keep young people from engaging in a particular sexual practice on the pretext that it was unusual, the court felt that it contravened section 15 of the Canadian Charter of Rights and Freedoms, which bans all forms of discrimination based on age. The justices noted that the legislature sought to justify its decision by "attempting to demonstrate the immoral nature of homosexual practices and expressing the fear that homosexuality is either an *acquired behaviour* or a *disease that children may contract*" (*Roy c. La Reine* (C.A.) [1998] R.J.Q. 1059, our translation, emphasis added). They observed that homosexuality was still heavily stigmatized in some official discourse, which presented it as a danger or risk from which children must be protected. The use of medical discourse as a tool of legitimization by Parliament seems quite obvious here.

Although both the Quebec and Ontario courts of appeal (in Ontario, *R. v. C.M.* (Ont. C.A.) [1995] 98 C.C.C. 481) declared section 159 of the Criminal Code unconstitutional, the federal courts had not yet reached consensus on the subject, mainly because of an opinion written by Justice Wilson of the Supreme Court of Canada: "The legislature has concluded that sodomy or buggery are forms of penetration that could be dealt with separately ... We are faced with distinctions aimed at *biologically different acts that go to the heart of society's morality and involve considerations of policy*. They are, in my view, best left to the legislature" (*R. v. Hess; R. v. Nguyen*, [1990] 2 S.C.R. 906, 59 C.C.C (3d) 931, emphasis added). According to Justice Wilson, "normal" sexuality, by all evidence, does not include anal intercourse. This ruling left the lower courts free rein when they dealt with the constitutionality of the statute. William A. Schabas (1995, 95-97) cites the example of two contradictory opinions: one by Judge Corbett of the Ontario Court (General Division), who concluded that section 159 was a violation of the fundamental principles of Canadian justice under section 7 of the Canadian Charter of Rights and Freedoms (*R. v. M.* (O.C., G.D.) [1992] 75 C.C.C. 556, 565-67); and one by Judge Wallace of the Supreme Court of British Columbia in *R. v. Khadikian,* which used the same reasoning as Justice Wilson's (*R. v. Khadikian,* (1968) 29 C.C.C. (3d) 154, 17 W.C.B 115, 159-60 (BCSC)). In short, an analysis of section 159 of the Criminal Code of Canada indicates that there is still a form of legal discrimination with regard to anal intercourse, which has long been associated with homoerotic lifestyles. On the other hand, as rulings in the Quebec and Ontario courts of appeal attest, Canadian jurisprudence is tending to gradually eliminate this discrimination.

The Quebec Charter of Human Rights and Freedoms: A World First

Quebec is an ambassador and pioneer, both in Canada and abroad, with regard to legal protection of homosexuals from discrimination based on sexual orientation. Quebec homosexuals' quest for legal recognition took a huge step forward in 1977 with adoption by the Quebec government of section 10 of the Charter of Human Rights and Freedoms, which explicitly protects homosexuals against all forms of discrimination linked to sexual orientation.[14] It was adopted by the National Assembly on 14 December 1977 and took effect one week later. The Quebec government thus became the first to ban discrimination against gays and lesbians.[15] Section 10 of the Charter stipulates,

> Every person has a right to full and equal recognition and exercise of his human rights and freedoms, without distinction, exclusion or preference based on race, colour, sex, pregnancy, sexual orientation, civil status, age except as provided by law, religion, political convictions, language, ethnic or national origin, social condition, a handicap or the use of any means to palliate a handicap.

The Quebec Charter, however, applies only in areas of provincial jurisdiction. Thus, even though Quebec took advantage of its right to opt out of section 15(1) – a section that did not include sexual orientation on its list of bases for discrimination – when the Canadian Charter of Rights and Freedoms was adopted in April 1982, it could not intervene against discrimination due to sexual orientation when a federal jurisdiction was involved.[16] It was not until 1995, through the Supreme Court of Canada's ruling in *Egan and Nesbit,* that Canada prohibited discrimination due to sexual orientation.[17] In that ruling, Justice Gerard Vincent La Forest wrote, on behalf of the four justices in the majority, on the definition of marriage,

> Marriage has from time immemorial been firmly grounded in our *legal tradition,* one that is itself a reflection of long-standing philosophical and *religious traditions.* But its ultimate *raison d'être* transcends all of these and is firmly anchored in the *biological and social realities that heterosexual couples have the unique ability to procreate,* that most children are the product of these relationships, and that they are generally cared for and nurtured by those who live in that relationship. *In this sense, marriage is by nature heterosexual.* (emphasis added)

In 2005 this opinion was reversed!

The Quebec Charter nevertheless did not offer full legal recognition for homosexuals. It was limited by the existence of certain derogations to the principle of interdiction on discrimination (Duplé 1984, 826). For example, before 1995 the Charter allowed discrimination in areas such as contracts and insurance, pension, retirement, and social benefits plans. Because the legislature used negatives in the wording of the Charter, Nicole Duplé (1984, 826) sees the effect as a ban on discrimination rather than an affirmation of equality. For instance, a homosexual might have been refused access to a private club due to his sexual orientation, and the court could not intervene under the Quebec Charter since section 15 forbade only discrimination in access to public places and services. Another limitation of the Charter, Duplé (1984, 829, our translation), continues, was that "the purported victim of discrimination has the task of establishing that it is due to a reason included on the closed list of bases of discrimination that he or she has been the object of a prohibited distinction, exclusion, or preference." Louise Letellier (1993, 111) explains, however, that the Charter defined discrimination as much by its effects as by its foundation, and therefore the victim did not have to prove the intentional nature of a discriminatory action. In other words, an unintentional infringement of the right recognized in section 10 was still illegal. In addition, according to the Human Rights Tribunal and jurisprudence, the restrictive interpretation of the exceptions regime of the Charter (section 20) prevailed. This rule stipulated, "In case of doubt in interpretation of the law, the decision must be made in the sense given in the Charter" (Letellier 1993, 111, our translation).

The example of clause 1 of section 20 is interesting, as it permits "a distinction, exclusion or preference based on the aptitudes or qualifications required for an employment, or justified by the charitable, philanthropic, religious, political or educational nature of a non-profit institution or of an institution devoted exclusively to the well-being of an ethnic group." In a ruling made in 1980 regarding a ban on homosexuals joining the Big Brothers Association – an association that recruits men to serve as father substitutes and stable male role models for boys without fathers – the tribunal ruled

> that homosexuality in itself should not deprive someone of the right to respond to the needs of a child. It should be only one fact among others. The Tribunal would find justified, considering the nature of the association, that a homosexual pedophile would be excluded. But outside of this hypothesis, it is of the opinion that section 20 does not permit the association to discriminate globally against all homosexuals. (Duplé 1984, 838, our translation)[18]

Finally, no Quebec statute was now allowed to contravene sections 1 to 38 of the Quebec Charter, "unless the legislature expressly indicates its intention to override the Charter statute" (Duplé 1984, 834, our translation). A statute that established a distinction based on sexual orientation would be judged invalid and of no force or effect.

From Common-Law Spouses to Civil Union: Marriage by Another Name

After eliminating discrimination against homosexuals in certain areas in 1995, on 6 May 1999 the Quebec legislature adopted Bill 32, modifying Quebec statutes (other than the Civil Code) "so that same-sex common-law spouses had the same rights and obligations as opposite-sex common-law spouses" (Labrèche 1999, 507, our translation). The statute, which came into effect on 16 June 1999, reformed the Workers' Compensation Act, the Automobile Insurance Act, the Insurance Act, the Taxation Act, the Labour Standards Act, the Quebec Pension Plan, the Supplemental Pension Plans Act, and other legislation. The modifications did not apply, however, to family-related issues such as adoption and food allowances, which were reserved for legally married spouses. Since Bill 32 did not expand the definition of "spouses," all of the rights and obligations applying to legally married spouses under the Civil Code did not apply to common-law spouses, either opposite-sex or same-sex. Marriage was defined in section 364 of the Quebec Civil Code as a union between a man and a woman, and this definition remained under federal jurisdiction. Because the Quebec legislature could not change the content, it had jurisdiction only to solemnize it.

Full legal recognition of same-sex couples' right to marry came on 7 June 2002, after many months of consultations. Through the Act Instituting Civil Unions and Establishing New Rules of Filiation, adopted unanimously by the National Assembly, the Government of Quebec eliminated all legal discrimination concerning common-law spouses. More than fifty provincial statutes were modified to integrate the notion of civil union, which, as a civil contract between two people, gave homosexuals the same rights and obligations as people united in marriage. Civil union requires the parties to live conjugally, be faithful to each other, and provide help and assistance, whereas nothing of this sort binds common-law couples. Although the surviving spouse in a civil union becomes de facto the main heir in the absence of a will, the surviving spouse in a common-law couple must be designated as heir. Moreover, in addition to the traditional registrars and religious ministers, the statute on civil unions authorizes notaries, mayors, and counsellors as recognized celebrants. Before the bill was adopted in April 2002, the minister of justice, Paul Bégin, stated, "It will be marriage in everything but name." In the first six months following the statute's coming into effect (July to December), the Institut de la statistique du Québec listed 150 same-sex couples who chose civil union to celebrate

Table 5.1

Civil unions, opposite-sex and same-sex couples, Quebec, 2002-04

Civil unions	Sex of the spouses			
	1 man + 1 woman	2 men	2 women	Total
2002 (July–December)	11	83	67	161
2003	68	141	133	342
2004 (January–August)	72	32	24	128

Source: Institut de la statistique du Québec.

their relationship (eighty-three gay couples and sixty-seven lesbian couples) (see Table 5.1).

Toward Civil Marriage between Same-Sex Spouses

In September 2002, the Superior Court of Quebec became the second court in Canada (after the Ontario Superior Court on 12 July 2002) to invalidate the traditional definition of marriage, which "may be contracted only between *a man and a woman* expressing openly their free and enlightened consent" (emphasis added). According to Justice Louise Lemelin, this restrictive definition was an unjustified violation under section 15 of the Canadian Charter of Rights and Freedoms. The court also ruled that procreation should not be considered the only characteristic of marriage. This decision was validated on 19 March 2004 by the Quebec Court of Appeal, the province's highest court, which unanimously rejected an appeal by the Catholic Civil Rights League. Quebec thus became the third province, after Ontario (10 June 2003) and British Columbia (8 July 2003), to legally authorize marriages between same-sex partners. The first gay marriage in Quebec was performed in Montreal on 1 April 2004. Michael Hendricks and René Lebœuf said their "I do's" three years to the day after the first same-sex marriage was celebrated in the Netherlands. Following this judicial trend, on 26 November 2004, the Ontario Court of Appeal unanimously ruled that the Canada Pension Plan Act was unconstitutional and ordered the Government of Canada to pay pensions retroactively (to 1985) to surviving spouses of same-sex couples. The estimated total disbursement amounted to almost $140 million, to be shared among approximately 1,300 people.

Thereafter, over a period of just one year starting in July 2004, courts in the majority of provinces and territories concluded that the traditional definition of marriage was unconstitutional (see Figure 5.1). Only Alberta, Prince Edward Island, the Northwest Territories, and Nunavut, together representing about 10 percent of Canada's population, did not allow same-sex marriage before the federal government legislation in July 2005.

The federal government estimates that there are about 34,000 same-sex couples in Canada and that 2,500 homosexual marriages have been celebrated since the courts made their rulings. The first of these was the ruling by the Ontario Court of Appeal in *Halpern v. Toronto (City)* ([2003]), in which the court opined that the common-law definition of marriage, which

Figure 5.1
Recognition of same-sex marriage in Canada by provinces and territories

Province or territory	Date of recognition
Ontario	10 June 2003
British Columbia	8 July 2003
Quebec	19 March 2004
Yukon	14 July 2004
Manitoba	16 September 2004
Nova Scotia	24 September 2004
Saskatchewan	5 November 2004
Newfoundland and Labrador	21 December 2004
New Brunswick	23 June 2005
Prince Edward Island	20 July 2005
Alberta	20 July 2005
Northwest Territories	20 July 2005
Nunavut	20 July 2005
Canada	20 July 2005

excludes homosexual marriages, contravenes section 15 of the Charter. Marriage, the court ruled, should be redefined as the "voluntary union for life of two persons to the exclusion of all others," and homosexual couples should have the right to marry.

Following this ruling, Parliament asked the Supreme Court of Canada to rule on the constitutionality of same-sex marriage by answering the following questions:

1 Is the annexed *Proposal for an Act respecting certain aspects of legal capacity for marriage for civil purposes* within the exclusive legislative authority of the Parliament of Canada? If not, in what particular or particulars, and to what extent?
2 If the answer to question 1 is yes, is section 1 of the proposal, which extends capacity to marry to persons of the same sex, consistent with the *Canadian Charter of Rights and Freedoms*? If not, in what particular or particulars, and to what extent?
3 Does the freedom of religion guaranteed by paragraph 2(*a*) of the *Canadian Charter of Rights and Freedoms* protect religious officials

from being compelled to perform a marriage between two persons of the same sex that is contrary to their religious beliefs?

4   Is the opposite-sex requirement for marriage for civil purposes, as established by the common law and set out for Quebec in section 5 of the *Federal Law-Civil Law Harmonization Act, No. 1*, consistent with the *Canadian Charter of Rights and Freedoms?* If not, in what particular or particulars and to what extent?

The court's opinion was handed down on 9 December 2004. "Our Constitution is a living tree," it read, "which, by way of progressive interpretation, accommodates and addresses the realities of modern life ... Read expansively, the word 'marriage' in s. 91(26) does not exclude same-sex marriage." By answering questions 1 and 2 in the affirmative, the court left it up to the House of Commons to decide how marriage would be defined in Canada. Although they recognized the right of churches to refuse to celebrate marriages for same-sex couples (question 3), the justices avoided giving an opinion on the constitutionality of the traditional definition of marriage (question 4).[19] On 2 February 2005, the government tabled Bill C-38, concerning certain basic conditions for civil marriage, for first reading. The bill redefined marriage to include same-sex couples, the wording being that civil marriage is "the lawful union of two persons to the exclusion of all others." It also stipulated that religious authorities would have the right to refuse to celebrate such unions without contravening the Charter (section 3 of the bill). The vote for second reading took place on 4 May 2005. In a free vote, the House of Commons agreed, by 164 to 137, to send the bill to legislative committee before third and final reading.[20]

The large number of petitions supporting the sanctity of traditional marriage between a man and a woman, as well as the heated debates that surrounded second reading, underlined the highly controversial nature of same-sex marriage in Canada.[21] A number of members of Parliament (MPs) fiercely defended the traditional definition of marriage. Most of them felt that same-sex marriage posed a threat to the family and to the education of children. Here are some examples of what was said during the parliamentary debates: "It is a far cry from ... saying that I will be silent as we deconstruct marriage and open up the threat to marriage and the family" (Pat O'Brien, Liberal Party, 3 May 2005); "I believe that we need to promote marriage and reserve it exclusively for partners of the opposite sex to help ensure stability and support for children" (Gurbax Malhi, Liberal Party, 3 May 2005); "A restrictive marriage definition is required to protect children in Canadian society" (Léon Benoit, Conservative Party of Canada [CPC], 3 May 2005); "Would Parliament be acting consistent with jurisprudence if it justified a statutory definition of marriage ... on the basis that it would serve the best interests of children?" (Stockwell Day, CPC, 3 May 2005); "[Marriage] is a stable environment for the procreation and raising of children" (Rob Anders, CPC, 3 May 2005); "Marriage is a child centred union of a man and a woman" (Stephen Harper, leader of the Opposition, CPC, 16 February 2005). References to the protection of children were front and centre in the arguments of proponents of traditional marriage; the world "child" was used 351 times during the second reading's debates alone, and the word "family" was used 211 times. Newspapers such as the *National Post* also raised the spectre of protection of minors: "Canada is one of only three places on earth poised to endorse the use of children as social guinea pigs without their consent. And all because our intellectual and political elites haven't ever really thought about it?"[22]

Others felt that homosexual marriage was a vice and that the Charter was being used as a promotional tool for this type of perversion:

I am flabbergasted in the sense that this whole issue of the charter argument keeps coming up time and time again. If we sit back and look at it and analyze what is happening with the use of the charter in this country, the Liberals, the NDP and whoever else supports this kind of initiative, it is being used by them to cover up a myriad of sins. When I say a myriad of sins, look at it: decriminalization of marijuana, decriminalization of prostitution and same sex marriage ... It is to the detriment of this country. (Art Hanger, CPC, 5 April 2005)

[John Stuart Mill says that] we can prohibit a mischievous act if it is injurious to others and that such an act should be subject to reprobation and social stigma. He talks about putting "restraints upon the inclinations when the consequence of their indulgence is a life or lives of wretchedness and depravity to the offspring, with manifold evils to those sufficiently within reach to be in any way affected by their actions." I want it to be clearly understood that John Stuart Mill would never have advocated for unions ... Edward Gibbon ... cite[s] several things that made for the decline of the Roman Empire. One of these, the first that he cites, was the immorality that destroyed the integrity of family life. (Rob Anders, CPC, 4 April 2005)[23]

A reading of the parliamentary debates shows, however, that the majority of MPs, even those unreceptive to the idea of allowing marriages between same-sex partners, remained somewhat favourable to the idea that homosexual spouses should have the same rights and obligations as married people, except, perhaps, for the right of adoption. However, this was simply a form of compromise meant to preserve the sacred nature of traditional marriage and was, in fact, the alternative proposed by the leader of the Opposition, Stephen Harper. Apparently, the crux of the problem was the sanctity of the institution of marriage and its role in the education of children. Interestingly, these arguments (and fears) were the same as those used in France during the debates over adoption of the Pacte civil de solidarité (Pacs). Daniel Borrillo (1999, 163, our translation) has taken on the task of listing these arguments by subject in order of frequency: the reproductive purpose of marriage, nature, the danger to children, the danger to culture, retribution, and so on. Such arguments give "a glimpse of the nostalgia for the traditional family model – presented, moreover, as a guarantor of social cohesion and gauge of child development." As had been the case several times throughout history, the child, that most precious of assets, once again became the ultimate argument for limiting complete equality between heterosexual and homosexual couples. My partial analysis of parliamentary discourse would indicate that it was not so much marriage between same-sex partners that was upsetting to the community conscience as it was the implicit filiation. Minors were, as ever, to be protected.[24]

It is also of interest to observe that anxiety about same-sex marriage transcended political parties. Ninety-five of the ninety-nine Conservative MPs voted against the bill, as did thirty-five Liberals and seven Bloc Québécois MPs. One New Democrat MP abstained and promised to vote against Bill C-38 in third and final reading. The historic vote in the House of Commons was held on 28 June 2005 (see Figure 5.2). The passage of Bill C-38 – adopted in the House by a vote of 158 to 133 and in the Senate (on 19 July 2005) by a vote of 47 to 21, with royal assent granted on 20 July 2005 – made Canada the fourth country to allow same-sex marriages, after the

Netherlands (1 April 2001), Belgium (adopted 30 January 2003 and came into effect 1 June 2004), and Spain (30 June 2005). This final vote showed once again the contentiousness of gay marriage. Within the minority Liberal government, thirty-two Liberal MPs voted against the bill, with Joe Comuzzi submitting his resignation to Prime Minister Paul Martin since ministers were obliged to support the bill. Six Bloc Québécois MPs also voted nay, as did the entire Conservative caucus. As he had promised when the bill was adopted, Conservative leader Stephen Harper returned to this thorny question during the December 2005 election campaign.

The Catholic Church fiercely opposed the bill. New Democrat MP Joe Comartin, who gave marriage-preparation classes, resigned from this position in order to vote in favour of gay marriage. Monsignor Ouellet, cardinal of the Catholic Church in Canada, justified in these terms the decision made by the bishop in London, Ontario: "When a person has a leadership and teaching position on behalf of the Catholic Church, he must represent church doctrine, not his own divergent opinion. The bishop is right to say that until he changes his opinion, he shall not have the responsibility of teaching in the church's name" (quoted in *Le Droit*, 14 July 2005, our translation). Abroad, Colombian cardinal Alfonso Lopez Trujillo stated, following the first synod of the pontificate of Pope Benedict XVI, that "politicians and legislators must know that by proposing or defending projects for iniquitous laws, they have a serious responsibility and must find a remedy for the evil done." With regard to same-sex marriage, the cardinal felt that "this whole tendency, which could invade many

Table 5.2
Marriages of same-sex couples, Quebec, 2004-08

Marriages	Sex of the spouses		
	2 men	2 women	Total
2004 (March)	148	97	245
2005	278	173	451
2006	349	272	621
2007	251	216	467
2008	262	193	455
Total	1,288	951	2,239

Source: Institut de la statistique du Québec.

Figure 5.2
Chronology of legal recognition of gays in Quebec

27 June 1969	The House of Commons adopts the Omnibus Bill (Bill C-150) (takes effect 1 July 1969), marking the beginning of decriminalization of sexual practices conducted in private.
15 December 1977	The National Assembly of Quebec includes sexual orientation as a reason for discrimination in its Charter of Human Rights and Freedoms (section 10).
6 May 1999	Adoption of Bill 32, which changes Quebec law (except for the Civil Code) "so that same-sex common-law spouses have the same rights and obligations as opposite-sex common-law spouses" (our translation).
20 May 1999	A ruling by the Supreme Court of Canada (*M. v. H.* [1999] 2 S.C.C. 3) recognizes homosexual common-law unions.
7 June 2002	The Quebec government unanimously adopts the statute instituting civil union, which eliminates all legal discrimination against same-sex spouses.
12 July 2002	The Ontario Superior Court invalidates the traditional definition of marriage in *Halpern et al. v. Canada.*
6 September 2002	The Quebec Superior Court becomes the second court in Canada to invalidate the traditional definition of marriage, which "requires the free, enlightened consent of *a man and a woman* who take each other as spouses" (emphasis added, our translation), in *Hendricks v. Quebec,* 2002, R.J.Q. 2506.
10 June 2003	The Ontario Court of Appeal invalidates a definition of marriage that excludes homosexual marriages under section 15 of the Canadian Charter (*Halpern v. Canada,* 2003, 26403 (ON C.A.)).
19 March 2004	The Quebec Court of Appeal in its turn invalidates the traditional definition of marriage (*Ligue catholique pour les droits de l'Homme v. Hendricks,* 2004, 20538 (QC C.A.)).
1 April 2004	First same-sex marriage in Quebec, between Michael Hendricks and René Lebœuf.
29 April 2004	A bill introduced by MP Svend Robinson, modifying the Criminal Code (hate propaganda), receives royal assent. Now, section 718.2 of the Criminal Code of Canada, which considers offences motivated by prejudice or hate based on sexual orientation to be an aggravating circumstance, is applied to sections 318 and 319 of the Criminal Code.

▶

◄   Figure 5.2

7 October 2004	The House of Commons asks the Supreme Court of Canada to give an opinion on the constitutional foundation of the bill authorizing same-sex marriages.
9 December 2004	Opinion handed down by the Supreme Court that "the word 'marriage' in s. 91(26) does not exclude same-sex marriage."
1 February 2005	Bill C-38, legalizing same-sex marriage, is tabled in the House of Commons.
4 May 2005	Second reading in the House of Commons of Bill C-38. The bill is passed by 164 to 137.
28 June 2005	Bill C-38 is adopted by the House of Commons in third and final reading (158 to 133).
19 July 2005	Bill C-38 is adopted in the Senate (47 to 21).
20 July 2005	Royal assent respecting Bill C-38 is obtained.

nations, is clearly contrary to divine law, to God's commandments, and is a negation of natural law."[25] George Pell, archbishop of Sydney, Australia, felt that homosexuality posed a greater risk to health than did tobacco. He therefore refused to give communion to defenders of homosexual rights. The line between lobbying and threat seemed very thin.

Nevertheless, the statute was incontestably popular among gays and lesbians. Between the date that it came into effect, March 2004, and the end of 2008, almost 2,240 same-sex marriages were performed (see Table 5.2).

Legal Protection that Does Not Impede Forms of Repression

Apparently, homosexuals were now recognized and protected legally in Quebec and Canada. Was there a concurrent evolution in legal and police practice? In the late 1960s, after a period of intense debate surrounding adoption of the Omnibus Bill, police repression of homosexuals subsided somewhat. This period of relative calm ended suddenly in 1975, when thirty men were arrested at the Sauna Aquarius in Montreal. For the first time, charges were laid under the section of the Criminal Code that concerns bawdy houses. "Up to then," observes Higgins (1999, 122, our translation), "this statute had always been used against heterosexual brothels, so it was a surprise that it was invoked against a gay sauna, where there was no question of prostitution." Curiously, this case made jurisprudence, and courts subsequently used it in other cases involving gay saunas. Stuart Russell (1982, 299-300) points to *R. v. Walsh* as "another case of a prosecution for keeping a homosexual steam bath as a common bawdy-house involving the same defendant." In the Sauna Neptune case, the judge stated, "Sauna Neptune [is] therefore a recognized place where ... one [may] easily find partners for performing indecent acts ... The proof is overwhelming that an innumerable quantity of indecent acts were performed" (quoted in Russell 1982, 300).

The wave of repression swelled in 1976, mainly because of the clean-up campaign conducted in advance of the Olympic Games to be held in Montreal that year: "Using the propaganda theme 'Visitors are coming,' the municipal authorities took advantage of the upcoming Olympic Games to intensify repression of all marginal people. Unprecedented control measures were used. Soldiers joined federal, provincial, and municipal police forces: the media spoke of 20,000 men in arms in Montreal" (Sivry 1998, 240, our translation).

Arrests and cases of police harassment multiplied. A number of raids were conducted on gay saunas and bars. In January 1976, thirteen men were arrested at the Sauna Club, and thirty-five were brought in for questioning from the Club Baths sauna. On 11 February the target was Sauna Cristal. In May police raids intensified. "From May 13th to 15th, the Sauna Cristal, three men's bars, and the only discotheque for lesbians in Montreal, Jilly's, were raided" (Higgins 1999, 125, our translation). A police sweep at Sauna Neptune led to the arrest of eighty-nine men. According to Jean-Michel Sivry (1998, 240, our translation), "Things like this had not been seen since the October Crisis." To the surprise of the homosexual community, the print press presented the affair as a police operation that had led to the dismantling of a major prostitution ring.

Police repression was so heavy that it provoked the first large-scale gay demonstration in Montreal. On 19 June 1976, almost three hundred gays and lesbians marched through the city's streets (Adam 1995, 125). In the fall, the Association pour les droits des gais du Québec (ADGQ) was founded. Police harassment continued throughout the year. Higgins (1999, 128, our translation) describes how police officers armed with machine guns burst into Studio I, a Montreal bar, and relates that "other 'visits' took place at Truxx and Bud's." It was the raids on the Truxx and Le Mystique bars, on 21 October 1977, that brought many Montreal gays out of the closet. This police operation was so violent – the police descended on Truxx wielding machine guns and arrested 144 men for being in a bawdy house or gross indecency – that the next day 2,000 gays and lesbians poured out onto St. Catherine Street.[26] When the police tried to disperse the crowd, there was a riot, later dubbed "Quebec's Stonewall." For the first time, gays and lesbians had the support of the news media. Following this demonstration and upon request of the ADGQ, in December 1977 the Parti québécois adopted Bill 88, protecting homosexuals against all forms of discrimination on the basis of sexual orientation under the Charter of Human Rights and Freedoms (see Adam 1995; Bureau and Papy 2007; Noël 1998; Sylvestre 1979).

Thus, by the end of 1977, homosexual rights were relatively guaranteed in Quebec, thanks mainly to the province's Charter. Quebec gays and lesbians began to come into the public eye through their political organizations and media appearances. A study by Benoît Migneault (2001), of the Government of Quebec's division of magazines, newspapers, and government publications, illustrates the evolution in how publications dealt with the homosexual issue. The number of articles on the theme rose from an annual average of 1.6 for the period 1970-75 to around fifteen in the early 1980s. In 2001 the Montreal newspaper *La Presse* alone printed more than four hundred articles on gay subjects. Today, it is difficult to keep track of all of the television programs that deal with the homosexual issue every week. All Quebecers now have access to representations of gays and lesbians.[27] Both the quantity and the content of articles encourage a broader acceptance of gay issues in Quebec by demystifying them for the general public. Robert Schwartzwald (1997, 135, our translation) observes that, unlike in the United States, where in the 1980s homosexuals were associated with promiscuity and AIDS, in Quebec, "the portrayals of homosexuals in novels, television series, and movies resisted this association."

The visibility of gays in the Quebec media landscape and the development of the Gay Village in Montreal certainly made it easier for gays and lesbians to live openly. On the other hand, for some Montrealers, the Gay Village became synonymous with debauchery and perversion. As Frank

W. Remiggi (1998, 268, our translation) rightly notes, "All indications were that the concentration of gay businesses, customers, and residents contributed to an increase in homophobic violence"; in fact, gays and lesbians constituted the third-largest group targeted by hate propaganda in Canada, after blacks and Jews (Demczuk 1998, 401). The Commission des droits de la personne du Québec (1994, 88-91) described the scope of the problems linked to discrimination and violence against homosexuals in its report *De l'illégalité à l'égalité: Rapport de la consultation publique sur la violence et la discrimination envers les gais et lesbiennes*. The report recommended that awareness-raising, training, and public education campaigns be instituted on sexual orientation, heterosexism, and homophobia in order to put an end to the clichés and stereotypes that still negatively affected homosexuals. On the legislative front, it advocated – recommendations 26 to 29 – that sections 318 of the Criminal Code, on hate propaganda, and 319, on public incitement to hate, be modified to include homosexuals as victims. This change was made on 29 April 2004, when the bill on hate propaganda shepherded by MP Svend Robinson received royal assent. Since then, section 718.2 of the Criminal Code, which regards as an aggravating circumstance the fact that an offence is motivated by prejudice or hate based on sexual orientation, has been applied to sections 318 and 319 (Bill C-250, Robinson, 2004, c. 14. s. 1). Despite the end of judicial repression in Quebec, however, much research has found that social homophobia was still in evidence, especially in schools and the workplace (Bastien-Charlebois 2009; Chamberland, Bernier, and Lebreton 2009; Émond 2009; Rose 2009; Ryan 1999).

A Léger Marketing poll published in June 2001 ("Canadian Perceptions of Homosexuality," 22 June 2001) showed that homosexuals could expect greater tolerance and acceptance in Quebec than they could elsewhere in Canada: 85.5 percent of Quebecers (compared to 75.5 percent of all Canadians) felt that homosexuals should have the same rights as heterosexuals; 88.9 percent believed that gays and lesbians were the same as other people. Furthermore, 57.1 percent of Quebecers felt that gay couples should be allowed to adopt children. In comparison, in response to a similar question in France in September 2001, "68 percent of people questioned were not in favour, including 44 percent who were strongly opposed – a high level – and only 30 percent were in favour."[28] Higgins (1999, 140, our translation) believes that the increased tolerance and acceptance of gays had sources other than the sexual revolution and was "due to development of a dynamic urban life, the advent of new forms of communications, and new economic structures that created a society radically different from the one that preceded it." It is indeed possible that many new retail businesses in Quebec were trying to attract a gay clientele, considered well-off and big spenders, by more freely associating themselves with the gay cause – putting the lie to the old adage that money doesn't buy happiness! Finally, on 1 July 2004, the Centre for Research and Information on Canada noted that 57 percent of Canadians were in favour of same-sex marriage. Even more interestingly, 77 percent of people between the ages of eighteen and twenty-nine were in favour of same-sex marriage, compared to 37 percent of those aged over sixty. Paradoxically, the results of a Léger Marketing poll released on 1 June 2005 ("Perceptions and Opinions of Canadians Regarding Homosexual People") indicated that 49 percent of Canadians still considered homosexuality an abnormal state! This poll also revealed that Quebecers were more positively disposed toward homosexual marriages than were other Canadians (63 percent of those in Quebec were in favour, compared to, for example, only 41 percent in Alberta; the Canadian average was around 57 percent). On 15 November 2005, the Parti québécois elected the openly gay André Boisclair as party leader. What conclusions can be drawn from all of this? Perhaps simply, as Serge Bouchard and Bernard Arcand (1996, 146, our translation) humorously observe, that statistics, although they don't lie, may be made to say anything since "the numbers are as dumb as oysters. Furthermore, they do nothing but respond to the needs of our practices and theories!"[29]

Homosexuals in France: More Problematic Legal Recognition

In France the homosexual movement really took shape in the early 1970s with the formation of the Front homosexuel d'action révolutionnaire (FHAR), a social movement whose primary goal was to fight all conventions and to proclaim, loud and clear, the right of homosexuals to exist. The first gay demonstration took place on 1 May 1971 – somewhat submerged within the crowds of unionists and leftists (Girard 1981, 95) – and the public declaration of the "homosexual revolution" was presented by Guy Hocquenghem on 10 January 1972 in *Le Nouvel Observateur*. With FHAR, the long march of French homosexuals toward decriminalization of homoerotic lifestyles began.

Judicial Repression in the 1970s

The growing presence of homosexual movements in the public space did not impede judicial repression and press censure of the "homosexual fact." Under the statute on indecent assault (section 28), adopted in 1881 and modified in 1956, it was still possible to forbid publication of certain "homosexual" articles. Frédéric Martel (1999) and Jacques Girard (1981) give a number of examples. One was issue 12 of the magazine *Tout!* (23 April 1971), devoted in part to homosexuality but also to abortion and the right of minors to sexual freedom. Its editor, Jean-Paul Sartre, was found guilty of indecent assault and pornography by the minister of the interior at the time, Raymond Marcellin. The vice squad executed a search warrant on the premises of the Vive la Révolution movement and seized 10,000 copies of the offending issue, and some vendors of the magazine were taken to court. On the other hand, for the first time, the Conseil constitutionnel declared infringements on freedom of expression and association to be unconstitutional. The media furore surrounding issue 12 of *Tout!* also gave FHAR new energy. Other publications later seized for indecent assault included the magazine *Partisans* in July 1972 and the special issue of the journal *Recherches* titled "Trois milliards de pervers," published in March 1973. Its editor was taken to court and found guilty of indecent assault in May 1974. In 1977, an ordinance issued by Marcellin's successor as minister of the interior, Michel Poniatowski, forbade retailers from selling most homosexual magazines (*Gaie Presse, In, Andros, Dialogues,* and others). In 1979, the magazine *Libération* was, in its turn, found guilty of publishing classified ads catering to homosexuals.

Two sections of the French Penal Code of 1960 were explicitly dis-criminatory with regard to sexual relations between people of the same sex under twenty-one years of age: section 331, on indecent unnatural acts, and section 330, on indecent exposure. Clause 3 of section 331 stated that any homosexual act committed with a minor under twenty-one years of age was punishable by imprisonment. The jurisprudence also allowed for two homosexual minors caught in the act together to be reciprocally found guilty for cuts and injuries! This section was modified slightly in 1974 with the lowering of the age of sexual majority to eighteen years, but it did not eliminate the "two different minor ages in penal coverage: the one of fifteen years for heterosexual relations, the other of eighteen years for homosex-ual relations" (Lascoumes 1998, 110). According to Pierre Lascoumes (1998,

110-18), maintenance of this discriminatory regime was legitimized mainly by the need to protect families and children.

Penal Statistics on Homoerotic Lifestyles between 1972 and 1982

The criminal statistics in *Aspects de la criminalité en France en 1982 constatée par les services de police et de gendarmerie d'après les statistiques de police judiciaire* (1982) include 371 indecent assaults by homosexuals and 125 cases of homosexuality with minors out of a total of 16,076 morals and sex crimes – 3.09 percent of all crimes listed.[30] These statistics show that after 1972, indecent assaults committed by homosexuals dropped by 12.71 percent and offences of homosexuality with a minor plummeted by 48.56 percent. Over the same period, morals offences grew by 42.59 percent. In 1982 there were 7,185 molestations, a rise of 29.23 percent over 1972. It may be that more homosexuals were found guilty of this offence. A comparison of the indecent assaults committed by homosexuals with those committed by others shows that this hypothesis is shaky. Whereas the former constituted only 2.3 percent of morals crimes (371), the latter represented 33.66 percent (5,411). "Looking back," notes Jean Danet (1998, 102, our translation) "we can say that the fight [against homoerotic lifestyles] was waged with lukewarm determination and, in any case, more and more inconsistently. The statistics on numbers of convictions as a quantum of penalties are convincing in this regard."

In penal doctrine, the classification adopted in *Aspects de la criminalité en France* (1982, 7, our translation, emphasis added) notes that indecent exposure was considered a form of delinquency – that "as harmful and detrimental as it is, it nevertheless represents a *problem of minor importance.*" Homosexual acts with a minor were defined as being of medium criminality and were grouped among offences deemed "somewhat serious, both due to the *insecurity that they are likely to induce* and due to the *harm to the individual* that they provoke." In this category were also infanticide, child abuse, rape, and indecent assault. Morals offences among consenting adults (for example, procuring and use of pornography) were regarded as simple delinquency. Consistent with my hypothesis that the hate once directed at homosexuals was now displaced toward pedophiles and those who attacked children, it appears that crimes involving minors were more disturbing to the justice system than were homoerotic behaviours in themselves. The number of cases involving children had been on the rise since 1972; by 1982, offences against minors had increased by 21.94 percent, other offences against children and families by 9.83 percent, and incitement of minors to debauchery by 26.81 percent.

However, this hypothesis must be viewed with caution. Georges Vigarello (2001), Jean-Claude Guillebaud (1999), and Jenkins (1998) note, rightly, that incest and pedophilia, two serious crimes against children, were not demonized until the mid-1980s. From the 1970s until that time, Western societies had a relatively neutral opinion of pedophilia and incest. In France, more specifically, there was a considerable drop in convictions for homosexuality with a minor – by 48.56 percent – between 1972 and 1982. It is therefore correct to say that sexual behaviours, homoerotic or not, dropped in importance on the level of judicial intervention as the sexual revolution took hold. In fact, morals offences represented only 0.54 percent of overall criminality in France in 1982.

Decriminalization in the Early 1980s

Finally, in 1980, France began to modify its legislation to eliminate penal discrimination against homosexuals, although not without dithering. After almost two years during which the Assemblée nationale and the Senate reviewed the thorny dossier of discrimination against homosexuals, homosexual indecent assault became a simple offence, and section 330-2, which exacerbated homosexual indecent assault, was abrogated on 19 November 1980. In Martel's (1999, 133) view, "This key vote marked the end of all discriminatory measures related to homosexual acts between adults," but Lascoumes (1998, 110) maintains that, under the cover of protection of minors, some members of the Assemblée nationale likened homosexuality to pedophilia and used the precedent of proselytizing to indirectly discredit all homoerotic behaviours. It is worth remembering that on the very day that section 330-2 was abrogated, an amendment was passed to maintain the offence of homosexual relations with a minor under eighteen years of age. Section 331-2 provided that, "without prejudice to more serious penalties set out in the previous clause or in section 332 of the present code, an indecent or unnatural act with a minor individual of the same sex shall be punished with imprisonment of six months to three years and a fine of 60 to 20,000 francs." As Girard (1981, 168, our translation, emphasis added) remarks, the Conseil constitutionnel stated on 19 December 1980 that "the statute on repression of rape and certain morals offences may, without breaching the principle of equality, *distinguish, for the protection of minors,* acts performed between persons of the same sex from those performed between persons of different sexes." Once again, youth protection was the public authorities' primary concern.

With the election of François Mitterrand as president of France in 1981, the movement to eliminate discrimination against homosexuals gained momentum. In August 1981 Mitterrand granted amnesty to more than 150 homosexuals convicted of indecent assault or unnatural acts under section 330-2, which had been abrogated the preceding year. Then, through a circular issued by his minister of the interior, Gaston Defferre, Mitterrand directed police departments to eliminate all forms of discrimination and suspicion regarding individuals' sexual orientation. He recommended that the department specializing in "homosexual lifestyles" be disbanded and that homosexual filings be limited. The minister of health, Jack Ralite, announced, "France would no longer recognize the World Health Organization's classification of homosexuality as a mental illness" (quoted in Martel 1999, 132). France had hewn to this definition since 1968.

In December 1981, the Assemblée nationale began debate on reform of the Penal Code to eliminate all forms of homosexual discrimination. Abrogation of section 331 of the Penal Code and adoption of Act No. 82-682, which set fifteen years as the age of sexual majority for all types of sexual relations, were passed on 27 July 1982 (see Act No. 82-683 of 4 August 1982 and sections 227-22 and 227-27 of the New French Penal Code). Debate, sometimes heated, lasted almost nine months, to August 1982. "The climate was not one of consensus," Lascoumes (1998, 111, our translation) observes, "and the bill went back and forth between the Assemblée nationale and the Senate no fewer than three times before, finally, the government imposed section 45, clause 4, of the Constitution to ask the Assemblée nationale to give final assent."

From Decriminalization to the Pacs: Greater Judicial Recognition

Although homoerotic behaviours were decriminalized in the early 1980s, French homosexuals still had few rights. The French legislature rapidly filled this gap by adopting a series of measures to improve protection of homosexuals from discrimination. On 25 July 1985 the Assemblée nationale passed Act 85-772, on discrimination based on lifestyles – that is, sexual orientation. Section 225-1 of the Penal Code established a general principle banning discrimination against homosexuals under the morals category. Clause 2 of the section punished this form of discrimination with a fine of 200,000 francs. Section L.122-45 of the Labour Code protected homosexuals against discrimination based on lifestyle. Under this section (our translation), "no individual may be excluded from a recruitment process, and no employee may be disciplined or dismissed due to his or her origins, sex, or lifestyle."[31] Section L.122-35 ensured that homosexuals would not suffer discrimination through internal corporate rules.

On the other hand, until the Pacte civil de solidarité (Pacs) was adopted, in the fall of 1999, homosexual couples suffered various forms of social rights discrimination. In the absence of laws regulating partnership, jurisprudence had the force of law. Two rulings handed down by the Cour de cassation on 11 July 1989 – known as the *Air France* case – invalidated legal recognition of the status of gay and lesbian couples. The court ruled that "two people who have decided to live together as spouses, without benefit of marriage – this may concern only a couple composed of a man and a woman" (quoted in Bach-Ignasse 1998, 126, our translation), and also stipulated that Air France was not obliged to give the same social benefits to homosexual couples as it did to heterosexual couples. On 17 December 1997 this court ruled similarly in a case regarding same-sex couples' right to a lease, deeming that the expressions "cohabitation" and "marital life" were reserved solely for heterosexual couples. For homosexual couples, the expression "shared life" had to be used, and the decision on whether to issue a shared-life certificate to homosexuals fell under the jurisdiction of local administrations – that is, mayors (Leroy-Forgeot 1997, 109); in 1996, 243 bestowed such certificates (Martel 2000, 610). Some organizations in both the private and public sectors also began to offer homosexual couples benefits similar to those granted to heterosexual couples. This expression of goodwill did not, however, lead to legal recognition of the certificates, which was necessary to guarantee such benefits.

Nevertheless, homosexuals did gain some rights through governmental measures and jurisprudence. On 27 January 1993 the Assemblée nationale adopted section 78, which provided that an individual who has lived with someone on social security for twelve consecutive months and is dependent upon this individual has the right to receive social security, as does the person with whom he or she is living in a marital relationship (Code de la Sécurité sociale, section L.161-14, clauses 2 and 3). This measure overrode the 1989 court ruling by recognizing the status of cohabiting same-sex couples. Then, in a ruling handed down in July 1995, the Belfort Court ordered an insurance company to pay damages and interest, for moral and economic prejudice, to a lesbian whose spouse had been killed in a car accident twenty years before. The court based its decision on Act 1382 of the Civil Code and on a ruling of 27 February 1970 by the Cour de cassation, which determined that it was not necessary to establish a legal connection between the deceased person and the person asking for compensation for the death; the verdict was based "solely on criteria of the stability and duration of the relationship, as well as the reality of the prejudice suffered" (Leroy-Forgeot 1997, 120). According to Leroy-Forgeot (1997, 120), this was the first step toward legal recognition of same-sex couples.

On the other hand, in 1996, the head of the youth-protection department made a contrary ruling: because French law authorized adoption only for married couples, he blocked the adoption of a child by a homosexual despite the applicant's spotless social credentials. This decision was upheld by the president of the Council of Paris at the time, Jacques Chirac. According to Chirac, the "life choice" of the petitioner did not present "sufficient guarantees as to the conditions for housing a child" (quoted in Bach-Ignasse 1998, 133). The Administrative Court of Paris reversed this decision. Applying section 8 of the European Convention on Human Rights and section 9 of the Civil Code, the court ruled that "deciding under these conditions, by one judge's ruling, that a single homosexual man does not present sufficient guarantees to adopt a child amounts to introducing discrimination not intended by the legislature" (Borrillo and Pitois 1998, 142-43, our translation). The court cited the right of custody, the right of access, and the exercise of parental authority granted to homosexual parents after a divorce. The government's commissioner appealed to the State Council, which, on 9 October 1996, revoked the Administrative Court's decision, stating, "Given his living conditions and despite his definite human and academic qualities, [M.F.] does not present sufficient guarantees on the *family, educational, and psychological* fronts to house an adopted child" (quoted in Bach-Ignasse 1998, 134, our translation, emphasis added).[32]

The argument that the family as an institution and its preponderant role in the education of children had to be protected was used constantly during debates over the adoption of the Pacs. "Contrary to the few analyses by those who were more sensitive to public freedoms and discrimination," Borrillo (1999, 162, our translation) observes, "privatist doctrine did not hesitate to call upon tradition, the symbolism of marriage, the interest of the child, and the sensitivity of rural France to justify discrimination against same-sex unions." As in the past, science was used to support discrimination; this time, it was family experts whose opinions were sought. Éric Fassin (1999, 89ff) has shown how human sciences such as sociology, anthropology, and psychology became sources of legitimization for politicians and jurists debating the Pacs regime. Supporting, in a way, my hypothesis regarding the evolution of scientific discourse throughout history, Fassin (1999, 101, our translation) notes, "Divine authority was not invoked, but recourse was taken to the expertise of human sciences, the laws of psychism, and culture – to the 'anthropological foundations' of the 'symbolic order.'"[33] The key role accorded to youth protection is very obvious here.

The Pacte civil de solidarité: Marriage "Lite"[34]

The Pacs – which arose from a bill on civil union contracts, tabled in 1992, and was first called the Contrat d'union sociale and then the Pacte d'intérêt commun – was adopted in fourth reading in the Assemblée nationale on 13 October 1999 (315 in favour, 249 against) after thirteen months and more than 120 hours of debate.[35] The Constitutional Council confirmed ruling no. 99-419 DC on 9 November 1999, and the president of the Republic promulgated Act no. 99-944 on 15 November 1999 (see Figure 5.3). Under this statute, "a civil pact of solidarity is a contract entered into by two physical major persons, of different or same sex, to organize their common life" (section 515-1, Pacs, our translation). It enabled same-sex couples to forge a contractual union that obliged them to support each other materially and morally, and it permitted them to benefit from certain rights granted to couples. Partners united in a Pacs became jointly responsible for common debts that were governed by the regime of undivided co-ownership. They also had to submit joint tax returns as of three years after they concluded their Pacs. "Pacsed" employees could arrange to have their vacation at the same time as their spouse's vacation, take time off for the partner's family events, and, in the case of "Pacsed" civil servants, benefit from assignment priorities. As described by Alia Aoun (2000, 112, our translation),

The Pacs Act defines general rules by referring to notions inspired by the rules for marriage such as mutual and material assistance and solidarity of third parties for debts contracted for the needs of daily life ... Partners bound by a Pacs, unless specific sections of the statute provide otherwise, will benefit from the rights recognized in jurisprudence to people cohabiting, such as the right to spousal death benefits.

Unlike those in a cohabitation relationship, which is a common-law union without regard to age, individuals had to have reached the age of majority to enter into a Pacs. Adult homosexuals could now claim the status of cohabitant previously reserved solely for heterosexual couples and thus avail themselves of the same rights and benefits as heterosexual couples who were cohabiting or joined in a Pacs. Since 15 November 1999, cohabitation has been defined as a "common-law union, characterized by two people of different sexes or the same sex living together as a couple in a stable, continuous relationship" (our translation). This statute abrogated the Cour de cassation jurisprudence of 1989 and 1997, mentioned above (see Mécary 2000, 112; Mécary and Leroy-Forgeot 2001, 87-90). On the level of judicial doctrine, there was parity. Mécary and Leroy-Forgeot (2001, 121, our translation) note that this set the new legislation apart since homosexual unions had long been "held as immoral and rejected by law."

Notwithstanding the Pacs, homosexual couples were not able to marry, and they therefore did not have access to the benefits of marriage. "Although attractive at first glance," Mécary and Leroy-Forgeot (2001, 10, our translation) observe, "the Pacs offered fewer guarantees than those under marriage; it seemed much more complex, in terms of both formation and dissolution, than is the institution of marriage." Adoption of the Pacs did not completely eliminate the numerous inequalities that remained in French law. Among those noted by experts are that homosexual couples did not have the right to full adoption, medically assisted procreation techniques, surviving spouse's pension, surviving spouse's annuity, French citizenship for a foreign partner, judicial or extrajudicial representation between partners, international recognition of the status of spouse, family reunification, and freedom of movement as a couple.[36] According to Borrillo (2000, 117, our translation),

The rights of inheritance *ad intestat* in the case of death, shared parental authority, protection against deportation of the foreign partner, the possibility of donations between partners without a waiting period, the possibility to benefit from organ donations from a living person, and allocation of a housing loan, to cite just a few examples, remained prerogatives reserved exclusively for married couples.

Further, Borrillo feels that the Pacs constituted a "submarriage" that created a "subtle form of segregation of one category of couples." Claude Weill and his colleagues (1998, 7, our translation) conclude that this amounted to marriage "lite" – that is, the formalities of entering and leaving were less cumbersome, and the legal effects were attenuated and sometimes even deferred. With the Pacs, individuals' family ties remained separate; whereas "marriage links two families, grafting two genealogical trees and committing the descendants," this did not occur for "Pacsed" couples. Jean-Loup Vivier (2001, 149, our translation) remarks about all of these legal distinctions,

> As it is currently presented, the Pacte civil de solidarité is a compromise. Some provisions have been eliminated ... The pact remains well short of marriage when it comes to the partner's social status. There are few benefits offered to partners in the Labour Code. The Social Security Code does not guarantee the right of the surviving partner to a survivor's annuity. Furthermore, partners in general have no right to adopt a child, and homosexual partners have no right to use medically assisted procreation. This legal situation is felt by the interested parties to be intolerable discrimination.

Despite the numerous criticisms, in less than one year – between 16 November 1999 and 20 September 2000 – 23,000 couples (of all types) decided to avail themselves of the Pacs. Jean-Paul Pouliquen, president of the Collectif pour le contrat d'union sociale et le Pacs, estimates that 70 percent of Pacs unions in Paris involved homosexuals, compared to 40 percent in the provinces. After examining the largest court registries in France, Sophie Des Déserts (2000, 55) reaches the same conclusion. Thus, although it was not totally equitable, the Pacs seemed to be attractive for same-sex couples who wished to obtain some form of legal recognition.

Statistics gathered in 2008, however, show that today the Pacs is used mainly by heterosexual couples; same-sex couples accounted for only 5.6 percent of all French people in a Pacs union – 8,141 couples (4,742 gay couples and 3,399 lesbian couples) out of the 144,730 couples entering a Pacs union in that year.[37]

Certain major effects collateral to the debates over the Pacs should be noted. The announcement made by Mutuelle générale de l'Education nationale regarding the opening of benefits to homosexual couples was one notable example, as was Air France's decision to offer same-sex partners of the company's employees access to a group of privileges granted to heterosexual partners, as well as to offer Pacs partners its couples fares. Other improvements were to follow; in 2005, the Ministry for the Economy, Industry, and Employment eliminated the three-year delay that had been required for joint taxation of Pacs couples and aligned it with those for married taxpayers, starting with the 2004 tax year.[38] The rules for dissolution of a Pacs were also changed: the members of the couple did not immediately become personally taxable, as the 1999 Pacs provided, but continued to be taxed jointly until the union was dissolved. Finally, since 2007, couples in a Pacs union and married couples have had the same rights to exemption from succession taxes for the surviving spouse.

In the wake of the Pacs, other bills were tabled to fill the gaps in French law. Among these gaps, as Borrillo (2000, 118, our translation) notes, was the absence of a law protecting homosexuals from hate speech (a law that does exist in Canada). He presents several striking public examples (all our translation): "Homos can go to hell," a statement by Michel Maylan, of the Union pour la démocratie française (UDF); the definition of the Pacs as a "means of spreading AIDS," by Senator Emmanuel Hamel; and a tract published by a Christian sect with a print run of more than a hundred thousand copies that said, "What characterizes unions between inverts, in addition to the nauseating unnatural acts, is the great instability ... Sodomists and free-love supporters count on your apathy." The anti-homophobia bill tabled by then prime minister Jean-Pierre Raffarin on 23 June 2004, to modify the statute of 29 July 1881, was rejected by the Assemblée nationale thanks to lobbying by anticommunitarians. Nevertheless, the government introduced the main provisions of this bill in amendments to the bill on creation of the Haute autorité de lutte contre les discriminations et pour l'égalité. The bill, adopted by the Assemblée nationale and the Senate on 31 December 2004, stipulates, in section 20 (our translation),

> After clause 8 of section 24 of the statute of 29 July 1881 on freedom of the press, the following clause is inserted: "Those who, by the same means set out in the preceding clause, provoke hate or violence toward a person or a group of persons because of their sex, their sexual orientation, or their disability, or who provoke discrimination as provided in sections 225-2 and 432-7 of the Penal Code, shall be punished with the same penalties as set out in the preceding clause."

Section 21 reads (our translation),

> 1) After the second clause of section 32, the following clause is inserted: "Defamation committed by the same means of a person or group of persons because of sex, sexual orientation, or disability will be punished with the penalties set out in the preceding clause." 2) After the third clause of section 33, the following clause is inserted: "Abuse committed under the same conditions toward a person or group of persons because of sex, sexual orientation, or disability will be punished with the penalties set out in the preceding clause."[39]

The only problem was that, unlike under the initial bill, the burden of proving discrimination fell to the victim. Nevertheless, a first lawsuit for homophobia was brought against Christian Vanneste, member of the Assemblée nationale for the Union pour la majorité présidentielle, on 13 December 2005. Vanneste had stated in *La Voix du Nord* and in *Nord Éclair,* "Homosexuality is a threat to humanity ... I did not say that homosexuality is dangerous, I said that it is inferior to heterosexuality. If one pushed it to the limit, it would be dangerous to humanity" (our translation).[40] Thus yesterday's rhetoric was brought up to date! Judgment was reserved.

The March toward Social Acceptance
In a period of just under thirty years, there were significant improvements in the legal situation of French homosexuals. Can the same be said for levels of tolerance and social acceptance? Here is a brief history of the civil and social liberation of French gays.

From 1968 to the Early 1980s: Steps toward Normalization

As mentioned above, the first demonstration by French homosexuals, organized by the Front homosexuel d'action révolutionnaire, took place on 1 May 1971, amid the gatherings of leftists and unionists. In the early 1970s numerous protest groups were formed and dissolved. FHAR, created spontaneously, disappeared in the same way due to its "[refusal to] base itself on social reality, its rejection of all structure, and its lack of desire to fight repression" (Girard 1981, 111, our translation).[41] It also proved difficult to create political and action-oriented cohesion among homosexual action groups, and conflicts were not uncommon. Girard (1981, 108) discusses several examples, including one in which FHAR burned the director of the Arcadie group in effigy in a public square.

Nevertheless, gays were more and more in evidence, especially on television. On 21 January 1975 the program *Les Dossiers de l'écran* on Antenne 2 broadcast a debate on homosexuality after its screening of the film *Les Amitiés particulières,* adapted from a novel by Roger Peyrefitte that had previously been censored. More than 19 million viewers watched the program, and it received good reviews in the national and regional press. On 27 March 1976, 600 homosexuals participated in the first public gay festival in the sixteenth arrondissement. Next came a week-long festival in April 1977, with 10,000 attending (see Girard 1981, 115, 123, 142). Gradually, the media granted homosexuals more airtime, despite still-hostile scientific and judicial discourses.

In 1980, a *Le Nouvel Observateur* survey showed that 49 percent of the French population still considered homosexuality a social evil. Although 27 percent felt that it was an acceptable way of life, 34 percent saw it as a disease and 26 percent saw it as a sexual perversion. Despite these alarming statistics, homosexuals' visibility increased considerably. As Martel (1999, 136) notes about the 1980s, "Homosexuals seemed to be winners on every score and could even allow themselves a few fantasies. Gays played a role in fashion trends." In 1983, Jean Genet, a homosexual, won the Grand Prix national de littérature; the government's minister of culture, Jack Lang, lifted the censorship on a number of homosexual works of art; and the statute section requiring public-sector employees to have "good morals and good morality" was abrogated.

Between 1981 and 1984 gay life went public in France. Gay clubs, saunas, and "backrooms" had been burgeoning since the mid-1970s, to the point that every city with a population of 50,000 had its sauna. In fact, the sex industry as a whole underwent unexpected growth.[42] The creation of the Marais (literally, "swamp") neighbourhood in the third and fourth arrondissements of Paris crowned the era of gay liberation. French homosexuals were well on the way to social recognition and acceptance. A Sofres poll published in December 1984 showed that in just four years the proportion of French citizens who considered homosexuality an acceptable way of life had grown by 11 percent, to 41 percent. Nevertheless, 47 percent of French citizens continued to see homosexuality as either a perversion (19 percent) or a disease (28 percent).

The AIDS Years: A Step Backward

The period of euphoria proved to be short-lived, as the advent of the AIDS epidemic in the mid-1980s burst the bubble. Because the epidemic emerged at the very time when numerous gay saunas, bars, and backrooms – often viewed as places of constant cruising and multiple sexual relations – were being opened, French society, with a complacent press, quickly associated AIDS with homoerotic lifestyles.[43] Much ink was devoted to the "gay cancer epidemic," and the image of homosexuals quickly began to suffer (*Libération*, 19 March 1983). In 1987, 50 percent of respondents to a Sofres-*Le Nouvel Observateur* poll felt that AIDS was a consequence of the homosexual lifestyle, and 51 percent saw homosexuality as a disease or perversion. To the question, "In your opinion, are homosexuals responsible for the propagation of AIDS, including to people who are not homosexual?" 38 percent of respondents said yes, and 42 percent said no.

Paradoxically, only 19 percent of respondents claimed to feel anxious about homosexuals, which meant that 81 percent were indifferent or sympathetic to them. Among the other findings on the image of homosexuals during the AIDS crisis, 60 percent of respondents found it unacceptable for their children's teacher to be a homosexual, 48 percent did not want a homosexual to be the mayor of their municipality, and 57 percent did not want a homosexual as the president of the Republic. It is interesting to observe that the aspect of medical discourse dealing with reversibility of homosexuality influenced the respondents. In 1987, 53 percent of French citizens would have tried to change the sexual behaviour of their son if he were gay. Two conclusions can be drawn from these statistics, which admirably measure and weigh the facts but never make value judgments

(Bouchard and Arcand 1996, 145): first, there was not yet complete and full social acceptance of homosexuals in the AIDS era, and second, medical discourse had something to do with it.

Given the risks posed by AIDS, the French government intervened. In 1983, it published a ministerial circular that asked blood donors to fill out a form in order to exclude members of at-risk groups, one of which was homosexuals. Homosexual militants likened this to the pink star that identified gays under the Nazi regime and condemned it as a step backward when it came to their integration into society. Martel (1999, 197) considers this reaction irrational given the scope of the epidemic. However, as Olivier Fillieule (1998, 83) notes, it is important to place homosexual groups' reactions in context. First, knowledge of the disease was still limited. Second, homosexual movements, freshly struck off the list of social evils, still mistrusted the standardizing, globalizing medical discourse. Third, homosexuals' suspicion that there was a discriminatory plot is explained, more or less, by a press that sought to find the causes of the spread of AIDS solely in homoerotic lifestyles. In addition, French homosexual movements were not alone in their initial denial of the AIDS crisis; American homosexuals reacted similarly (see, notably, Bayer 1989; Wachter 1991).

In any case, with the epidemiologic context lending their actions legitimacy, the police began to close the backrooms. Starting in 1984, in both Paris and the provinces, the drug and prostitution squads shut down a number of these "sex rooms." Numerous heterosexual spouse-swapping clubs met the same fate. The police used section 334, clause 6, of the Penal Code, on public debauchery, to make their moves, reminiscent of how the Montreal police used the law to repress gay saunas in the mid-1970s. Martel (1999, 246) feels that these closures were motivated more by a general tightening of public morality than by concern about the propagation of HIV.

Thus, by 1987, there reigned a general climate of censorship of "bad morals," conveyed mainly by the Catholic Church and extreme-right groups. The ensuing years marked a step backward in gays' march toward social acceptance, as the church spread the idea of a link between homosexuality and AIDS. With discourse of these two political and moral forces "came a rhetoric of hatred, exclusion, moral depravity, and fear of the other" (Martel 1999, 246). Among the direct consequences of the rise of moral radicalism were measures instituted by the minister of the interior,

Charles Pasqua, to control and regulate "bad morals." Martel (1999, 246-47) also notes that Parisian prosecutors were asked to investigate "pink" messenger services, and the director of public freedoms received a request to monitor and censor, if necessary, the publication of certain works. The sale of the magazine *Gai pied* to minors was banned, as were posters advertising it. Ten other titles received similar treatment. These attempts at censorship, however, were rejected unanimously by the political class.

The 1990s: A Leap Forward

After a period of lethargy at the beginning of the decade, the homosexual movement became active and structured due to the AIDS epidemic, despite the fractured nature of French society with regard to communitarianism. ACT UP, an organization fighting AIDS, acted as the spearhead for this associative renewal.[44] In the 1990s, the homosexual fact gradually became less extraordinary for various reasons. Homosexual movements gained visibility, as did individual gays, on the political, social, cultural, and art scenes. There was also a form of desexualization of the homosexual identity, coinciding with a change in heterosexual lifestyles: "Whereas homosexuals were once the only demographic outlaws and society called them 'queers,' an increasingly broad spectrum of the population at large has now become 'deviant' and 'wild,' rejecting the confines of marriage as an institution" (Martel 1999, 314).[45] Martel (1999, 313) adds that there was a transformation in concepts of masculinity, and certain sexual practices, up to then considered exclusively homosexual, became widespread. He gives the example of sodomy, which was seen more and more as a sexual activity practised by heterosexual couples; almost 30 percent of men and 24 percent of women admitted that they had performed it at least once, and 15 percent of men and 13 percent of women did so regularly. In comparison, among homosexuals, sodomy was practised by 36 percent as the active partner and 28 percent as the passive partner. Regardless of the accuracy of these statistics (cited in Martel 1999), what must be noted is a change in attitude regarding sexual activities once considered "impure" and reserved almost exclusively for gays.

These changes in attitudes and sexual practices favoured the spread of gay and lesbian lifestyles, and the tolerance threshold rose. Various opinion polls presented a clear increase in acceptance of homosexuality among the public. In 1995, 51 percent of French people were in favour of homosexual marriage (and 48 percent were in 2002), and 63 percent agreed that homosexuals should have the same benefits as common-law couples (in 2002, 70 percent of respondents were in favour of the Pacs). Also in 1995, 65 percent of the French population felt that it was not a shock to see two homosexuals holding hands in public, and 41 percent of parents would accept having a homosexual child (19 percent had this opinion in 1973). In 1997, 55 percent of French citizens felt that homosexuality was an acceptable form of sexuality; 24 percent had held this opinion in 1973. Finally, the election in 2001 of a gay mayor of Paris proved that things had changed since 1987, when 48 percent of French people said that they would find such a situation unacceptable. According to Sofres (2001), the massive support of the Pacs by the French "is concrete testimony to the greater tolerance of homosexuality in France."

In short, since the 1970s, homosexuals have made considerable advances in social and judicial recognition. Today, French society is more and more accepting of gays and lesbians, and the law defines and recognizes same-sex couples, even though this legal recognition is not completely egalitarian, as shown by the difference between the Pacs system and traditional marriage, reserved for heterosexuals. However, the issue of parentality for same-sex couples is far from being settled in France, despite the fact that in November 2009 the majority of French people were in favour of it and despite the Besançon court's ruling that a lesbian couple may adopt a child.[46]

Some Comparisons: A Time Gap

It is difficult to compare the elements of legal recognition of homosexuals in Quebec and in France from the 1970s to the present. Both societies decriminalized homoerotic behaviours and sought to protect homosexuals against different forms of social and legal discrimination. In both social contexts, the sexual liberation movement of the 1970s played an important role in the legislative shift toward recognition and acceptance of all forms of sexuality, which became a private affair, situated beyond the control of the judicial system. However, some government members were resistant to the idea of decriminalization and greater legal recognition of homoerotic behaviours. Old prejudices, which associated homosexuality with corruption of minors or degeneration of the nation, persisted. In both Quebec and France, a portion of society (the Catholic Church, for example)

Figure 5.3
Chronology of legal recognition of gays in France

1810	The Penal Code ceases to repress homosexuality in itself.
6 August 1942	Certain homoerotic behaviours are recriminalized, notably by creating discrimination with regard to the age of sexual majority (fifteen years of age for heterosexuals versus twenty-one for homosexuals).
8 February 1945	Ordinance No. 45-190 (section 331, paragraph 3) represses all "immodest and unnatural acts" between individuals of the same sex and under twenty-one years of age.
1 February 1949	An ordinance by the prefect of Paris forbids men to dance together.
18 July 1960	The Mirguet Amendment, which includes homosexuality on the list of social evils, is adopted.
25 November 1960	The ordinance on indecent exposure makes the homoerotic act an aggravating circumstance (section 330, paragraph 2).
1968	France adopts the World Health Organization classification according to which homosexuality is a form of mental disease.
5 July 1974	The age of sexual majority is lowered to eighteen years with regard to homosexuality, whereas that for heterosexual relations remains at fifteen years.
June 1981	End of official filings of homosexuals according to a circular of the Ministère de l'Intérieur, and France no longer considers homosexuality a mental disease.
4 August 1982	Paragraph 2 of section 331 of the Penal Code is abrogated, thus ending the criminalization of homoerotic behaviours. Sexual majority is now fifteen years of age for all French citizens.
25 July 1985	Adoption of Act 85-772, which protects individuals against discrimination related to lifestyles. Section 225-1 of the Penal Code establishes, as a general principle, the banning of discrimination against homosexuals, and section L.122-45 of the Labour Code protects against discrimination based on lifestyles.
11 July 1989	Two rulings by the Cour de cassation (*Air France* case) invalidate legal recognition of the status of gay and lesbian spouses.
15 November 1999	The president of the Republic promulgates Act 99-994 on the Pacte civil de solidarité (Pacs).

associated homosexuality with pedophilia or, at least, depravation of minors (see "Pour le n.2 du Vatican, il y a 'une relation entre homosexualité et pédophilie,'" *Têtu*, 13 April 2010, www.lepost.fr). Medical discourse, matched with the return to a conservative view of the family and sexuality, legitimized these associations. The AIDS epidemic provided the rationale for the part of society that saw homosexuality as a social evil and a danger to the nation's health. On the legal front, the AIDS crisis was not transformed into repressive reform but simply slowed gays' and lesbians' march toward legal recognition. It is interesting, in fact, to note the growing place of homosexuals on the political scene: both the mayor of Paris and the leader of the Parti québécois were openly gay.

Recognition and legal protection occurred at different times in Quebec and France. In Quebec, in the late 1970s, the Charter of Human Rights and Freedoms (1977) protected homosexuals against most forms of discrimination. When Bill C-38 was adopted, on 28 June 2005, Canada authorized same-sex marriages. In France, this legal protection developed a bit later, starting in the mid-1980s (Act of 25 July 1985 regarding discrimination based on lifestyle); the Pacs, adopted in 1999, does not guarantee the same legal benefits as married couples enjoy.

Many legislative improvements were nevertheless made, notably with regard to taxation. The first homosexual marriage in France was performed on Saturday, 5 June 2004. This union was annulled by the court of first instance in Bordeaux on 27 July 2004, as it went against the directive issued by the Republic's attorney general. The mayor of Bègles was suspended for a month by the minister of the interior. But this series of events relaunched the debate on the issue of gay and lesbian marriage in France, a debate that the president promised to hold publicly. The legalization of marriage between same-sex spouses and homoparentality were two of the main themes of the Gay Pride March in Paris on 25 June 2005. A ruling by the court of first instance of Paris on 2 July 2004 made official the parental authority of a lesbian couple over their three daughters conceived by artificial insemination, even though at the time French singles did not have this authority. As Daniel Borrillo wrote in *Le Monde* on 22 September 2004 (our translation), "It was a true advance in the area of parentage, as the Pacs was in the sphere of marriage." In the same edition of *Le Monde*, Caroline Mécary commented (our translation), "This decision, still exceptional today, enabled the natural mother to cede her parental authority to the adoptive parent, although she continued to exercise it in practice. It thus allowed a link of parentage to be added that went toward greater protection of the child."

Another distinction is that the movement toward legal recognition and protection of gays resulted in Quebec from a series of repressive waves by the Montreal police in the mid-1970s. These violent actions brought homosexuals out of the closet through large public demonstrations and the creation of the Association pour les droits des gais du Québec (ADGQ). ADGQ's demands forced the Quebec government to adopt a law protecting gays and lesbians against discrimination. In France homosexual movements did not see legal protection as their highest priority in the 1970s and early 1980s. "Repression is not so much in the laws as in people's minds," FHAR declared (quoted in Girard 1981, 94), "what we must change are opinions." Girard (1981, 105, 134, our translation) observes that FHAR "never sought to fight legal repression affecting relationships with minors" and that other groups, such as Politique et Quotidien, saw it as a secondary issue. On the whole, these homosexual groups were more focused on a global struggle against established social norms. In the 1990s French gays demonstrated specifically for judicial recognition for same-sex couples, a recognition that they obtained through the Pacs in 1999. Finally, it should be noted that neither the French Pacs nor Quebec's civil union targeted homosexuals specifically. These laws concerned all unmarried couples whose uncertain legal status had to be clarified. In 2006, according to the 2006 Canadian Census, one-third of Quebecers were living in common-law relationships with no legal protection, particularly with regard to taxation, financial issues, and the sharing of family patrimony. Thus, homosexuals fell within the more general context of the management of new family dynamics.

Conclusion

FROM ONE SEXUAL PERVERSION TO ANOTHER?

It is an understatement to say that between 1970 and the mid-80's, for fifteen years, public opinion was lenient toward the role of adult pedophiles; these adults whose misdeeds are now denounced in the major press while their arrests are hailed as a valorous victory.

> – Jean-Claude Guillebaud, *The Tyranny of Pleasure*

It is not the vocation of science to say what is the norm; it is up to society to invent it – and, why not, in the name of equality.

> – Daniel Borrillo and Éric Fassin, *Au-delà du PaCS*
> (our translation)

Catholic politicians and lawmakers must feel their consciences particularly aroused ... by the heavy social responsibility of presenting and supporting iniquitous laws. There is no Eucharistic coherence when legislation is promoted that goes against the integral good of mankind, against justice and natural law.

> – Proposition 46, 1st Synod of the Pontificate of Pope
> Benedict XVI, in reference to homosexual marriage

The history of judicial repression of homoerotic behaviours in France and Quebec reveals certain differences in how each society has managed the "homosexual problem." Until the mid-eighteenth century the criminal justice system in New France was essentially an extension of the one in France. Both societies had been governed by Louis XIV's Grande Ordonnance since 1670. Criminal law, for the most part, fell within common law, and sentences varied widely according to judges' whims. The justice system was based principally on the postulates of vengeance and terror, with torture and exemplary sentences serving as a political ritual. The system was intended to maintain order, of course, but its main purpose was to keep the population aware of the sovereign's power and, as a corollary, aware of a certain conception of the social hierarchy. At the top sat the king, heir to divine will, and at the bottom were the subjects, loyal servants, joined in a single fate. By this very fact, an attack on the society became a direct attack on God, represented on Earth by the king, and he wrought vengeance on both individuals and the community.

Inherited in good part from the Middle Ages, legal doctrine in both the colony and the parent country strongly condemned sodomists. Their sin went counter to the divine nature of man and merited a punishment equal to the crime, an exemplary sentence drawn from divine justice – the stake. It was the moral crime par excellence, a "crime of divine lèse-majesté," in Durkheim's (1900) terms. Nevertheless, as in the Middle Ages, sodomy, as a *nefandum crimen,* was rarely punished in public. It was preferable to conceal this detestable crime rather than to risk teaching it to the faithful. Sodomists were punished openly only when their crime was combined with a blood crime or an attack on a minor. In these cases, the violence of the assault (murder or rape) was veiled behind the unnatural act. In other words, the sentence totally excluded the violent act to concentrate only on the sodomy, the crime against religion that upset public morality. Since violence was common in the Ancien Régime, and since children were not yet seen as full human beings, universal individuals, it was better to highlight what was more repugnant to the public conscience.

After the British Conquest in 1760, the two societies took different paths with regard to the workings of their justice systems. Now under the British, the colony was subjected to another strongly repressive penal system, particularly in terms of public morality. In French Canada, as in New France preceding it, homoerotic behaviours were presented to the community as impure acts – crimes against nature – due mainly to the omnipresence of the Catholic Church in all spheres of social life, especially starting in the 1840s. Religious discourse dominated the lifestyles and morality of French Canadians throughout the nineteenth century. Through its insistence on a "retraditionalized" family, the church shaped the French Canadian collective identity. Criminal law in French Canada was also largely influenced by religious discourse, and exemplary sentences were the rule. Homoerotic behaviours, consenting or not, were heavily repressed by penal doctrine; capital punishment for these offences was not officially abolished until 1861. Nevertheless, no exemplary sentence was handed down for sodomy in French Canada during the nineteenth century.

France, guided by the Enlightenment philosophers, began its long march to the revolution, when the Ancien Régime's administration of the penal system and its justification for sentences disappeared.[1] In a wave of universal reason, French society and its justice system gradually became laicized, with ecclesiastic discourse giving way to "scientific" and "rational" discourses. At the same time, the hierarchy of crimes changed: those with a religious or moral connotation tended to disappear from the Penal Code, replaced by those that affected individuals and their possessions. Consenting individuals performing sex acts in private, including homoerotic ones, left the penal field, even though homoerotic lifestyles were viewed with anxiety by the public authorities. With massive secularization of French society, in which the physician gradually took over from the priest as counsellor and spiritual guide – first in urban areas and then in the countryside – the religious conception of public morality dissolved. Instead, it was fear of contagion, associated with deviant lifestyles, that upset the community – more precisely, the rising middle class. Medical discourse reflected the fantasies of the bourgeoisie and, at the same time, imposed its economic, managerial, and arithmetical vision of sexuality.[2] The public-health current, advocated and abundantly employed by the emerging medical authority, encouraged the bourgeoisie to protect itself against the risk of widespread depravation of morals to which degeneration of the nation would lead.

In other words, whereas in the previous century the sodomist was *punished* because he had dared to affront the divine order, the very core of the common conscience, now society sought to *control* him due to the risks that he posed to individuals, who had recently been elevated to the supreme value of the community. The penal system's target quietly shifted from the delinquent act to the delinquent personality, to use the terms of Garapon and Salas (1995). In modern criminal law, the dialectic of crime and punishment was rapidly supplanted by "that of symptom and treatment, the criminal appearing more as a patient than a villain" (Garapon and Salas 1995, 147, our translation). This marked the beginning of the psychologization and pathologization of the deviant, and the invert, the new (essentially male) figure created by the legal-medical discourse, was no exception. Society undertook to treat him if he suffered from any psychic or physical disorder or to rehabilitate him if he had been struck down by an incurable degenerative disease. Punishment was intended no longer to expiate him (repressive law) but to control him in the name of protecting society and the individuals within it. Thus what I have termed preventive law – that is, repressive intervention (deprivation of freedom, castration, and so on) – was instituted, but this was done in the name of an ideal of rehabilitation and restitution of the deviant to "normal"; criminal law was authorized to intervene on behalf of the general interest, whether there was a victim or not, and to impose on "deviant victims" – victims of their own disease – treatments appropriate to that disease.

The precepts of rehabilitation and dissuasion with a view to limiting recidivism existed well before the penal reforms of the Enlightenment. What was new, Michel Foucault (1979) observes, was that prevention began to take precedence, and it became the true stake in the economics of punishment in nineteenth-century penal philosophy. Of course, behaviours legally defined in the Penal Code were still being judged in the courts. However, passions, instincts, maladaptations, deviances, and effects of environment or heredity were simultaneously being assessed. From physical torture, the interest of justice turned to healing the soul, and a wide range of techniques were developed in an attempt to understand and treat the new deviants. The mechanisms of conflict resolution, which were once based solely on the supposed knowledge of rational authorities, now had to integrate the polemics of expertise. This was the explosion of technoscience as defined by Olivier Clain (1989).[3]

Because social problems were myriad and individualized, punitive practice also became more and more individualized. From general and deductive punishment, the penal system turned toward what Michel Freitag (1986) has termed the "decision-making–operational mode of regulation," in which each particular case was judged independently of the others and in the moment. The law, like the punitive function, was adapted to the specific aspects of individuals who were more and more differentiated. These new extrajudicial elements were superimposed on the power to punish and continued to operate as nonjudicial (nonrepressive) elements but within the punitive penal system. Behind a face of rehabilitation, of "reinstatement," the new penal therapy legitimized judicial intervention that was, in short, very repressive. This incursion by the justice system into therapy with regard to homosexuals continued and evolved throughout the first three-quarters of the twentieth century (Corriveau 2007).

Starting in the mid-twentieth century, Quebec began to accede to modernity as it underwent intensive secularization, urbanization, and industrialization and was liberated from ecclesiastical discourse. The justice system saw a similar transformation starting in 1969, with quiet but full decriminalization of homoerotic acts conducted in private among consenting adults. Over a ten-year period Quebec decriminalized all of these sexual practices and set in motion a broad-based trend toward recognition and legal protection of homosexuals. As had occurred in France in the previous century, in Quebec individuals became distinct from a common conscience up to then governed by religious discourse. In the name of universality of the human being, homosexuals were recognized to have the right to demand full recognition of their specificities.

Meanwhile, after 150 years of no repression in its criminal doctrine, France took a leap backward by recriminalizing, specifically and in themselves, certain homoerotic sexual practices. Following the traumas of war, especially the economic, demographic, and political losses, traditional Christian values were revalorized, and puritanism was seen as the path to reclaiming the nation. "Work, Family, Homeland," declared Philippe Pétain. Criminal law was reformed to respond to the prerogatives of the pro-birth and nationalist policies in force since the end of the First World War. In line with the trend toward moral strictures, Charles de Gaulle placed homosexuality on the list of social evils in 1960. This climate of judicial segregation of homosexuals lasted until 1982, when all homoerotic behaviours conducted among consenting adults in private were decriminalized. It was not until the Pacs was instituted, in 1999, that same-sex couples were legally recognized, although they did not obtain parity with married heterosexual couples.

Today, homoerotic lifestyles are beyond the scope of repressive law in both France and Quebec. At the same time as homoerotic behaviours were decriminalized, the figure of the homosexual, with his own identity and specificities, was recognized in law. As newly recognized individuals who could conduct their private life as they wished, homosexuals sought acknowledgment of all of their specificities under general principles of human rights.[4] To this effect, gays (and lesbians) defined themselves and formed pressure groups to claim and highlight each of their particular characteristics.[5] A number of Western countries have addressed the question of same-sex marriage in recent years. After the Netherlands on 1 April 2001 and Belgium on 1 June 2003, Spain became the third country in the European Union to legalize same-sex marriages, through a Senate vote, on 30 June 2005. The senators approved the bill, which also allows adoption by gay couples, by a majority of forty (187 votes for, 147 against, and 4 abstentions). On 5 December 2005, the United Kingdom legalized gay marriage, and the first same-sex marriage in the United Kingdom was celebrated on 19 December 2005 in Belfast, Northern Ireland. Forecasts call for some eleven thousand unions to be pronounced by 2010. In the United States the Massachusetts Supreme Court authorized gay marriage in 2003, and a court in the State of Washington confirmed its legality on 4 August 2004. In Canada, following the initiative of nine of the thirteen provinces and territories, Parliament finally came down in favour of same-sex marriage on 28 June 2005. The statute came into force on 20 July 2005. From the stake to town hall – that is the extent of the reversal of judicial logic with regard to homosexuality in the West.

From Homosexual to Pedophile?

The historical study of the repression of homosexuals has highlighted the recurrence of certain themes in how these "deviant" lifestyles have been controlled since the Middle Ages. Aside from the grip of ecclesiastical discourse (even today), the interdependence, or even correlation, between social crises and repression of homoerotic lifestyles has been underlined. Periods of upheaval marked by low birth rates, war, and economic crisis have coincided with a resurgence of repression in which the homosexual was the scapegoat used to calm public opinion or justify political action. On the other hand, this repression was not directed strictly against homosexuality. All "dangerous classes" were controlled by the "dominant classes" following economic and social crises, as the latter defended their social privileges through regulation of deviance. The predominant role played by the family in the control of homosexuality and, more generally, of sexuality among children, has also been observed.

In this regard, history gives a glimpse of how the social perception of the sex pervert has changed. Society seems to have transferred its abhorrence from sodomists to pedophiles. In my research, I observed that when society "discovered" children as separate beings, universal persons, the justice system made sure to repress anything that could impede their development. Of course, the evolution of the concept of the child, protection of children, and the "moral panic" that surrounds this is not linear – to the contrary! Philip Jenkins (1998) brilliantly shows the cyclic nature of societal attitudes toward protection of children in North America over the past century. Nevertheless, it is of interest to apply the typology of the figure of the child formulated by Daniel Dagenais (2008, 91) to the history of repression of homoerotic lifestyles. According to Dagenais, the figure of the child evolved as follows. First, in traditional societies, the child seemed to be attached to the family's economic reproduction; although he was the family's heir, little attention was paid to his particular needs. Then, with modernity, the child became an individual on his own who needed protection in the same way as all universal subjects did. Finally, in contemporary societies, the child is presented as an "increasingly rare commodity," a projection of the self through whom the adult perceives his or her own completion.

At the same time, the history of the repression of homoerotic lifestyles shows that up to the seventeenth century, France meted out severe punishment to sodomists accused of murder, rape, or assault on children. However, society considered the child permanently perverted by this type of sexual assault and sanctioned him at the same level as the accused. With the "discovery" of the child in the eighteenth century and the philosophy of youth protection that endured throughout the nineteenth century, the child became the object of sustained attention, and everything that might interfere with his or her development was disturbing. In this regard, it is relevant to note that the image of the homosexual also began to change in the nineteenth century. It was no longer homosexuality in itself that upset the community but the risks attributed to it, mainly depravation of the morals of minors. Inversion was seen as a sort of contagious degeneration, and it was feared that it would be transmitted to children. The homosexual's choice of sexual object, very often associated with youth in the collective imagination, thus made him potentially dangerous.

As Duclos (1997) observes, childhood is now subjected, more than ever, to community protection. Protection of youths against all forms of violence has become a predominant community issue that illustrates perfectly the context in which the new representation of pedophilia occurs. Jean-Claude Guillebaud (1999) and Jenkins (1998) posit that pedophilia is supplanting all other fears in the collective imagination as "news items of a sexual nature become a recurring scenario in modern times" and as "each new instrument of communication helps to disseminate this unremitting fear" (Guillebaud 1999, 255). To this, I must add as a possible avenue for research that it is mainly fear of increased contact with and reciprocal recognition of pedophiles facilitated by the Internet and its global reach that explains and legitimizes the recent legislative activity with regard to cyberspace. Internationally, good examples are the creation of the Children's Rights Committee within the United Nations by the ministers of justice of the G8 countries in Paris in May 2003 and the formulation of national and international strategies aimed specifically at protecting children against sexual exploitation on the Internet. Similarly, in the *Speech from the Throne to Open the First Session of the 37th Parliament,* the Canadian government promised to intervene "to safeguard children from crime, including criminals on the Internet," by creating new criminal offences such as luring a child on the Internet (section 172) and a ban on access to juvenile pornography (section 163.1(4.1)). Similarly, in France, section 227-23 of the Penal Code criminalizes pornography featuring a minor, and section 227-24 bans the manufacture, transfer, and dissemination "by any means and on any medium of a violent or pornographic message."

It appears that the hate once focused on sodomists has simply been displaced toward pedophiles, the new sexual pariahs par excellence for a society in which the interests of the child are paramount in the collective conscience. Antoine Garapon and Denis Salas (1996, 87, our translation) note in this regard that the "penalization of community life finds its acme in the figure of the sexual pervert, who has made his appearance in political debate in recent years." In Quebec an article in the Quebec City newspaper *Le Soleil* on 31 January 2003 (our translation) evoked the scandal of child prostitution sweeping the city, where "things have reached the point that the mayor is likening the current situation to a bad western in which people are lynched in the public square with no other form of trial." The reporter added that "rumours in the city that condemn one and all [have reached an extraordinary] level of collective hysteria."[6]

Could it be that Western societies have simply shifted their cult object from the family to the child? The history of legal repression of homo-erotic lifestyles leads me to think that it has. First, religion represented the sodomist as a threat to the traditional family, the heart of the community; then, medicine designated the risks that the invert posed to the health of the nation; finally, the state, medicine, the human sciences, and the clergy all raised the dangers inherent in the corruption of minors' morals and the importance of the family in educating children. By chance or not, in the early twenty-first century, with homosexuals' rights legally guaranteed, we are seeing, as a corollary, a hunt for pedophiles and incestuous fathers. From one sexual pervert to another – is this the unconscious logic under-lying the evolution of the penal system with regard to management of human sexuality? Does this mean that René Girard (1986) is right to sug-gest that family seeks and always finds a guilty party, a substitute pervert, in order to divert insatiable societal violence toward a sacrificial victim?

Notes

Chapter 1: Ancient Greece to the Seventeenth Century

1 See, on this subject, the many warnings by Boswell (1980, 1994).

2 Éribon (2004, 156) observes, "A cultural and historical gaze turned toward Greece served for a long time (up until quite recently) as a way for gay people (mostly from privileged backgrounds, of course) to provide themselves with a set of references that justified what Christian culture, social prejudices, and even the law condemned to silence." For example, he explains in a note on page 379 that, according to Georges Dumézil, "Bernard Sergent tends to believe too easily that what he finds in the texts allows him to know what was going on in reality."

3 The origin and diffusion of pederastic customs in Greece was apparently the result mainly of Doric influence – more specifically, the military organization of the Doric states. Dover (1978, 185) notes that although the currently available data do not allow us to determine beyond all doubt that Sparta and the Doric states were the point of origin for diffusion of homoerotic eros throughout ancient Greece, it is irrefutable that the Greeks gave homoeroticism social acceptance and exploited it artistically. As a consequence, the Doric states influenced, even if slightly, the Greek territory as a whole. It would be a mistake, however, to believe that homoerotic lifestyles "evolved" in a linear and homogeneous fashion throughout Greece, and attempting to build an image of these lifestyles solely according to how they are presented in philosophical and literary tradition is a matter more of fantasy than of empirical reality. As Éribon (2004, 161) warns, "It seems more likely that the image we have, rather than being a true picture of daily life in a given society, is the product of acts of literary adjustments, ideological justification, or philosophical representation."

4 As Veyne (1978, 55, our translation) notes, if the Romans were puritanical with regard to sex, marriage, and reproduction, they were even more so with regard to virility: "Virility (*virtus*) being the duty of the freedman, the mark of his power, failure was marked by shame and visions of demons. The only model of Roman sexuality was *dominatio* by the *dominus* over everything else. Rape within inferior statuses was the

norm. Sex without putting one's power to the service of another was respectable."
See also Hupperts (2006, 49ff).

5 On this subject, Lever (1985, 27, our translation) states, "Roman aristocrats were
highly infatuated with Greek fashions and customs but never managed to do more
than plagiarize them maladroitly. If they practised pederasty, it was only through
snobbery, with an eye to fashion and distinction."

6 The historical reconstruction of repression of homoerotic behaviours in the Middle
Ages is a difficult enterprise, as attested to by the paucity of research produced
on the subject. Aside from the substantial work by Boswell (1980, 1994), very few
researchers have attempted an in-depth exploration of this field of study, which is
strewn with methodological obstacles. This explains why I often refer to Boswell.
Even the exhaustive study by Gauvard (1991) on criminality in the Middle Ages refers to it very rarely (see pages 597-98 on homosexuality and bestiality). Among the
methodological difficulties encountered, Boswell underlines that prejudices against
homoerotic lifestyles no doubt encouraged the deliberate falsification of historical
data. In addition, due to the private nature of homoerotic lifestyles, the majority
of available sources that deal with the subject are official documents, particularly
repressive legislative and religious measures. As a consequence, it is risky to draw
conclusions solely from these sources without having established "the extent to which
such laws are honoured, supported, or generally approved" (Boswell 1980, 22). Finally,
not only did the Middle Ages extend, as a historical period, for almost one thousand
years, but obviously Christian influence was not perceived in the same way or with
the same intensity everywhere. See also Hergemöller (2006).

7 Although some historians have questioned Procopius's true intentions with this
critique of Justinian, Boswell (1980, 173-74) states, "Procopius records the criminalization of homosexuality as one of several programs the emperor undertook chiefly to
get money from the persecuted and lists it among the oppression of the Samaritans,
the pagans, unorthodox Christians, and astrologers." For more details on the secret
history of Procopius, see Procopius (1961).

8 Hergemöller (2006, 57) notes, "Those whom we today call 'homosexuals' were
grouped together with others who had sex with animals, who engaged in anal or
oral intercourse, or who practised contraception or abortion."

9 Bishop Burchard set out punishments only for homosexuality perpetrated by married men. See, on this subject, Boswell (1980, 205) and Spencer (1995, 108).

10 The close relationship with the destruction of Sodom seems obvious here.

11 According to Gauvard (1991, 598; our translation), "Testimonials confirm the difference between north and south with regard to the hierarchy of sins."

12 For more about Henry III's homosexuality, see Godard (2001, ch. 2) and Teasley (1987,
27), who writes, "Henry was charged with being unnaturally passive, effeminate, and
addicted to the company of his male cronies rather than that of his wife ... But there
was much more to the charge, for it became associated with a host of other sins: ir-

religion, atheism, sorcery, treason, rape, tyranny, monstrous animalistic behaviour, and the killing of children."

13   "Of the 1,500 judgments pronounced in the French Parliament during the reign of Saint Louis, only 1 refers to sodomists" (Bullough 1974a, 186).

14   For more details on this complex historical period, which it would be erroneous to call neutral with regard to the issue of repression of homoerotic lifestyles, see two very interesting works: Godard (2001) and Poirier (1996). See also Puff (2006).

15   Courouve (1979) found thirty-nine cases of capital punishment carried out between 1317 and 1783. See also Sibalis 2006a).

Chapter 2: The Grande Ordonnance of 1670 to the British Conquest

1   Two manuscripts conserved at the Bibliothèque nationale de France, titled *Procès faits à divers sodomites jugés au Parlement de Paris* (under call numbers 10969 and 10970), form the general documentary basis for academic and historical research on the repression of homoerotic lifestyles under the Ancien Régime. Collected by an eighteenth-century compiler, these two registers, containing proceedings of trials for sodomy and bestiality in the sixteenth, seventeenth, and eighteenth centuries, constitute a detailed legal source with fascinatingly precise testimonies. For instance, the two short books by Dr. Ludovico Hernandez published in 1920 and the more recent study by Lever (1985) use evidence from these two anecdote-rich documents. Although the second manuscript is devoted entirely to the famous sodomist Benjamin Deschauffours, the first lists, out of a total of ninety-eight trials, only ten for pederasty; the rest dealt with bestiality. Researchers have also had a chance to work from the archives of the Bastille conserved at the Bibliothèque de l'Arsenal (manuscripts 10254 to 10260). This archival collection comprises a corpus of seven boxes that relate the police memoranda written between 1723 and 1749 (the years 1749 to 1780 are missing). Although these memoranda do not tell us about the arrests that led to the public convictions, they describe the legal decisions that I researched for this book, as it seemed important to retrace the discourse of power as presented and represented to its subjects. On this subject, see Merrick and Ragan Jr. (2001, 52-75). For this section on repression of homoerotic lifestyles in France, I am very grateful to my fellow historian and friend Pascal Bastien for his methodological advice and work on the archives.

2   In *Les Institutes au droit criminel* (1757, our translation), Muyart de Vouglans defines sodomy as the group of sexual acts not oriented toward procreation: "It is also committed by a man with a woman when they do not use the ordinary path to generation. Finally, it is committed by a man on himself."

3   Pastoureau (1999, 189) notes, however, that for bestiality trials, only the transcripts, and sometimes just copies rather than the original documents, were burned.

4   According to Rey (1989, 142), two hypotheses might be advanced to explain the application of this exemplary punishment. First, "judged directly by the judges of

Chatelet, and not by the lieutenant-general, the two men could have been the victims of the smouldering conflict between the magistracy and the police." Second, because there had been riots in the spring of 1750 following the rumour that the police had assaulted a child, this was an attempt to appease the masses.

5 The term *mouche* was coined for the first spies engaged for the Court of François I by Antoine de Mouchy. See Lever (1985, 263).

6 For a detailed history of how the Parisian police dealt with "sodomites," see Rey (1982, 1987, 1989, 1991).

7 According to Rey (1989, 131), "Many of the accused declared that this situation was peculiar to Paris: there were no *mouches* deployed elsewhere (at Rouen or in Brittany, for example)."

8 With regard to denunciation and the use of mouches in legal practice, Farge (1993, 13) notes, "The hunt for loose talk, comment and rumour was one of the essential preoccupations of the government of the capital. The attachment of so much import-ance to this activity, as in the planning of *mouches* and official observers whose job it was to 'seize' anything said in public places, shows well enough how useful a tool the spoken word was for the police. It was in fact a tide to be harnessed and stemmed." See also Sibalis (2006a, 221), Lever (1985, 263), and Rey (1989, 131ff).

9 It was the same for other sex "crimes," including cohabitation. Usually, family mem-bers served as "enemies." See Farge (1993).

10 According to Merrick and Ragan Jr. (2001, 31), the police "morals squads" questioned almost a thousand individuals in the gardens of Luxembourg, Palais-Royal, and the Tuileries.

11 According to Sibalis (2006a, 212), "French law courts tried sodomites infrequently and rarely imposed the death sentence."

12 Here is an example given by Rey (1989, 133): "He [Haimier, officer of the Provoship and general marshalsea of the Île-de-France] quite readily set free young men, men with families, and those involved in business. He showed his respect for those societal units (family, parish, neighborhood) that could set back on the straight path those who had strayed from it." Although Pierrat (1996, 148, our translation) mentions that "noblemen convicted of sodomy benefited from a system of favour: they were garrotted secretly – that is, out of the public eye," it should be noted that the practice of *retentum* (a tacit clause or proviso) was not reserved solely for the nobility. See Bastien (2006, 103-6).

13 Merrick and Ragan Jr. (2001, 31) note that the police "collected information about and apprehended thousands of individuals, including members of the nobility and clergy, whom they usually released or at least treated with some deference, and large numbers of artisans and servants, who were much more likely to be punished."

14 However, as Rey (1989, 142) mentions, "no clear traces [of banishment] remain in the police archives of such penalties, undoubtedly because such were usually imposed only after the accused had already been imprisoned in Bicêtre."

15 It is amusing to observe that the statute of 31 March 1928 on army recruitment stipulated that homosexuals condemned "to one year in prison for indecent assault were to be incorporated, obligatorily and directly, into light infantry battalions" (Girard 1981, 20, our translation)!

16 The situation seemed to be quite similar in the church: a gap persisted between repressive discourse and actual practice.

17 The exceptions were Jean Diot and Bruno Lenoir, who, as Rey (1989, 141-42) notes, should have been sent to Bicêtre. According to Sibalis (2006b, 110), this execution remained the exception: "The police ordinarily released arrested sodomites with a simple warning or, at worst, after a few weeks of administrative detention."

18 As Bastien (2005, 50) notes, the crime was presented under its biblical name, sodomy, rather than the more laicized term, pederasty, a term that did appear, however, in jurisprudence treatises in the eighteenth century.

19 For more details on legal rituals in France, see Bastien (2005; 2006).

20 As Cellard (1991, 27, our translation) notes, "The parent country had managed to establish in North America a typically French society in terms of its population, institutional and legal framework, behaviours, beliefs – in short, its mentality." For more on criminal justice in New France, see Boyer (1966) and Cellard (2000).

21 Crimes and offences listed in New France may be broken down into five categories. I use the classification of Lachance (1978, 1984), who based his groupings on the classifications of criminalists of the time (D. Jousse and M. de Vouglans) and on those of twentieth-century criminologists (D. Szabo and G.M. Sykes). The five categories are crimes of "divine lèse-majesté," offences against religion (heresy, witchcraft, etc.); crimes of "human lèse-majesté," offences against the king's authority or the public order; crimes against the person or the honour (rape, homicide, injury, etc.); crimes against property, offences ranging from theft to setting fires, forgery, and being in possession of stolen property; and crimes against morals.

22 The sources used for this section were mainly *Jugements et délibérations du Conseil souverain de la Nouvelle-France (1663-1716)*, (Quebec City: Imprimerie A. Côté, 1885-1891), *Journal des Jésuites*, Boyer (1966), Hurteau (1991), Lachance (1984), and Séguin (1972).

23 *Journal des Jésuites* (1893), 116. It should be noted that Boyer (1966, 227, 330, our translation), relying on the *Jugements et délibérations du Conseil souverain*, does not mention the name of the guilty party but notes only that he "was found guilty of a crime against nature *(convictus crimine pessimo)*." He was the first white man (settler) to be accused of crimes against nature. In the seventeenth century Aboriginals were not yet fully subjected to colonial law, although the presence of berdaches within Aboriginal tribes indicates that certain homoerotic customs were practised. See also Hurteau (1991).

24 "In reparation for which he is banished from this country in perpetuity and enjoined to keep his banishment for a life penalty, [and pay] two hundred pounds of alms,

half to the poor of Hôtel Dieu and the other to the Bureau of the Poor" (*Jugements du Conseil souverain,* vol. 3, 558, our translation).

25 "The Council in deliberation has sentenced and sentences said la Roze and Dubois to serve in His Majesty's country, to wit, said La Roze for three years and said Dubois two years; Mr. Governor being asked not to give them parole for this time. Bochart Campigny/Depeiras" (*Jugements du Conseil souverain,* vol. 3, 558, our translation).

26 The "recruited soldier accused of the Crime of Bestiality" (*Jugements du Conseil souverain,* vol. 4, 110, our translation).

27 The court "discharges said François Judicth dit Rencontre of the accusation and sets him free and orders that his trial will be closed and sealed to be opened only upon arrest" (*Jugements du Conseil souverain,* vol. 4, 110, our translation).

28 "We wish, however, for you to make it more difficult to be absolved for the greatest sins, especially those that have a censure attached, such as setting fires, magic, sodomy, bestiality, incest" (Mandements des Évêques de Québec, "Circulaire avant départ pour la France," 1690, *Têtu I,* 285, quoted in Hurteau 1991, 73, our translation). See also Sylvestre (1983, 15).

29 Mandements des Évêques de Québec, "Statuts publiés dans le second synode tenu à Ville-Marie," 10 and 11 March 1694, article 21, *Têtu I,* 319, quoted in Hurteau (1991, 74).

30 *Rituel du diocèse de Québec publié par l'ordre de Mgr l'évêque de Québec* (Paris: Simon Langlois, 1703), referenced in Hurteau (1991, 74).

31 As Seifert (2001, 45) notes, "This repression contributes in many cases to a fascination with the 'sodomite' and sodomy, a fascination that is amply expressed in songs and poems of the *Chansonnier Maurepas.*"

32 For a complete and fascinating history of the different meanings of the words "pederast" and "pederasty," see Féray (2004). As he notes (2004, 60, 67, our translation), although "pédérast" and "pédérastie" first appeared in the French language in the sixteenth century, "it must be observed that at the time they were part of the vocabulary of the literate and scholarly," and it was not until the "early nineteenth century that the majority of French-language dictionaries and encyclopaedias generally had a more complete definition of the word 'pédéraste.'" Moreover, the word appeared more frequently in police memoranda in the mid-nineteenth century. According to Féray (2004, 50, our translation), "To the police confidences were added the indiscretions of another profession, auxiliary to the justice system: that of forensic physicians."

33 Vigarello's (2001, 57) conclusions on rape are similar to mine with regard to sodomy, for which court cases were rare and generally limited to child rape. See also Farge and Revel (1991).

34 Although it is difficult to obtain exact data on the population of Paris, demographers estimate that it grew from 430,000 in 1650 to about 510,000 in 1700. See, in particular, Dupâquier (1988, 94).

35 Lever further notes, "It was also normal to enlist lay sodomists, once they had served their sentence, in the king's army."

Chapter 3: The British Conquest to the Late Nineteenth Century

1 The St. Lawrence Valley was the part of New France conquered in 1760. It was also called the Province of Quebec. It was not until later that other parts of New France were defeated or surrendered, as Louisiana was by Napoleon in 1803. The expression "part of Canada called New France" designates the territory that became Lower Canada in 1791. Thus it is anachronistic to use the term "Lower Canada" before that year.

2 For more details on this case, see Merrick (2001). As Sibalis (1999, 13) notes, five of the seven Parisian sodomists burned in the entire eighteenth century had committed "other serious crimes, like rape and murder."

3 It should be noted in passing that "the new revolutionary legislation of 1791 partially introduced the adversarial system, while preserving certain rules of the inquisitorial system, including written information ... [Later], the Code d'instruction criminelle of 1808 was presented as 'a work superimposing opposing provisions of two previous statutes, the Ordinance of 1670 and the statutes of 1791.' This was the mixed system in which the first phase of the trial, the investigation, was inquisitorial, while the judgment phase adopted the adversarial model" (Tulkens and van de Kerchove 1993, 372, our translation). For an excellent analysis of how adoption of the Declaration of the Rights of Man and the Citizen affected the judicial system, see Tulkens and van de Kerchove (1993, 65-70).

4 In 1784, Mouffle d'Angerville related that a certain commissioner, named Foucault, had "a thick book in which were written all the names of pederasts reported to the police; he claimed that there were in Paris almost as many [pederasts] as there were prostitutes – that is, around 40,000." In the eighteenth century, "out of a population that ranged from 600,000 to 650,000 between the beginning and the end of the century, the lieutenant general estimated that there were 20,000 sodomists around 1725" (Lever 1985, 249-50, our translation).

5 According to Peniston (2001, 183), "In the eighteenth century, the police rarely enforced these laws, which called for the death penalty for sodomites. Instead, they developed a policy of surveillance and harassment which treated same-sex sexual behavior as a misdemeanor. In the nineteenth century, they continued to keep under surveillance and to harass men who engaged in such behavior by interpreting broadly the new laws against public offenses against decency, incitement of youth to debauchery, and sexual assaults, and applying these laws loosely."

6 For more details on the Penal Code of 1791 and 1810, see Sibalis (1996).

7 In his study on homosexuality and prostitution in Paris between 1870 and 1918, Revenin (2005, 11, 166) shows that male prostitution and homosexuality were often associated and combined in judicial, literary, police, religious, and other discourses. Thus, in the absence of penalization of homosexuality per se, legislative means were used to repress homosexuals through the offences of vagrancy, soliciting, or indecent exposure, which were often associated with prostitution.

8 According to Tamagne (2001, 62, our translation), "The effeminate homosexual became a specific literary character on his own, found, for example, in novels of formation, in which he was a grotesque, enterprising figure whom the hero met on his path and tried to avoid."

9 For more information on the emergence of medical authority and its effects on penal rationality, see Corriveau (2004) and Foucault (1990).

10 This trend emerged in the witchcraft trials. "Now ecclesiastical power itself appeals to medicine in order to rid itself of this problem," observes Foucault (2003, 221).

11 For a detailed examination of forensic medicine in France in the nineteenth century, see Chauvaud (2000) and Guillaume (1996, 100).

12 For a better understanding of the connection between the criminal justice system and medico-legal expertise in France in the nineteenth century, see Foucault (1982). See also Peniston (2004) and Sibalis (1996).

13 On his list of pathological deviations of the venereal appetite, Dr. Michéa placed Greek love in the top position. "Greek love" was then subdivided into pedophilia and lesbianism. For more information, see Courouve (1985, 180-81). See also Hekma (1994, 183).

14 At the time, the church still played an important role in the state. For example, the budget for the clergy was twice as large as that for teachers, and the number of churches grew from 36,000 in 1830 to 42,000 in 1869. See Hahn (1979, 53).

15 For this section, the traditional sources of law – statutes, jurisprudence, and doctrine – have been used. I analyze the perception of homoerotic lifestyles in French Canada under the English regime mainly through commentators on British law. The deficiencies in the criminal justice apparatus with regard to police intervention, the extent of the territory, and, especially, self-regulation of the crime by local communities make it difficult to use penal statistics as quantitative sources for analysis of criminality. It is therefore plausible that the penal statistics are not always representative of social regulation in the colony as a whole, as the rural way of life was still very important at the time. See Boyer (1966) and Fecteau (1985).

16 According to Désaulniers (1977, 142), there are indications that French criminal statutes were abrogated neither at the time of the Conquest nor at the time of the Royal Proclamation of 7 October 1763, nor even in the Ordinance of 17 September 1764, which established the courts of justice in the colony. Opinions on this subject differ.

17 "Without falling into stereotypes, one may reasonably posit that in the adversarial system, settlement of conflicts is managed by individuals, citizens; the state intervenes little. The trial takes place according to the rules of the civil process: it is set in motion by an accuser who is generally the victim and proceeds under the management of the parties themselves. The judge's function is to arbitrate debates and settle conflicts. The adversarial system is set up to protect individual freedom. The presumption of innocence is, in this sense, at the heart of the adversarial system" (Tulkens and van de Kerchove 1993, 371-72, our translation).

18 "The British penal laws deserved the epithet 'Bloody Code' because of the readiness to invoke hanging: the number of crimes leading to hanging went from about 50 in the 17th century to more than 200 by the end of the 18th century. In England, as here, for that matter, the death penalty was applied somewhat erratically. Simple infringements of conduct such as the theft of turnips, stealing a shilling or damaging a fish pond could lead directly to hanging" (Cellard 2000, 9).

19 Under the Test Act, French Canadians were required to renounce Catholicism and their allegiance to the pope. Concretely, the Act was aimed at excluding Catholics from the public service.

20 See *R. v. Alfred Métayer dit St-Onge,* Court of Sessions of the Peace 1876 11 18, MJ n. 84; *R. v. Calixte Desjardins,* Court of Sessions of the Peace 1879 01 17, MJ n. 10.

21 For more details on Bentham and the influence of his writings, compulsory reading is Borrillo and Colas (2005, 222-33) and Crompton (1978; 1998).

22 For more details on the Catholic Church's influence over the French Canadian population, see Hamelin and Gagnon (1984).

23 Province of Canada Statutes, *An act for consolidating and amending the Statutes in this Province relative to Offences against the person,* 4-5 Vict. (1841), c. 27, s. 15.

24 Starting in 1840, even though the term "Lower Canada" was still widely used, official documents used the term "Canada East." In 1867 it became the Province of Quebec.

25 Dagenais explains that settlers who moved to New France came mainly from regions of France that, from the point of view of family structure, were the most modern in the country. For more details, see the excellent work by Dagenais (2008, 128-41).

26 In Jarrell's (1987, 43) view, the Catholic Church's grip on French Canada was a phenomenon unmatched in other nations.

27 "Aside from Montreal, with a population of about 250,000, and Quebec City, which had barely 60,000 inhabitants, Quebec had only nine towns with 5,000 to 13,000 inhabitants. The rest of the population lived in hundreds of dispersed localities" (Hamelin and Gagnon 1984, 27, our translation).

Chapter 4: The Late Nineteenth Century to the Sexual Revolution

1 A 1950 English court ruling states, "In order to constitute the offence of gross indecency between male persons, actual physical contact is not essential." See *R. v. Hunt,* 34 Cr. App. R. 135.

2 Before the Criminal Code of 1954-55 was enacted, the sentence of whipping was mandated for only twelve charges: those in sections 80 (attack on sovereignty), 135 (rape), 137 (attempted rape), 138 (carnal knowledge of a girl under fourteen years of age), 141 (indecent assault on a female person), 142 (incest), 148 (assault by a man on another man), 218 (suffocation, giving drugs for the purpose of overcoming resistance to a criminal act), 289 (theft), 292 (theft), 289 (breaking and entering with a weapon), 292 (assault on a woman causing bodily harm), and 299 (gross indecency).

However, whipping was handed down as a sentence only once for an indecent assault by a man on another man. For more information, see Parker (1964-65).

3 The section on gross indecency was not modified during the general revisions of the Criminal Code in 1906 and 1927 but simply taken up in its entirety under section 206. In 1953-54 the offence of gross indecency was transformed by section 149. See S.C. 1954, c. 51, s. 149.

4 Section 293 replaced section 260 in 1906 and was abrogated in its turn in 1953-54 by section 148.

5 About the statute on sexual psychopaths in the United States, Jenkins (1998, 87) observes, "Homosexuals all too easily qualified for inclusion under the new legislation because of the inclusion of sodomy in the lists of offenses meriting psychopath status."

6 See Vigarello (2001). As he notes (2001, 150), "The immediate suspicion of a woman regarded as too 'free' was no longer expressed in the legal texts, as under the ancien regime, but it remained implicit, diffused and very present in penal practice."

7 See *R. v. Belt* (B.C.A.C.) [1944] 84 C.C.C. 403. This case offers an example of a life sentence handed down for an act of sodomy.

8 Section 147 was abrogated for the first time in 1906 and replaced by section 202.

9 *R. c. Joseph Clément*, Sessions de la paix, Montréal (1897-05-28), MJQ/CPA, n. 65; *R. c. Victor Brunette*, Sessions de la paix, Montréal (1897-11-16), MJQ/CPA, n. 161.

10 "The first step to this acquired homosexuality, however, was masturbation" (Bullough 1974b, 107). See also Arcand (1993, ch. 8) and Tamagne (2004, vol. 2, 32). As Tamagne notes, "In the authors' minds, solitary masturbation must lead to mutual masturbation."

11 For more details on the situation in the United States, see Chauncey (1994b). On the situation in Europe, see Tamagne (2004, vol. 2).

12 On the debates surrounding the nature and causes of homosexuality, highly recommended sources are Dorais (1994) and Koertge (1981).

13 Dorais (1994, 108) notes that in the past fifty years, studies on hormonal causes of homosexuality have been contradictory. Some propose that homosexuals have a higher hormonal level than do heterosexuals, whereas others suggest the contrary. He concludes that these studies do not prove any "significant difference in hormonal level between the homosexual population and the heterosexual population."

14 On castrations performed in the United States, see Duffy (1965).

15 I would like to thank Isabelle Perreault for sharing her research conducted for her postdoctoral project, *Les thérapies de choc au Canada entre 1925 et 1960. L'Hôpital Saint-Jean-de-Dieu à Montréal comme exemple des savoirs et des pratiques des psychiatres franco-canadiens.*

16 For more on this issue, see Engelhardt and Caplan (1987, esp. chs. 16 and 17). See also Thuiller (1989, 1128).

17 For a detailed analysis of this subject, see Kinsman (1996, 183ff).

18   "Fruit Machine" was the name given to the project by RCMP agents. See Gentile and Kinsman (2008).

19   I do not have statistics for 1948. See *Annuaire du Québec* (1954, 218; 1959, 229).

20   According to Linteau and colleagues (1991, 308), "In the strict sense, the Quiet Revolution generally refers to the political, institutional and social reforms undertaken between 1960 and 1966 by the Liberal government of Premier Jean Lesage. Some writers trace the beginning of the Quiet Revolution to a slightly earlier date – the death of Maurice Duplessis and the accession to power of Paul Sauvé in 1959."

21   See Rouillard and Goulet (1999, 86, our translation): "Fifteen hundred new officers swelled the ranks of the police force."

22   A methodological problem arises when one wishes to use criminal statistics in France. To begin with, I was not able to uncover, as I could for Quebec, explicit penal statistics on the repression of homoerotic behaviours for the period 1942-68. The only detailed statistics, listed in *Aspects de la criminalité en France en 1982 constatée par les services de police et de gendarmerie d'après les statistiques de police judiciaire*, cover from 1970 to 1982. This data-collection system was created in 1971 and applied in 1972 in order to give a more accurate and complete picture of criminality in France. Previously, criminal statistics had not been classified according to offence. For example, the statistics give only the number of offences for all crimes against morals, without specifying the nature of the crime. In *Crimes et villes*, Denis Szabo (1960, 64, our translation) notes, "It is thus not surprising that criminologically and sociologically valid data are extremely rare in the criminal statistics published after 1945. We have, per department, the number of criminal charges and defendants. But neither offences nor infractions are listed, only the nature of the crime, categorized as offences against the person, property, and the public good."

23   Tamagne's (2004) work, originally a doctoral dissertation, is an essential reference for this historical period in France.

24   In Revenin's (2005, 149-50, our translation) view, "It should be noted that although police surveillance of Parisian homosexuals was as active during the Belle Époque as during preceding decades, police raids in homosexual establishments were much rarer during the Belle Époque than during the 1870s, which were marked by the ultraconservative and clericalist policy called the 'moral order.'"

25   See Revenin (2005, 166-73), who lists the different statutes used against homosexuals, including vagrancy, begging, public exposure, indecent assault with violence, and habitual incitement of minors to debauchery.

26   Ironically, homosexuals were associated with the Vichy regime, although this very regime re-established legal repression against homosexuality by raising the age of consent for homosexuals to twenty-one years.

27   The age of majority for heterosexuals was set at fifteen years in 1945. See implementing order no. 45-1472 of 4 July 1945, p. 4072.

28   For details on the use of common-law provisions, see Boninchi (2005, 161-74).

29 For an excellent summary of the origins of section 334, see Boninchi (2005, 152-56).
30 Boninchi (2005, 149, our translation) also notes that the idea of castration had been advanced to control recidivist homosexuals but was quickly rejected as "contrary to Christian principles."
31 For an idea of the debate on the 1960 bills, see Dallayrac (1968, 234-37). See also Girard (1981, 15ff).
32 "In an article appearing in *Le Monde* on 23-24 July 1961, the minister of public health, Mr. Chenot, wrote, 'In reality, there are two causes of this: microbes' increased resistance to antibiotics [and] the considerable expansion of homosexuality in all countries ... How can we fight this resurgence? By imposing stronger sentences on homosexuals'" (Girard 1981, 16, our translation).
33 For a detailed description of the evolution of these concepts, see Courouve (1985) and Corriveau (2004).
34 On the evolution of treatment as penal philosophy, see Quirion (2006).
35 I am grateful to Olivier Clain for having pointed me in this direction in my research.

Chapter 5: The 1970s to the Present

1 For a remarkable analysis of the development of gay and lesbian movements, see Adam (1995).
2 Very likely, the term "gay" has existed since the nineteenth century. It was used in the 1920s by homosexuals so that they would recognize each other. For more details, see Courouve (1985, 111-12).
3 I consider sexual orientation not to be immutable and set for life but to be constructed and modulated in individuals throughout their lives according to their experiences and environment. In other words, the categories "homosexual" and "heterosexual" are social labels and do not correspond to a psychological or medical reality.
4 For an excellent summary of the subject, see Dorais (1994).
5 Cohen-Jonathan (2002, 110) gives details of the *Dudgeon* case, as well as the *Norris* case (26 Oct. 1988, A. n. 142).
6 On France, see Aoun (2000), Bach-Ignasse (1998), Borrillo (1995, 1998), Leroy-Forgeot (1997), Martel (2000), Mécary (2000), Mécary and Leroy-Forgeot (2001), and Meyer (1998). On Quebec, see Duplé (1984), Demczuk and Remiggi (1998), Goreham (1984), Letellier (1993), Richard and Seguin (1988), and Schabas (1995).
7 For further details on the debates around Quebec's entry into modernity, see the excellent collected work by Elbaz and colleagues (1996).
8 Section 147 of the Criminal Code of 1953-54 had been abrogated and replaced by section 155.
9 It is also possible that it was Trudeau's political courage that was mainly responsible for adoption of the Omnibus Bill. See Corriveau (2007).
10 It is interesting to observe the evolution of this expert knowledge with regard to the homosexual "question." Fassin (1999, 89ff) and Borrillo (1999, 161ff) discuss this in the

context of the debates surrounding adoption of the Pacte civil de solidarité (Pacs) in France. I strongly suggest that the reader refer to these authors for an understanding of how anthropology, sociology, and psychoanalysis, in turn, tried to explain and legitimize the proposed legislative changes. As Fassin (1999, 108, our translation) brilliantly summarizes, "Politicians tried to justify their rejection by referring to experts."

11 According to Smith (1999, 45), it seems that the governments of Manitoba (1974), Saskatchewan (1976), and Alberta (1976) also legitimized some of their legislative modifications with a medical model that promulgated the idea of an innate, immutable sexuality.

12 *R. v. Hunt,* 34 Cr. App. R. 135; *R. c. Whissel,* R.J.P.Q. 85-121 (C.S.P) (our translation). Furthermore, in *R. v. Lavallée,* [1975] C.A. 547, the court stipulated that fellatio fell under the definition of gross indecency.

13 *R. v. M.* (M.H.), (1994) 91 C.C.C. (3d) 504, 516 (N.S.C.A.).

14 L.Q. 1975, c. 6; L.R.Q. 1977, c. C-12, modified by L.Q. 1982, c. 61. The Charter of Human Rights and Freedoms was promulgated by Robert Bourassa's government in 1976, but at that time it made no mention of sexual orientation.

15 Some state that the Danish government was the first to ban discrimination based on sexual orientation. However, the Danish Criminal Code was modified only on 3 June 1987 (Act 357, 3 June 1987). The new statute, which came into effect on 1 July 1987, reads, "Persons who publicly or deliberately disseminate statements or other reports by which any group of people are threatened, ridiculed or degraded on account of their racial origin, skin colour, national or ethnic origin, beliefs or sexual orientation, are liable to fines, short-term detention or imprisonment for up to two years." On the other hand, the Danish government was the first to recognize unions between same-sex spouses, in 1989. For more information, see the report of the International Lesbian and Gay Association (http://www.ilga.org).

16 It is interesting to note that France also decriminalized homosexuality in 1982. Was it a sign of the times?

17 According to Smith (1999, 3-4), "Almost twenty-five years later the Supreme Court of Canada, in a narrow decision, held that even though the Canadian Charter of Rights and Freedoms prohibited discrimination on the grounds of sexual orientation James Egan and Jack Nesbit, a gay couple, were not entitled to spousal benefits under the Old Age Security program. The court found that the denial of benefits was a reasonable limit on the rights of lesbian and gay citizens." On Canada, see the tremendous work by Smith (2008).

18 See also the ruling by Judge Marc Beauregard, who, in *Association des gais du Québec c. Commission des écoles catholiques de Montréal,* 1980 C.S. 93, invalidated the use of the exceptions regime for religious motives.

19 For the full opinion, see http://www.scc-csc.gc.ca.

20 This procedure was exceptional since bills are normally reviewed by parliamentary committees.

21 The debates on the second reading of Bill C-38 on 16-18 February 2005, 21 March 2005, 24 March 2005, 4-5 April 2005, and 3 May 2005 give a good view of MPs' diverging positions on the definition of marriage.

22 Barbara Kay, "It's Time to Think about the Children," *National Post,* 5 February 2005, A16.

23 For comparison, here is the commentary by jurist Philippe Malaurie (quoted in Borrillo 1999, 168, our translation) during the debates over the Pacs: "If we want to impede pedophilia, drugs, violence, and chaos in the schools and in the suburbs, we cannot count only on the police, judges, prisons, and chemical castration. We should not destroy the invisible sentinels that maintain the coherence of our society: the difference between man and woman and family stability. These bills damage social cohesion and our family structures."

24 On the subject of parentality of gay couples, see L'Archevêque, Julien, and Ryan (2009) and Corriveau (2009).

25 See http://www.vatican.va/roman_curia/pontifical_councils/family/documents/ rc_pc_family_doc_20051007_trujillo-synod_en.html.

26 See Higgins (1999, 130). According to Sivry (1998, 243), there were 144 arrests for being in a bawdy house in the Le Mystique and Truxx bars. Five years later, 120 of those arrested were cleared of all charges.

27 On this subject, see the series of articles titled "Homosexualité: La télé est sortie du placard" in the "Arts Magazine" section of *Le Soleil* (19 January 2009). The articles talk about how Quebec television, unlike television in the United States, portrays "homosexuality as part of daily life, far from the clichés of the past" (our translation).

28 See "Les Français, le PaCS et l'adoption d'enfants par les homosexuels," 5 September 2001, http://www.Sofres.com.

29 For an excellent critique of the use of polls and other statistics, see the classic work by Robert and Faugeron (1980).

30 The "morals and sex crimes" category was divided as follows: (1) rape, (2) molestation, (3) indecent assault by a homosexual, (4) indecent assaults by other individuals, (5) homosexuality with minors, and (6) incitement of minors to debauchery. The facts recorded include "all crimes and offences observed and discovered throughout the territory by the Gendarmerie nationale and the national police (urban police, judicial police, general information, air and border police, territorial surveillance)" (5, our translation).

31 In section 225-1 the French Penal Code also banned all forms of discrimination based on sex, family situation, state of health, disability, political opinion, race, nationality, religion, and union membership.

32 This tends to show antihomosexual prejudices. For more on this ruling, see Borrillo and Pitois (1998).

33 Fassin (1999) observes that the church also turned to expert discourses.

34   The Pacs has been the subject of extensive legal analysis by a number of authors; see
Aoun (2000), Mécary (2000), Mécary and Leroy-Forgeot (2001), and Vivier (2001).
Therefore, here I present only the general outline of the enabling statute.

35   For a detailed history of the debates on adoption of the Pacs, see Borrillo and Fassin
(1999), Martel (2000, ch. 18), and Moutquh (1999). For a history of the inception of
the Pacs, see, among others, Lanez (1998), Mécary and Leroy-Forgeot (2001, ch. 3),
and Weill et al. (1998).

36   For a critical analysis of the effects and paradoxes of the Pacs, notably compared
to common-law marriage, see Borrillo (2000, 117), Mécary (2000), Mécary and
Leroy-Forgeot (2001), and Vivier (2001). See also Pisier (2000), who argues that the
statute, by refusing the right to marriage and filiation, maintains the primacy of the
heterosexual family through the symbolism of sexual differentiation.

37   See http://www.ined.fr/fr/pop_chiffres/france/mariages_divorces_pacs/pacs.

38   See http://www.bpbfc.banquepopulaire.fr/acef/Lettre_2005-04/pfis_arch.asp.

39   See http://www.legifrance.gouv.fr/WAspad/UnTexteDeJorf?numjo=SOCX0400130L.

40   See Stéphane Durand Souffland, "Le premier procès pour homophobie tourne au
débat philosophique," *Le Figaro,* http://www.lefigaro.fr/actualite/2006/05/17/01001-
20060517ARTWWW90315-le_premier_proces_pour_homophobie_tourne_au_debat
_philosophique.php.

41   For more details on the evolution of French homosexual groups, see Girard (1981).

42   Martel (1999, 178) estimates that the revolutionary homosexual movements (FHAR,
Groupes de libération homosexuels, Comité d'urgence anti-répression homosexuelle)
"had a concrete effect on homosexual emancipation only after they had been appropriated by business, and when sex itself became communal." According to Martel,
the change of opinion on homosexuality was produced with very little help from
militant gay groups. Not having a gay political community, France was home to a
community of sexual pleasure. However, Girard (1981, 7, our translation) is of the
opposite opinion: "Homosexual struggles never were and never will be reduced to
their organized form, known as the homosexual movement. A wide network of
microcommunities raised voices that permeated all levels of society; the taking of
individual positions played a significant role in the evolution of opinion."

43   "Not one week goes by that the mainstream press does not gush sensational headlines
on a disease that is overwhelming us poor pederasts. It's stronger than the plague
and gangrene combined ... One thing is certain: homosexuality sells," remarked Dr.
Lejeune in 1982 (quoted in Filleule 1998, 82, our translation).

44   Filleule (1998, 86, our translation) gives a good explanation of the emergence of
ACT UP, which defines itself as "an association of people affected by AIDS. Through
intense lobbying and direct action (demonstrations, zaps, die-ins, etc.), the organization tries to pressure governments and sectors responsible to various degrees for
managing the disease to wage a more effective and less discriminatory fight against
AIDS."

45 "With all these single-parent families, blended families, and single-person house-
holds, the idea of a 'natural' family – simple and universal – has been discredited.
Marriage, where it survives, is often redefined as a contractual bond, with all the
precariousness and fragility characteristic of such bond. As the classical family model
has weakened, it has been replaced by recognition of sexual pleasure at the expense
of fertility alone. The heterosexual with multiple partners has become more visible.
The image of masculinity has also changed" (Martel 1999, 315-16).

46 See http://www.lefigaro.fr/actualite-france/2009/11/21/01016-20091121ARTFIG00069-
les-homosexuels-bousculent-les-regles-de-l-adoption-.php; and http://www.lefigaro.
fr/actualite-france/2009/11/10/01016-20091110ARTFIG00482-feu-vert-a-l-adoption-
pour-un-couple-d-homosexuelles-.php. On the issue of homosexual parentality in
France, see the excellent work edited by Cadoret and colleagues (2006).

Conclusion: From One Sexual Perversion to Another?

1 It is interesting to note that Voltaire was strongly opposed to homosexuality. Borrillo and Colas (2005, 158, our translation) note that although Voltaire was a great
defender of human rights, he nevertheless defined love between men as an "infamous
attack against nature and destructive of the human species," using biologicizing and
moralizing rhetoric that was difficult to reconcile with a philosopher of reason.

2 See Guillebaud (1998, 270).

3 Clain (1989, 126, our translation) defines "technoscience" as the "different disciplines
[that] exchange interpretive models (based on an existing analogy between related
disciplines) that no longer have their own foundation ... The other disciplines are
subdivided in a completely 'nonconceptual' way into particular spheres of research,
which, precisely because they belong to a number of existing disciplines, are institutionalized into new disciplines. Each new discipline is thus defined only as the sum
of the areas of intervention that it brings together institutionally and academically."
This idea of disciplines that are either multidisciplinary or clinical – that is, likely to
respond in a specialized way to certain social demands – also refers to what Gagné
(1999, 35-36, our translation) presents as "research based on the assembly of a plur-
ality of specialties around a single objective," with a view to "producing in-depth
knowledge of the phenomenon."

4 On the legal front, some difficulties remain for homosexuals to obtain the same
legal recognition as heterosexuals, notably with regard to parentality. See Gross and
colleagues (2005), Chamberland, Gagné, and Paquin (2006), Herbrand (2008), and
Corriveau (2009).

5 Freitag (1992, 48, our translation, emphasis added) observes that with "the new logic
of legitimization of the diversity of empirical interests and thus of conflicts of interests
or objectives in society ... the 'interests' in question ended up being stated no longer
in the flat universalist language of 'interests' but in the *immediately concrete language
of the claim of recognition of particular identities,* themselves based on whatever kind

of difference." Paraphrasing Gagné (1992, 730), we could say that because they were recognized by the authorities and captured in retrospect by positive law, the rights of gays and lesbians were transformed into human rights. Luhmann (1989, 60) concurs, noting that new judicial formulas such as "proportionality" and "balance of interests" open the legal system to adaptation to the particularities of each individual case.

6   See also Greco (2009), who shows that the Toronto media have twisted reality in their accounts of luring children through the Internet.

References

Adam, Barry. 1985. Structural Foundations of the Gay World. *Comparative Studies in Society and History* 27: 658-71.

–. 1995. *The Rise of a Gay and Lesbian Movement*. 1987. Reprint, New York: Twayne.

Allen, Luther A. 1998. L'aventure sexuelle clandestine: Le cas du Mont Royal. In *Sortir de l'ombre. Histoires des communautés lesbienne et gaie de Montréal,* ed. Irène Demczuk and Frank W. Remiggi, 81-102. Montreal: VLB édition.

Annuaire du Québec. Quebec City: Bureau de la statistique du Québec, 1930-39, 1954, 1959.

Aoun, Alia. 2000. *Le Pacs.* Paris: Delma express and Dalloz.

Arcand, Bernard. 1993. *The Jaguar and the Anteater: Pornography Degree Zero.* Trans. Wayne Grady. London and New York: Verso.

Ariès, Philippe. 1962. *Centuries of Childhood: A Social History of Family Life.* New York: Vintage Books.

–. 1971. *Histoire des populations françaises et de leurs attitudes devant la vie depuis le XVIIIe siècle.* Paris: Seuil.

–. 1982. Saint Paul et la chair. In *Communications 35, Sexualités occidentales,* 52-55. Paris: Seuil.

Aron, Jean-Paul, ed. 1984. *Misérable et glorieuse. La femme du XIXe siècle.* Paris: Éditions complexe.

Aspects de la criminalité en France en 1982 constatée par les services de police et de gendarmerie d'après les statistiques de police judiciaire. 1982. Paris: La documentation française.

Assemblée Nationale. 1960. *Séance du 18 juillet 1960.* Paris: Assemblée Nationale.

Bach-Ignasse, Gérard. 1998. Familles et homosexualités. In *Homosexualité et droit. De la tolérance sociale à la reconnaissance juridique,* ed. Daniel Borrillo, 122-38. Paris: Presses Universitaires de France.

Badinter, Elisabeth, and Lydia Davis. 1995. *XY, on Masculine Identity.* Trans. Lydia Davis. New York: Columbia University Press.

Barbier, Edmond-Jean-François. 1726. Manuscrit français 10286. Bibliothèque nationale de France.

–. 1750. Manuscrit français 10289. Bibliothèque nationale de France.

–. 1857. *Chronique de la Régence et du Règne de Louis XV, ou Journal de Barbier.* 8 vols. Paris.

Bastien, Pascal. 2005. L'exécution publique: Peine ou pénitence? In *Le Châtiment. Histoire, philosophie et pratiques de la justice pénale,* ed. Christian Nadeau and Marion Vacheret, 39-62. Montreal: Liber.

–. 2006. *L'Exécution publique à Paris au XVIIIe siècle. Une histoire des rituels judiciaires.* Seyssel: Champ Vallon.

Bastien-Charlebois, Janik. 2009. Insultes ou simples expressions? Les déclinaisons de "gai" dans le parler des garçons adolescents ... In *Diversité sexuelle et constructions de genre,* ed. Line Chamberland, Blye W. Frank, and Janice Ristock, 51-74. Quebec City: Presses de l'Université du Québec.

Bayer, Ronald. 1989. *Private Acts, Social Consequences: AIDS and the Politics of Public Health.* New York: Free Press.

Bechtel, Guy. 1994. *La Chair, le diable et le confesseur.* Paris: Plon.

Bentham, Jeremy. 1785. *Essay on Paederasty.* See Louis Crompton. 1978. *Journal of Homosexuality* 3 (4): 383-88.

Bernier, Jacques. 1989. *La Médecine au Québec. Naissance et évolution d'une profession.* Quebec City: Presses de l'Université Laval.

Bertrand, Marie-Andrée. 1988. L'analyse du discours juridique. In *Homosexualités et tolérance sociale,* ed. Louis Richard and Marie-Thérèse Séguin, 143-52. Moncton: Éditions d'Acadie.

Bieber, Irving. 1987. On Arriving at the American Psychiatric Association Decision on Homosexuality. In *Scientific controversies: Case Studies in the Resolution and Closure of Disputes in Science and Technology,* ed. Hugo Tristram Engelhardt and Arthur Caplan, 417-37. Cambridge, UK: Cambridge University Press.

Blackstone, William. 1769. *Commentaries on the Laws of England.* Vol. 4. London. See http://www.lonang.com/exlibris/blackstone/bla-415.htm.

Bonello, Christian. 2000. Du médecin légiste à l'aliéniste: L'homosexualité sous le regard de la médecine au XIXe siècle. In *Homosexualités. Expression/répression,* ed. Louis-Georges Tin and Geneviève Pastre, 65-81. Paris: Stock.

Boninchi, Marc. 2005. *Vichy et l'ordre moral.* Paris: Presses Universitaires de France.

Borrillo, Daniel. 1995. Statut juridique de l'homosexualité et Droits de l'Homme. In *Un sujet inclassable? Approches sociologiques, littéraires et juridiques des homosexualités,* ed. Rommel Mendès-Leite, 99-116. Lille: Cahiers Gai Kitsch Camp, no. 28.

–, ed. 1998. *Homosexualité et droit. De la tolérance sociale à la reconnaissance juridique.* Paris: Presses Universitaires de France.

–. 1999. Fantasmes des juristes vs Ratio juris: La doxa des privatistes sur l'union entre personnes de même sexe. In *Au-delà du PaCS. L'expertise familiale à l'épreuve de l'homosexualité*, ed. Daniel Borrillo and Éric Fassin, 161-90. Paris: Presses Universitaires de France.

–. 2000. *L'Homophobie*. Paris: Presses Universitaires de France and Que sais-je?

Borrillo, Daniel, and Dominique Colas. 2005. *L'Homosexualité de Platon à Foucault. Anthologie critique*. Paris: Plon.

Borrillo, Daniel, and Éric Fassin, eds. 1999. *Au-delà du PaCS. L'expertise familiale à l'épreuve de l'homosexualité*. Paris: Presses Universitaires de France.

Borrillo, Daniel, and Thierry Pitois. 1998. Adoption et homosexualité: Analyse critique de l'arrêt du Conseil d'État du 9 octobre 1996. In *Homosexualité et droit. De la tolérance sociale à la reconnaissance juridique*, ed. Daniel Borrillo, 139-50. Paris, Presses Universitaires de France.

Boswell, John. 1980. *Christianity, Social Tolerance, and Homosexuality: Gay People in Western Europe from the Beginning of the Christian Era to the Fourteenth Century*. Chicago: University of Chicago Press.

–. 1994. *Same-sex Unions in Premodern Europe*. New York: Villard Books.

Bouchard, R.F, and J.D. Franklin. 1980. *Guidebook to the Freedom of information and Privacy Acts*. New York: Clark Boardman and Company.

Bouchard, Serge, and Bernard Arcand. 1996. *De la fin du mâle, de l'emballage et autres lieux communs*. Montreal: Boréal.

Bowman, Karl M., and Bernice Eagle. 1953. The Problem of Homosexuality. *Journal of Social Hygiene* 39 (1): 2-16.

Boyer, Raymond. 1966. *Les Crimes et châtiments au Canada français du XVIIe au XXe siècle*. Montreal: Cercle du livre de France.

Bullough, Vern L. 1974a. Heresy, Witchcraft, and Sexuality. *Journal of Homosexuality* 1 (2): 183-201.

–. 1974b. Homosexuality and the Medical Model. *Journal of Homosexuality* 1 (1): 99-110.

Bureau, Marie-France, and Jacques Papy. 2007. L'orientation sexuelle et la Charte des droits et libertés de la personne: Récit d'une trajectoire. In *La Charte Québécoise: Origines, enjeux et perspectives*, ed. Alain-Robert Nadeau and Revue du Barreau du Québec, 109-41.

Cadoret, Anne, Martine Gross, Caroline Mécary, and Bruno Perreau, eds. 2006. *Homoparentalités. Approches scientifiques et politiques*. Paris: Presses Universitaires de France.

Canada. 1958. Royal Commission on the Criminal Law Relating to Criminal Sexual Psychopaths. Report of the Royal Commission on the Criminal Law Relating to Criminal Sexual Psychopaths. Ottawa: Queen's Printer.

–. 1984. Committee on Sexual Offences against Children and Youth. *Sexual Offences against Children: Report of the Committee on Sexual Offences against Children and Youth* (the Badgley Report). 2 vols. Ottawa: Department of Supply and Services.

Carlier, François. 1981. *Prostitution antiphysique*. 1887. Reprint, Paris: Le Sycomore.

Carpentier, Jean, and François Lebrun, eds. 2000. *Histoire de France*. Paris: Seuil.

Cartuyvels, Yves, Françoise Digneffe, and Dan Kaminski. 1997. Droit pénal et déformalisation. In *Les Mutations du rapport à la norme. Un changement dans la modernité?* ed. Jean De Munck and Marie Verhoeven, 219-42. Brussels: De Boeck.

Cellard, André. 1991. *Histoire de la folie au Québec de 1600 à 1850.* Montreal: Boréal.

–. 2000. *Punishment, Imprisonment and Reform in Canada, from New France to the Present.* Trans. Eileen Reardon. Ottawa: Canadian Historical Association.

Chamberland, Line, Michaël Bernier, and Christelle Lebreton. 2009. Discrimination et stratégies identitaires en milieu de travail. Une comparaison entre travailleurs gais et travailleuses lesbiennes. In *Diversité sexuelle et constructions de genre,* ed. Line Chamberland, Blye W. Frank, and Janice Ristock, 221-62. Quebec City: Presses de l'Université du Québec.

Chamberland, Line, Frédérick Gagné, and Johanne Paquin. 2006. L'homoparentalité au Québec: Les changements législatifs et leurs impacts dans la sphère du travail. In *Homoparentalités. Approches scientifiques et politiques,* ed. Anne Cadoret, Martine Gross, Caroline Mécary, and Bruno Perreau, 143-56. Paris: Presses Universitaires de France.

Chauncey, George. 1998. Genres, identités sexuelles et conscience homosexuelle dans l'Amérique du XXe siècle. In *Les Études gay et lesbiennes,* ed. Didier Éribon, 97-108. Paris: Centre Georges Pompidou.

–. 2000. *Les Experts du crime. La médecine légale en France au XIXe siècle.* Paris: Aubier, 2000.

Chiffoleau, Jacques. 1990. Dire l'indicible. Remarques sur la catégorie du *Nefandum* du XIIe au XVe siècle. *Annales E.S.C.* 45: 289-324.

Clain, Olivier. 1989. Sur la science contemporaine. *Société* 4: 95-142.

Cohen-Jonathan, Gérard. 2002. *Aspects européens des droits fondamentaux. Libertés et droits fondamentaux.* Paris: Montchrestien.

Coke, Sir Edward. 1979. *The Third Part of the Institutes of the Laws of England.* 1625. Reprint, New York: Garland.

Commission des droits de la personne du Québec. 1994. *De l'illégalité à l'égalité. Rapport de la consultation publique sur la violence et la discrimination envers les gais et lesbiennes.* Quebec City: Commission des droits de la personne du Québec.

Corriveau, Patrice. 2004. Du sodomite au gai: Histoire et sociologie de la répression juridique des homosexuels masculins en France et au Québec de la Grande Ordonnance de 1670 à aujourd'hui. PhD diss., Université Laval and Université Picardie Jules Verne.

–. 2007. Discours religieux et médical au cœur du processus de légitimation du droit pénal. La gestion des mœurs homoérotiques au Québec (1892-1969). *Champ Pénal/ Penal Field,* http://champpenal.revues.org/document2282.html.

–. 2009. Le droit à la parentalité au Québec. Source de discrimination envers les couples gais? In *Diversité sexuelle et constructions de genre,* ed. Line Chamberland, Blye W. Frank, and Janice Ristock, 137-54. Quebec City: Presses de l'Université du Québec.

Courouve, Claude. 1979. Sodomy Trials in France. *Gays Books Bulletin* 1: 22-23, 26.

—. 1985. *Vocabulaire de l'homosexualité*. Paris: Payot.

Crémazie, Jacques. 1842. *Les Lois criminelles anglaises: Traduites et compilées de Blackstone, Chitty, Russell et autres criminalistes anglais telles que suivies en Canada arrangées suivant les dispositions introduites dans le code criminel de cette province ... province du Bas-Canada*. Quebec City: Imprimerie de Fréchette.

Crompton, Louis. 1978. Jeremy Bentham's Essay on Paederasty. *Journal of Homosexuality* 3 (4): 383-88.

—. 1998. *Byron and Greek Love*. Trowbridge, UK: Cromwell Press.

Dagenais, Daniel. 2008. *The (Un)Making of the Modern Family*. Trans. Jane Brierly. Vancouver: University of British Columbia Press.

Dallayrac, Dominique. 1968. *Dossier homosexualité*. Paris: Robert Laffont.

Danet, Jean. 1998. Le statut de l'homosexualité dans la doctrine et la jurisprudence françaises. In *Homosexualité et droit. De la tolérance sociale à la reconnaissance juridique*, ed. Daniel Borrillo, 97-108. Paris: Presses Universitaires de France.

d'Angerville, Mouffle. 1784. *Mémoires secrets pour servir à l'histoire de la République des lettres*. Vol. 23. Paris.

Deacon, Edward E. 1831. *A Digest of the Criminal Law of England*. Vol. 2. London: Saunders and Benning.

De Becker, Raymond. 1967. *The Other Face of Love*. Trans. Margaret Crosland and Alan Davantry. London: Spearman.

Delon, Michel. 1987. The Priest, the Philosopher, and Homosexuality in Enlightenment France. In *'Tis Nature's Fault: Unauthorized Sexuality during the Enlightenment*, ed. Robert Purks Maccubbin, 122-31. Cambridge, UK: Cambridge University Press.

Delumeau, Jean. 1992. *L'Aveu et le pardon. Les difficultés de la confession (XIIIe-XVIIIe siècles)*. Paris: Fayard.

Demczuk, Irène. 1998. À l'aube du prochain millénaire. In *Sortir de l'ombre. Histoires des communautés lesbienne et gaie de Montréal*, ed. Irène Demczuk and Frank W. Remiggi, 399-406. Montreal: VLB éditeur.

Demczuk, Irène, and Frank W. Remiggi, eds. 1998. Un demi-siècle de changements. In *Sortir de l'ombre. Histoires des communautés lesbienne et gaie de Montréal*, ed. Irène Demczuk and Frank W. Remiggi, 13-23. Montreal: VLB éditeur.

Demers, Robert. 1984. De la *lex scantina* aux récents amendements du Code criminel: Homosexualité et droit dans une perspective historique. *Les Cahiers de droit* 25 (4): 777-800.

de Rosset, François. 1619. *Histoires Tragiques*. Paris: Librairie générale de France.

Désaulniers, Claude. 1977. La peine de mort dans la législation criminelle de 1760 à 1892. *Revue générale de droit* 8: 141-84.

de Schutter, Olivier. 1993. Homosexualité, Discours, Droit. *Revue interdisciplinaire d'études juridiques* 30: 83-142.

Des Déserts, Sophie. 2000. Pacs: L'an 1 des nouveaux couples: Douze mois après la loi. *Le Nouvel Observateur* 1876 (19 October): 54-57.

Des Maisons, François. 1667. *Nouveau recueil d'arrests et reglemens du Parlement de Paris.* Paris: Chez Guillaume de Luynes.

Dorais, Michel. 1994. La recherche des causes de l'homosexualité: Une science-fiction? In *La Peur de l'autre en soi. Du sexisme à l'homophobie,* ed. Daniel Welzer-Lang, Pierre Dutey, and Michel Dorais, 92-146. Montreal: Éditions VLB.

Dover, Kenneth J. 1978. *Greek Homosexuality.* Cambridge, MA: Harvard University Press.

Duclos, Denis. 1997. Crimes, pédophilies et milices morales. L'enfance une espèce en danger? *Le Monde diplomatique,* January, 24-25.

Duffy, C. 1965. *Sex and Crime.* Garden City, NJ: Doubleday.

Dupâquier, J., ed. 1988. *Histoire de la population française.* Vol. 2, *De la Renaissance à 1789.* Paris: Presses Universitaires de France.

Duplé, Nicole. 1984. Homosexualité et droits à l'égalité dans les Chartes canadienne et québécoise. *Les Cahiers de droit* 25 (4): 802-42.

Durkheim, Émile. 1900. Deux lois de l'évolution pénale. *L'Année sociologique* 4: 65-95.

–. 1964. *The Division of Labor in Society.* Trans. George Simpson. 2nd ed. New York: Free Press.

Du Rousseau de la Combe, G. 1756. *Traité des matières criminelles suivant l'ordonnance du mois d'août 1670.* Paris.

Elbaz, Mickaël, Andrée Fortin, and Guy Laforest, eds. 1996. *Les Frontières de l'identité. Modernité et postmodernité au Québec.* Quebec City/Paris: Presses de l'Université Laval/L'Harmattan.

Émond, Gilbert. 2009. "Tous les garçons et les filles de mon âge ..." Attitudes, homophobie et tyrannie relative à l'homosexualité chez les adolescents des deux sexes dans les écoles. In *Diversité sexuelle et constructions de genre,* ed. Line Chamberland, Blye W. Frank, and Janice Ristock, 19-50. Quebec City: Presses de l'Université du Québec.

Engelhardt, Hugo Tristram, and Arthur Caplan, eds. 1987. *Scientific Controversies: Case Studies in the Resolution and Closure of Disputes in Science and Technology.* Cambridge, UK: Cambridge University Press.

Éribon, Didier, ed. 1998. *Les Études gay et lesbiennes.* Paris: Centre Georges Pompidou.

–. 2004. *Insult and the Making of the Gay Self.* Trans. Michael Lucey. Durham, NC: Duke University Press.

Falconnet, Georges, and Nicole Lefaucheur. 1975. *La Fabrication des mâles.* Paris: Seuil.

Farge, Arlette. 1993. *Fragile Lives: Violence, Power and Solidarity in Eighteenth-Century Paris.* Trans. Carol Shelton. Cambridge, MA: Harvard University Press.

Farge, Arlette, and Jacques Revel. 1991. *The Rules of Rebellion: Child Abductions in Paris in 1750.* Trans. Claudia Mieville. Cambridge, UK: Polity Press.

Fassin, Éric. 1999. La voix de l'expertise et les silences de la science dans le débat démocratique. In *Au-delà du PaCS. L'expertise familiale à l'épreuve de l'homosexualité,* ed. Daniel Borrillo and Éric Fassin, 89-110. Paris: Presses Universitaires de France.

Fecteau, Jean-Marie. 1985. Régulation sociale et répression de la déviance au Bas-Canada au tournant du 19e siècle (1791-1815). *Revue d'histoire de l'Amérique française,* 38 (4): 499-521.

Féray, Jean-Claude. 2004. *Histoire du mot pédérastie et de ses dérivés en langue française.* Paris: Quintes-feuilles.

Féré, Charles. 1904. *The Evolution and Dissolution of the Sexual Instinct.* Paris: Charles Carrington.

Fillieule, Olivier. 1998. Mobilisation gay en temps de sida. Changement de tableau. In *Les Études gay et lesbiennes,* ed. Didier Éribon, 81-96. Paris: Centre Georges Pompidou.

Flandrin, Jean-Louis. 1991. *Sex in the Western World: The Development of Attitudes and Behaviour.* Trans. Sue Collins. Philadelphia: Harwood Academic.

Fortin, Andrée. 1996. Les trajets de la modernité. In *Les Frontières de l'identité. Modernité et postmodernité au Québec,* ed. Mickaël Elbaz, Andrée Fortin, and Guy Laforest, 23-28. Quebec City/Paris: Presses de l'Université Laval/L'Harmattan.

Foucault, Michel. 1979. *Discipline and Punish: The Birth of the Prison.* New York: Vintage Books.

–, ed. 1982. *I, Pierre Rivière, Having Slaughtered My Mother, My Sister, and My Brother: A Case of Parricide in the 19th Century.* Trans. Frank Jellinek. Lincoln: University of Nebraska Press.

–. 1985. *The History of Sexuality.* Vol. 2, *The Use of Pleasure.* New York: Pantheon Books.

–. 1990. *The History of Sexuality.* Vol. 1, *An Introduction.* New York: Vintage Books.

–. 1991. Le pouvoir, une bête magnifique. In *Dits et Écrits,* vol. 3, 268-82. Paris: Gallimard.

–. 2003. *Abnormal: Lectures at the Collège de France, 1974-1975.* Ed. Valerio Marchetti and Antonella Salmoni. Trans. Graham Burchell. New York: Picador.

Fournier, Marcel, Yves Gingras, and Othmar Keel, eds. 1987. *Sciences et médecine au Québec, perspectives sociohistoriques.* Quebec City: Institut québécois de recherche sur la culture.

Freitag, Michel. 1986. *Dialectique et société.* Vol. 2, *Culture, pouvoir et contrôle: Les modes de reproduction formels de la société.* Montreal: L'Âge d'Homme.

–. 1992. L'identité, l'altérité et le politique. Essai exploratoire de reconstruction conceptuelle-historique. *Société* 9: 1-55.

Gagné, Gilles. 1992. Les transformations du droit dans la problématique de la transition à la postmodernité. *Les Cahiers de droit* 33 (3): 701-33.

–. 1996. Tradition et modernité au Québec: D'un quiproquo à l'autre. In *Les Frontières de l'identité: Modernité et postmodernité au Québec,* ed. Michaël Elbaz, Andrée Fortin, and Guy Laforest, 65-81. Quebec City: Presses de l'Université Laval.

–. 1999. "L'école au Québec: un système qui parasite des institutions." In *Main basse sur l'éducation,* ed. Gilles Gagné, 7-54. Montreal: Éditions Nota bene.

Garapon, Antoine, and Denis Salas. 1995. Pour une nouvelle intelligence de la peine. *Esprit,* October, 145-61.

–. 1996. *La République pénalisée.* Paris: Hachette.

Garnot, Benoît. 1991. *Société, cultures et genres de vie dans la France moderne, XVIe-XVIIIe siècle.* Paris: Hachette.

Gauvard, Claude. 1991. *De grace especial. Crime, État et société en France à la fin du Moyen Âge.* Paris: Publications de la Sorbonne.

Gauvin, Yvon. 1953. Problème de réhabilitation sociale des malades mentaux. PhD diss., Université de Montréal.

Gentile, Patrizia, and Gary Kinsman. 2008. "Fiabilité," "Risque" et "Résistance": Surveillance au Canada des homosexuels durant la Guerre froide. *Bulletin d'histoire politique* 16 (3): 43-58.

Gigeroff, Alex K. 1968. *Sexual Deviations in the Criminal Law: Homosexual, Exhibitionistic, and Pedophilic Offences in Canada.* Toronto: University of Toronto Press.

Girard, René. 1977. *Violence and the Sacred.* Trans. Patrick Gregory. Baltimore, MD: Johns Hopkins University Press.

–. 1981. *Le Mouvement homosexuel en France, 1945-1980.* Paris: Syros.

–. 1986. *The Scapegoat.* Trans. Yvonne Freccero. Baltimore, MD: Johns Hopkins University Press.

Godard, Didier. 2001. *L'Autre Faust. L'homosexualité masculine pendant la Renaissance.* Béziers: H et O éditions.

Goodich, Michael. 1976a. Sodomy in Ecclesiastical Law and Theory. *Journal of Homosexuality* 1 (4): 427-34.

–. 1976b. Sodomy in Medieval Secular Law. *Journal of Homosexuality* 1 (3): 295-302.

Goreham, Richard A. 1984. Le droit à la vie privée des personnes homosexuelles. *Les Cahiers de droit* 25 (4): 843-72.

Goubert, Jean-Pierre. 1982. 1770-1830: La première croisade médicale. In *La Médicalisation de la société française, 1770-1830,* ed. Jean-Pierre Goubert, 3-16. Waterloo, ON: Historical Reflections Press.

Gowing, Laura. 2006. Lesbians and Their Like in Early Modern Europe, 1500-1800. In *Gay Life and Culture: A World History,* ed. Robert Aldrich, 125-43. London: Thames and Hudson.

Greco, Christopher. 2009. Constructing "Reality": The Portrayal of Internet Child Luring by Toronto-based Newspapers (1998-2008). MA thesis, University of Ottawa.

Gross, Martine, Stéphane Guillemarre, Lilian Mathieu, and Caroline Mécary. 2005. *Homosexualité, mariage et filiation. Pour en finir avec les discriminations.* Paris: Syllepse.

Guillaume, Pierre. 1990. *Médecins, Église et foi depuis deux siècles.* Paris: Aubier.

–. 1996. *Le Rôle social du médecin depuis deux siècles (1800-1945)*. Paris: Association pour l'étude de l'histoire de la sécurité sociale.

Guillebaud, Jean-Claude. 1999. *The Tyranny of Pleasure*. Trans. Keith Torjoc. New York: Algora.

Guyot, M. (Joseph Nicolas). 1785. *Répertoire universel et raisonné de jurisprudence civile, criminelle, canonique et bénéficiale*. Vol. 16. Paris: Visse Libraire.

Hahn, Pierre. 1979. *Nos ancêtres les pervers*. Paris: Olivier Orban.

Halperin, David M. 1990. *One Hundred Years of Homosexuality: And Other Essays on Greek Love*. New York: Routledge.

Hamelin, Jean, and Nicole Gagnon. 1984. *Histoire du catholicisme québécois. Le XXe siècle*. Vol. 1, *1898-1940*. Montreal: Boréal.

Hekma, Gerk. 1994. L'histoire des homosexualités en France: Perspectives. In *Sodomites, invertis, homosexuels: Perspectives historiques*, ed. Rommel Mendés-Leite, 181-88. Lille: Cahiers Gai Kitsch Camp, no. 7.

Henderson, Jeffrey. 1991. *The Maculate Muse: Obscene Language in Attic Comedy*. New York and Oxford: Oxford University Press.

Herbrand, Cathy. 2008. Les normes familiales à l'épreuve du droit et des pratiques: Analyse de la parenté sociale et de la pluriparentalité homosexuelles. PhD diss., Université Libre de Bruxelles.

Hergemöller, Bernd-Ulrich. 2006. The Middle Ages. In *Gay Life and Culture: A World History*, ed. Robert Aldrich, 57-79. New York: Universe.

Hernandez, Ludovico. 1920. *Les Procès de sodomie aux XVIe, XVIIe et XVIIIe siècles*. Paris: Bibliothèque des curieux.

Higgins, Ross. 1998. Identités construites, communautés essentielles. De la libération gaie à la théorie "queer." In *Les Limites de l'identité sexuelle*, ed. Diane Lamoureux, 109-33. Montreal: Éditions du Remue-ménage.

–. 1999. *De la clandestinité à l'affirmation. Pour une histoire de la communauté gaie montréalaise*. Montreal: Comeau et Nadeau.

Higgins, Ross, and Line Chamberland. 1992. Mixed Messages: Gays and Lesbians in Montreal Yellow Papers in the 1950s. In *The Challenge of Modernity: A Reader on Post-Confederation Canada*, ed. I. McKay, 422-31. Toronto: McGraw-Hill Ryerson.

Hirschfeld, Magnus. 1936. *Sexual Anomalies and Perversions*. London: F. Aldor.

Hocquenghem, Guy. 1993. *Homosexual Desire*. Durham, NC, and London: Duke University Press.

Hupperts, Charles. 2006. Homosexuality in Greece and Rome. In *Gay Life and Culture: A World History*, ed. Robert Aldrich, 29-56. New York: Universe.

Hurteau, Pierre. 1991. Homosexualité, religion et droit au Québec. Une approche historique. PhD diss., Concordia University.

–. 1993. L'homosexualité masculine et les discours sur le sexe en contexte montréalais de la fin du XIXe siècle à la Révolution tranquille. *Histoire sociale* 26 (51): 41-66.

Jablonski, Olivier. 2001. The Birth of a French Homosexual Press in the 1950s. *Journal of Homosexuality* 41 (3-4): 233-48.

Jarrell, Richard A. 1987. L'ultramontanisme et la science au Canada français. In *Sciences et médecine au Québec, perspectives sociohistoriques*, ed. Marcel Fournier, Yves Gingras, and Othmar Keel, 41-68. Quebec City: Institut québécois de recherche sur la culture.

Jenkins, Philip. 1998. *Moral Panic*. New Haven, CT: Yale University Press.

Jugements et délibérations du Conseil souverain de la Nouvelle-France (1663-1716). 1885-1891. 4 vols. Quebec City: Imprimerie A. Côté.

Kinsey, Alfred C., Wardell B. Pomeroy, and Clyde E. Martin. 1948. *Sexual Behaviour in the Human Male*. Philadelphia and London: W.B. Saunders.

Kinsman, Gary. 1996. *The Regulation of Desire: Homo and Hetero Sexualities*. 2nd ed., rev. Montreal: Black Rose Books.

–. 2000. Constructing Gay Men and Lesbians as National Security Risks, 1950-70. In *Whose National Security? Canadian State Surveillance and the Creation of Enemies*, ed. Gary Kinsman, Dieter K. Buse, and Mercedes Steedman, 143-53. Toronto: Between the Lines.

Koertge, Noretta, ed. 1981. *Nature and Causes of Homosexuality*. Special issue, *Journal of Homosexuality* 6 (4). Binghamton, NY: Haworth Press.

Labrèche, Diane. 1977. Vers une stérilisation complète de la règle d'or. *Criminal Reports (C.R.N.S.)* 36: 368-78.

Labrèche, Louise. 1999. Résumé des différentes législations québécoises concernant les conjoints de même sexe. *Assurances* 67 (3): 507-9.

Lachance, André. 1978. *La justice criminelle du roi au Canada au XVIIIe siècle*. Quebec City: Presses de l'Université Laval.

–. 1984. *Crimes et criminels en Nouvelle-France*. Montreal: Boréal.

–. 1985. Le contrôle social dans la société canadienne du Régime français au XVIIIe siècle. *Criminologie* 28 (1): 7-18.

Lagrange, Hugues. 1995. *La Civilité à l'épreuve. Crime et sentiment d'insécurité*. Paris: Presses Universitaires de France.

Lance, Daniel. 2000. *Au-delà du désir, littératures, sexualités et éthique*. Paris: L'Harmattan.

Lanez, Émilie. 1998. Pacs: Polémique autour d'un mariage du troisième type. *Le Point* 1359 (3 October): 103-6.

Laqueur, Thomas. 1990. *Making Sex: Body and Gender from the Greeks to Freud*. Cambridge, MA: Harvard University Press.

L'Archevêque, Alexandre, Danielle Julien, and Bill Ryan. 2009. Contextes d'accès à la parentalité et intégration des identités homosexuelle et paternelle chez les pères gais. In *Diversité sexuelle et constructions de genre*, ed. Line Chamberland, Blye W. Frank, and Janice Ristock, 155-88. Quebec City: Presses de l'Université du Québec.

Lasch, Christopher. 1979. *The Culture of Narcissism*. New York: Warner Books.

Lascoumes, Pierre. 1998. L'homosexualité entre crime à la loi naturelle et expression de la liberté. La dépénalisation de l'attentat à la pudeur sur le mineur de 15 ans par une personne de même sexe. In *Homosexualité et droit. De la tolérance sociale à la reconnaissance juridique,* ed. Daniel Borrillo, 109-21. Paris: Presses Universitaires de France.

Le Goff, Jacques. 1991. Le refus du plaisir. In *Amours et sexualité en Occident,* ed. Georges Duby et al., 177-90. Paris: Seuil.

—. 1998. Le refus du plaisir. *Les Collections de l'histoire* 5: 36-41.

Lemieux, Lucien. 1989. *Histoire du catholicisme québécois. Les XVIIIe et XIXe siècles.* Vol. 1, *Les années difficiles*. Montreal: Boréal.

Lemieux, Raymond, and Jean-Paul Montminy. 2000. *Le Catholicisme québécois.* Quebec City: Les Éditions de l'IQRC.

Léonard, Jacques. 1992. *Médecins, malades et société dans la France du XIXe siècle.* Paris: Sciences en situation.

Leroy-Forgeot, Flora. 1997. *Histoire juridique de l'homosexualité en Europe*. Paris: Presses Universitaires de France.

Letellier, Louis. 1993. Homosexualité et droit: La quête de l'égalité. *Le Médecin du Québec* 28 (9): 105-15.

Lever, Maurice. 1985. *Les Bûchers de Sodome*. Paris: Fayard.

Linteau, Paul-André, René Durocher, Jean-Claude Robert, and François Ricard. 1991. *Quebec since 1930*. Trans. Robert Chodos and Ellen Garmaise. Toronto: James Lorimer.

Luhmann, Niklas. 1989. Le droit comme système social. *Droit et société* 11-12: 53-67.

Martel, Frédéric. 1999. *The Pink and the Black: Homosexuals in France since 1968.* Trans. Jane Marie Todd. Stanford, CA: Stanford University Press.

—. 2000. *Le Rose et le noir. Les homosexuels en France depuis 1968*. Paris: Seuil.

Mead, George H. 1918. The Psychology of Punitive Justice. *American Journal of Sociology* 23: 577-602.

Mécary, Caroline. 2000. *Droit et homosexualité*. Paris: Dalloz.

Mécary, Caroline, and Flora Leroy-Forgeot. 2001. *Le Pacs*. Paris: Presses Universitaires de France.

Merrick, Jeffrey. 2001. "Brutal Passion" and "Depraved Taste": The Case of Jacques-François Pascal. *Journal of Homosexuality* 41 (3-4): 85-103.

Merrick, Jeffrey, and Bryant T. Ragan Jr., eds. 2001. *Homosexuality in Early Modern France*. New York and Oxford: Oxford University Press.

Meyer, Catherine-Anne. 1998. L'homosexualité dans la jurisprudence de la Cour et de la Commission européenne des droits de l'homme. In *Homosexualité et droit. De la tolérance sociale à la reconnaissance juridique,* ed. Daniel Borrillo, 153-79. Paris: Presses Universitaires de France.

Migneault, Benoît. 2001. L'amour qui n'ose dire son nom dans les périodiques québécois des XIXe et XXe siècles. *À rayons ouverts* 55: 4-5.

Morris, Polly. 1989. Sodomy and Male Honor: The Case of Somerset, 1740-1850. In *The Pursuit of Sodomy: Male Homosexuality in Renaissance and Enlightenment Europe,* ed. Kent Gerard and Gert Hekma, 383-406. New York and London: Harrington Park Press.

Mosse, George L. 1988. Homosexualité et fascisme français. *Sociétés* 17: 14-16.

–. 1997. *L'Image de l'homme. L'invention de la virilité moderne.* Paris: Abbeville.

Moutouh, Hugues. 1999. L'esprit d'une loi: Controverses sur le Pacte civil de solidarité en France. *Les Temps modernes* 603: 189-213.

Muchembled, Robert. 1994. *Magie et sorcellerie en Europe: Du Moyen Âge à nos jours.* Paris: Colin.

Muyart de Vouglans, P.F. 1757. *Les institutes au droit criminel.* Paris.

–. 1780. *Les loix criminelles de France dans leur ordre naturel.* Paris: Merigot.

Noël, Roger. 1998. Libération homosexuelle ou révolution socialiste? L'expérience du GHAP. In *Sortir de l'ombre. Histoires des communautés lesbienne et gaie de Montréal,* ed. Irène Demczuk et Frank W. Remiggi, 187-206. Montreal: VLB éditeur.

Nye, Robert A. 1989. Sex Difference and Male Homosexuality in French Medical Discourse, 1830-1930. *Bulletin d'histoire médicale* 63: 32-51.

Parker, Graham E. 1964-65. Corporal Punishment in Canada. *Criminal Law Quarterly* 7: 193-211.

Pastoureau, Michel. 1999. Une justice exemplaire: Les procès faits aux animaux. In *Les Rites de la justice. Gestes et rituels judiciaires au Moyen Âge occidental,* ed. Claude Gauvard and Robert Jacob, 173-200. Paris: Léopard d'Or.

Peniston, William A. 2001. Pederasts, Prostitutes, and Pickpockets in Paris of the 1870s. *Journal of Homosexuality* 41 (3-4): 169-87.

–. 2004. *Pederasts and Others: Urban Culture and Sexual Identity in Nineteenth-Century Paris.* New York: Harrington Park Press.

Perreault, Isabelle. 2009. Sciences médicales, sciences sociales: La psychiatrie au Québec entre 1920 et 1950. Analyse des causes et diagnostics d'internement à Saint-Jean-de-Dieu dans une perspective de genre. PhD diss., University of Ottawa.

Pierrat, Emmanuel. 1996. *Le Sexe et la loi.* Paris: Arléa.

Pires, Alvaro P. 1998. La formation de la rationalité pénale moderne au XVIIIe siècle. In *Histoire des savoirs sur le crime et la peine,* ed. Christian Debuyst, Françoise Digneffe, and Alvaro P. Pires, 1-220. Montreal/Ottawa/Brussels: Presses de l'Université de Montréal/Presses de l'Université d'Ottawa/De Boeck University.

Pisier, Evelyne. 2000. Sexes et sexualités: Bonnes et mauvaises différences. *Les Temps modernes* 609: 156-75.

Plato. 2001. *The Banquet.* Trans. Percy Bysshe Shelley. Withefish: Kessinger Publishing.

Poirier, Guy. 1996. *L'Homosexualité dans l'imaginaire de la Renaissance.* Paris: Honoré Champion.

Poursin, Jean-Marie. 1992. La recherche démographique française: Le tournant. *Esprit*, January, 5-29.

Procopius. 1961. *Procopius of Caesarea: The Secret History*. Trans. Richard Atwater. 1927. Reprint, Ann Arbor: University of Michigan Press.

Puff, Helmut. 2006. Early Modern Europe, 1400-1700. In *Gay Life and Culture: A World History*, ed. Robert Aldrich, 79-102. New York: Universe.

Quignard, Pascal. 1994. *Le Sexe et l'effroi*. Paris: Gallimard.

Quirion, Bastien. 2006. Traiter les délinquants ou contrôler les conduites: Le dispositif thérapeutique à l'ère de la nouvelle pénologie. *Criminologie* 39 (2): 137-64.

Remiggi, Frank W. 1998. Le Village gai de Montréal: Entre le ghetto et l'espace identitaire. In *Sortir de l'ombre. Histoires des communautés lesbienne et gaie de Montréal*, ed. Irène Demczuk and Frank W. Remiggi, 267-89. Montreal: VLB éditeur.

Revenin, Régis. 2005. *Homosexualité et prostitution masculines à Paris, 1870-1918*. Paris: L'Harmattan.

Rey, Michel. 1982. Police et sodomie au XVIIIe siècle: du péché au désordre. *Revue d'histoire moderne et contemporaine* 29: 113-24.

–. 1987. Parisian Homosexuals Create a Lifestyle, 1700-1750. In *'Tis Nature's Fault: Unauthorized Sexuality during the Enlightenment*, ed. Robert Purks Maccubbin, 179-90. Cambridge, UK: Cambridge University Press.

–. 1989. Police and Sodomy in Eighteenth-Century Paris: From Sin to Disorder. In *The Pursuit of Sodomy: Male Homosexuality in Renaissance and Enlightenment Europe*, ed. Kent Gerard and Gert Hekma, 129-46. New York and London: Harrington Park Press.

–. 1991. Naissance d'une minorité. In *Amour et sexualité en Occident*, ed. Georges Duby, 309-16. Paris: Seuil.

Richard, Louis, and Marie-Thérèse Seguin, eds. 1988. *Homosexualités et tolérance sociale*. Moncton: Éditions d'Acadie.

Robb, Graham. 2004. *Strangers: Homosexual Love in the Nineteenth Century*. New York and London: W.W. Norton.

Robert, Philippe, and Claude Faugeron. 1980. *Les Forces cachées de la justice. La crise de la justice pénale*. Paris: Le Centurion.

Rocher, Guy. 1992. *Introduction à la sociologie générale*. Montreal: Hurtubise HMH.

Romi, Raphaël. 1988. Droit et homosexualité. *Actes* 64: 29-34.

Rose, Hilary A. 2009. A Contextual Model of Victimization of Sexual Minority Youth. In *Diversité sexuelle et constructions de genre*, ed. Line Chamberland, Blye W. Frank, and Janice Ristock, 75-102. Quebec City: Presses de l'Université du Québec.

Rouillard, Jacques, and Henri Goulet. 1999. *Solidarité et détermination. Histoire de la Fraternité ùdes policiers et policières de la Communauté urbaine de Montréal*. Montreal: Boréal.

Russell, Stuart J. 1982. The Offence of Keeping a Common Bawdy House in Canadian Criminal Law. *Ottawa Law Review* 14 (2): 270-313.

Ryan, Bill. 1999. S'accepter comme gai ou lesbienne: Pour en finir avec la honte. In Gouvernement du Québec, *Adapter nos interventions aux réalités homosexuelles*, vol. 1, *Les jeunes, leurs familles et leurs milieux de vie*, 41-52. Programme de formation, Ministère de la Santé et des Services sociaux.

–. 2003. *A New Look at Homophobia and Heterosexism in Canada.* Canadian AIDS Society.

Sartre, Maurice. 1991. L'homosexualité dans la Grèce antique. In *Amour et sexualité en Occident*, ed. Georges Duby, 53-68. Paris: Seuil.

–. 1998. Les amours grecques: Le rite et le plaisir. *Les Collections de l'histoire* 5: 14-19.

Saunders, D.E. 1967-68. Sentencing of Homosexual Offenders. *Criminal Law Quarterly* 10: 25-29.

Sawatsky, John. 1980. *Men in the Shadows.* Toronto: Doubleday Canada.

Schabas, William A. 1995. *Les Infractions d'ordre sexuel.* Montreal: Les éditions Yvon Blais.

Schmitt, Éric-Emmanuel. 1993. *Le Visiteur.* Paris: Magnard.

Schwartzwald, Robert. 1997. La fédérastophobie, ou Les lectures agitées d'une révolution tranquille. *Sociologie et sociétés* 29 (1): 129-43.

Séguin, Robert-Lionel. 1972. *La Vie libertine en Nouvelle-France au dix-septième siècle.* Montreal: Leméac.

Seifert, Lewis C. 2001. Masculinity and Satires of "Sodomites" in France, 1660-1715. *Journal of Homosexuality* 41 (3-4): 37-52.

Sergent, Bernard. 1986. *L'homosexualité initiatique dans l'Europe ancienne.* Paris: Payot.

Sibalis, Michael D. 1996. The Regulation of Male Homosexuality in Revolutionary and Napoleonic France, 1789-1815. In *Homosexuality in Modern France*, ed. Jeffrey Merrick and Bryant T. Ragan, 80-101. New York: Oxford University Press.

–. 1999. Paris. In *Queer Sites: Gay Urban Histories since 1600*, ed. David Higgs, 10-37. London and New York: Routledge.

–. 2001. The Palais-Royal and the Homosexual Subculture of Nineteenth-Century Paris. *Journal of Homosexuality* 41 (3-4): 117-29.

–. 2002. Homophobia, Vichy France, and the "Crime of Homosexuality": The Origins of the Ordinance of 6 August 1942. *GLQ Forum* 8 (3): 301-18.

–. 2006a. Homosexuality in Early Modern France. In *Queer Masculinities, 1550-1800: Siting Same-Sex Desire in the Early Modern World*, ed. Katherine O'Donnell and Michael O'Rourke, 211-31. Houndmills, UK: Palgrave Macmillan.

–. 2006b. Male Homosexuality in the Age of Enlightenment and Revolution, 1680-1850. In *Gay Life and Culture: A World History*, ed. Robert Aldrich, 103-24. New York: Universe.

Sivry, Jean-Michel. 1998. Traces militantes éphémères: L'ADGQ et Le Berdache. In *Sortir de l'ombre. Histoires des communautés lesbienne et gaie de Montréal*, ed. Irène Demczuk and Frank W. Remiggi, 235-66. Montreal: VLB éditeur.

Smith, Miriam. 1999. *Lesbian and Gay Rights in Canada: Social Movements and Equality-Seeking, 1971-1995.* Toronto: University of Toronto Press.

—. 2008. *Political Institutions and Lesbian and Gay Rights in the United States and Canada.* New York: Routledge.

Soman, Alfred. 1984. Pathologie historique: Le témoignage des procès de bestialité aux XVIe-XVIIe siècles. In *La Faute, la répréssion et le pardon: Actes du 107e congrès national des sociétés savantes,* Brest, 1982, 149-61. Paris: Comité des travaux historiques et scientifiques.

Sot, Michel. 1991. La genèse du mariage chrétien. In *Amour et sexualité en Occident,* ed. Georges Duby, 193-206. Paris: Seuil.

Spencer, Colin. 1995. *Homosexuality in History.* New York: Harcourt Brace.

Statistical Year Book of Canada. 1901. Ottawa: Government Printing.

Suyeux, Jean. 1983. Homosexualité, la fin d'une longue répression. *Psychologies* 2: 31-33, 64.

Sylvestre, Paul-François. 1979. *Les homosexuels s'organisent.* Ottawa: Homeureux.

—. 1983. *Bougrerie en Nouvelle-France.* Hull: Éditions Asticou.

Symonds, John A. 1983. *Male Love: A Problem in Greek Ethics and Other Writings.* New York: Pagan Press.

Szabo, Denis. 1960. *Crimes et villes.* Paris: Éditions Cujas and Bibliothèque de sociologie criminelle.

Tamagne, Florence. 2000. La répression de l'homosexualité dans les années 1920 et 1930: Étude comparative. In *Homosexualités. Expression/répression,* ed. Louis-Georges Tin and Geneviève Pastre, 82-90. Paris: Stock.

—. 2001. *Mauvais genre? Une histoire des représentations de l'homosexualité.* Paris: Éditions de La Martinière and Les Reflets du savoir.

—. 2004. *A History of Homosexuality in Europe: Berlin, London, Paris, 1919-1939.* 2 vols. New York: Algora.

Tardieu, Ambroise. 1995. *Enquête médico-légale des attentats aux mœurs.* Intro. Georges Vigarello. 1857. Reprint, Paris: Éditions Jérôme Millon.

Teasley, David. 1987. The Charge of Sodomy as a Political Weapon in Early Modern France: The Case of Henry III in Catholic League Polemic, 1585-1589. *Maryland Historian* 18: 17-30.

Théry, Irène. 1993. *Le Démariage, justice et vie privée.* Paris: Odile Jacob.

Thuiller, Pierre. 1989. L'homosexualité devant la psychiatrie. *La Recherche* 213: 1128-40.

Tin, Louis-Georges, and Geneviève Pastre, eds. 2000. *Homosexualités. Expression/ répression.* Paris: Stock.

Trumbach, Randolph. 1989. Sodomitical Assaults, Gender Role, and Sexual Development in Eighteenth-Century London. In *The Pursuit of Sodomy: Male Homosexuality in Renaissance and Enlightenment Europe,* ed. Kent Gerard and Gert Hekma, 407-29. New York and London: Harrington Park Press.

Tulkens, Françoise, and Michel van de Kerchove. 1993. *Introduction au droit pénal. Aspects juridiques et criminologiques*. Brussels: Kluwer Éditions Juridiques.

Veyne, Paul. 1978. La famille et l'amour sous le Haut-Empire romain. *Annales* 1: 35-63.

–. 1981. L'homosexualité à Rome. In *Amour et sexualité en Occident*, ed. Georges Duby, 69-78. Paris: Seuil.

–. 1998. Éloge de la virilité. *Les Collections de l'histoire* 5: 17.

Vigarello, Georges. 2001. *A History of Rape: Sexual Violence in France from the 16th to the 20th Century*. Trans. Jean Birrell. Malden, MA: Polity Press.

Vivier, Jean-Loup. 2001. *Le pacte civil de solidarité. Un nouveau contrat*. Paris: L'Harmattan.

Wachter, Robert M. 1991. *The Fragile Coaliton: Scientists, Activists and AIDS*. New York: St. Martin's Press.

Walsh, Anthony. 1994. Homosexual and Heterosexual Child Molestation: Case Characteristics and Sentencing Differentials. *International Journal of Offender Therapy and Comparative Criminology* 38 (4): 339-53.

Weeks, Jeffrey. 1980. Inverts, Perverts, and Mary-Annes: Male Prostitution and the Regulation of Homosexuality in England in the Nineteenth Century and Early Twentieth Century. *Journal of Homosexuality* 6 (1-2): 113-34.

Weill, Claude, Robert Marmoz, Isabelle Monnin, and Guillaume Malaurie. 1998. PaCS: Les nouveaux couples font la loi. *Le Nouvel Observateur* 1767 (17 September): 4-13.

Welzer-Lang, Daniel, Pierre Dutey, and Michel Dorais, eds. 1994. *La Peur de l'autre en soi. Du sexisme à l'homophobie*. Montreal: Éditions VLB.

Zeikowitz, Richard E. 2003. *Homoeroticism and Chivalry: Discourses of Male Same-Sex Desire in the Fourteenth Century*. New York: Palgrave Macmillan.

Index

Note: "(f)" after a page number indicates a figure; "(t)" after a page number indicates a table

Aboriginals, 176*n*23
abortion, 15, 144, 173*n*8
Act 4-5 Victoria c. 27 (1841 England), 66
Act 60-773 (social scourges) (France),
    110. *See also* Penal Code (France)
Act 85-772 (anti-discrimination)
    (France), 147-48, 160(f). *See also*
    Penal Code (France)
Act 99-944 (Pacs) (France), 150. *See
    also* Pacte civil de solidarité (Pacs)
    (France)
Act Instituting Civil Unions and
    Establishing New Rules of Filiation
    (2002 Quebec), 131
ACT UP (France), 158, 186*n*44
Administrative Court of Paris, 149
adoption and parenting: European
    Parliament, 120; France, 149-50, 151-
    52, 159, 187*n*4; France and Quebec
    compared, 161-62; opinion poll on
    (Quebec), 142; Quebec, 130-31, 136
adultery: Antonine law, 15; in Middle
    Ages, 20-21, 173*n*9; in New France, 40
age in regulation of pederasty, 10-11

age of consent/majority: in chronology
    (France), 160(f); European Parlia-
    ment, 120; France, 50, 54-55, 106, 109,
    144, 147, 182*nn*26-27; for Pacs, 151;
    Quebec, 81, 126. *See also* consensual
    and consent (in law)
AIDS: activism (France), 158, 186*n*44;
    as basis for repression, 111; in denial,
    157; France and Quebec compared,
    161; in Pacs debate, 153; Quebec and
    US compared, 141; revival of stereo-
    types and, 119; step backward
    (France), 156-58
Air France, 148, 153, 160(f)
Alberta, 132, 143, 184*n*11
Alexandrian rule, 19
Allen, Luther A., 98
American Psychiatric Association, 94,
    118
Les Amitiés particulières (Peyrefitte), 155
anal penetration/sexual relations: act
    not the focus, 78; under Criminal
    Code (Canada), 126-28; in definition
    of homosexual, 173*n*8; no gender

distinction, 20; proof as incrimination, 70; proof needed, 67; proof not needed, 71; regulated by courts, 125; use of term, 84, 125

Ancien Régime: break with (1791), 54, 60-61, 165; compared to Britain, 64; compared to Vichy regime, 106; discrepancy between doctrine and practice, 32, 35; historic record, 174*n*1; violence part of life, 36, 164

Anders, Rob, 135-36

Andros, 144

Angers Court of Appeal, 56

Annuaire du Québec (1930-39), 87

Antenne 2, 155

anthropology, 150

Antiquity and regulation of homo-eroticism, 8-14

Antonine law (96-192 CE), 15

Aoun, Alia, 150-51

Aquinas, Thomas, 67

Arabs, 25

Arcadie, 110

Arcadie group, 155

Arcand, Bernard, 143

Ariès, Philippe, 20

Aristotle, 22

Asian heretics, 24

Asians, 25

Aspects de la criminalité en France, 145-46, 185*n*30

assault with intent, 68, 71. *See also* crime and homoeroticism

Association pour les droits des gais du Québec (ADGQ), 140-41, 162

Athenagorus, 17

Athenian comedy, 12

Aurelius, Marcus, 15

Australia, 139

Automobile Insurance Act (Quebec), 130

Badinter, Elizabeth, 59

banishment, 33, 41, 44, 175*n*14, 176*n*24

Barbier, Edmond-Jean-François, 30-31, 35, 38, 44

Bastien, Pascal, 29, 30-31, 32, 33, 34

bawdy house charges (Montreal), 139-40, 185*n*26

beautiful vice, 51, 60, 103

Bégin, Paul, 131

Bègles, 161

Belfort Court, 149

Belgium, 137, 168

Benoit, Léon, 135

Bentham, Jeremy, 69

Bertrand, Marie-Andrée, 81, 124, 125

Besançon court's ruling, 159

bestiality: under British law, 66, 70; convictions of (1930-39 Quebec), 87; as indistinct from sodomy, 84, 85, 173*n*8; in Middle Ages, 20, 24, 173*n*8; in New France, 40, 41, 42, 43, 45; in Renaissance, 27

Bible and Scriptures: early influence of, 15-16; Genesis, 22; Leviticus, 7, 16; in Middle Ages, 18; Sodom and/or Gomorrah, 16, 36, 68, 173*n*10

Bicêtre Hospital, 30, 33, 35, 175*n*14, 176*n*17

Bieber, Irving, 92-93, 119

Big Brothers Association, 130

Bill 32 (Quebec), 130-32, 138-39(f)

Bill 88 (Quebec), 141

Bill C-38 (Canada), 134-37, 138-39(f), 161, 185*n*21

Bill C-150, 123. *See also* Omnibus Bill (1969)

Bill C-250 (Canada), 142

birth rate and demographics: associated with morality, 18, 103; dread of depopulation, 15, 57, 60, 108; mortality rates, 50; and repression of

homosexuality, 100, 111, 168; and
scapegoating, 88-89; statutes on anti-
birth propaganda (France), 107. *See
also* reproductive sexuality
bisexuality, 8, 26, 93
blackmail in 1700s France, 31
Blackstone, Sir William, 67-69
blight of homosexuality, 23, 60-61,
109-10. *See also* contagion
blood donation, 157
Boisclair, André, 143
Bonello, Christian, 53
Boninchi, Marc, 106, 107
Borrillo, Daniel, 69, 136, 150-53, 161,
163
Boswell, John, 11, 16, 18, 21, 173*nn*6-7
Bouchard, Serge, 143
bourgeoisie: destroyed in French
Canada, 77-78; fear of pederasty by,
53-54, 60-61; rise in France of, 4;
surveillance by, 49
Bowman, Karl M., 93
Boyer, Raymond, 42, 65
Britain: adversarial system, 64-65;
capital punishment, 64-65, 69-70,
165, 180*n*18; criminalization (1885
England), 73; Edward II, 25; entrap-
ment by police (1930s), 87; legalized
gay marriage, 168; media, 104;
national security and values, 107;
prosecutions and convictions (1945-
55), 107; sodomy in laws of, 66-69;
statistics on death penalty (1700-
1835), 70
British Columbia, 132, 133(t)
Brunette, Victor, 85
bubonic plague, 15
Bud's (Montreal), 141
buggery, 66, 84
Bulgarians, 24
Burchard, Bishop, 173*n*9

burning at the stake: carried out, 30,
33-34, 174*n*4, 176*n*17, 178*n*2; class and,
33; evidence as inaccurate, 26; by
Justinian, 15; not carried out, 30-32,
43-44; for violence or involving children, 52. *See also* capital punishment;
penalties for sodomy
Buxton, Sir Thomas Fowell, 64

Canada Pension Plan Act, 132
Canadian Charter of Rights and Freedoms, 127-28, 132, 184*n*17; Parliament
questions Court on same-sex marriage, 133-34; section 15(1), 128, 132-33
canon law, 17-19
capital punishment: between 1317
and 1789, 27, 174*n*15; abolished for
sodomy (England), 70; in British
law, 69-70, 165, 180*n*18; for buggery,
66; France 1600s, 33-34; French and
British system compared, 64-65; in
New France, 42; "no longer appropriate," 46; for passive homoerotic
behaviour (342 CE), 15; in Renaissance, 27. *See also* burning at the
stake; penalties for sodomy
capitalism, 89, 91-92
Carlier, François, 52-53
Caron, Jean, 89-90
Carpentier, Jean, 47
cases and trials
– CASES: *Air France* case, 148, 160(f);
*Association des gais du Québec c.
Commission des écoles catholiques
de Montréal*, 184*n*18; *Dudgeon* case
(EU), 119; *Egan and Nesbit* (Supreme
Court of Canada), 129; *Everett George
Klippert v. Her Majesty* (1967), 95,
123; *Fretté v. France*, 121; *Halpern et al.
v. Canada*, 138(f); *Halpern v. Canada*,
138(f); *Halpern v. Toronto (City)*,

132-33; *Hendricks v. Quebec,* 138(f);
Her Majesty v. Laprise, 73; *Ligue ca-
tholique pour les droits de l'Homme v.
Hendricks,* 138(f); *M. v. H.,* 138(f); *R.
c. Joseph Clément,* Sessions de la Paix,
Montréal, 181*n*9; *R. c. Victor Brunette,*
181*n*9; *R. c. Whissel,* 184*n*12; *R. v. Alfred
Métayer dit St-Onge,* 180*n*20; *R. v.
Belt,* 181*n*7; *R. v. Calixte Desjardins,*
180*n*20; *R. v. C.M.,* 127; *R. v. Hess,*
127; *R. v. Hunt,* 180*n*1, 184*n*12; *R. v.
Khadikian,* 128; *R. v. Lavallée,* 184*n*12;
R. v. M. (1992), 128; *R. v. M.* (1994),
184*n*13; *R. v. Nguyen,* 127; *R. v. P.,* 82;
R. v. Walsh, 140; *Roy c. La Reine,*
126, 127
– TRIALS: Besançon court's ruling,
159; Victor Brunette (1897 Montreal),
85; Jacques Chausson and Jacques
Paulmier, 46; Joseph Clément (1897
Montreal), 85; Court of King's Bench
(185-89), 65; Benjamin Deschauffours
(1700s), 35, 38, 46; Jean Diot and
Bruno Lenoir (France 1750), 30-31,
174*n*4, 176*n*17; Claude Fabre, 46;
René Huguet (Le Tambour), 41, 44;
Philippe Bouvet de La Contamine
(1677), 33, 46; Jean Baptiste Lebel,
46; Antoine Marouër, 46; Montreal
(1850-89), 73; Léonard Moreuil (1633),
33; Jean-François Paschal, 46, 52;
François Judicth dit Rencontre, 42,
44, 177*n*27; Nicolas Daucy dit Saint-
Michel, Jean Forgeron dit la Roze,
and Jean Filio dit Dubois, 41-42, 44,
177*n*25; Félix Simon (1650), 33, 46;
René du Tertre (1680), 34, 46;
Timarchus (364 BCE), 8-9; Isaac du
Tremble and Claude Fabre (1667),
34-35; Lambert Trippodière, 46;
Maurice Violain (1678), 33, 46. *See*

also crime and homoeroticism;
statistics
castration, 15, 93, 114, 115, 183*n*30
Cathars, 24
Catholic Civil Rights League, 132
Catholicism: canon law, 17-19; influence (Quebec), 121-22, 180*n*26;
influence in French Canada, 74-75,
76-79, 81, 82; influence in sentencing
(1600s), 35; in New France, 43; recognized in Union Act, 72; in same-sex
marriage debate, 137, 139. *See also*
Christianity; ecclesiastical and religious discourses; ecclesiastical power
Cellard, André, 39, 46, 54, 63, 75
censorship: church controlling information, 22; France post-1942, 102;
prosecution of homosexuality in
publications, 144; of public homosexual representations, 104, 110;
reaction to AIDS, 158; reversal of,
155. *See also* media
Centre for Research and Information
on Canada, 143
Champs-Élysées, 55
Chansonnier Maurepas, 177*n*31
Charcot, Jean-Martin, 113
Charter of Fundamental Rights (EU),
120-21
Chauncey, George, 86
Chausson, Jacques, and Jacques
Paulmier, 46
Chenot, Mr., 183*n*32
Chiffoleau, Jacques, 23, 24, 27
children and minors: in cases of,
177*n*33; charged in Paris (1850-70),
52-53; and church (post-Second
World War Quebec), 92; corruption
of, 83, 123; criminal relations with
(France), 146-47; early attitudes
toward, 49-50; fear of contagion

(1850-70), 53, 58; France and Quebec compared, 159, 161-62; gross indecency charges (1961 Toronto), 99; in history of repression of homosexuality, 169-70; indecent assaults with (France), 145-46; indecent unnatural acts (France), 144-45; in law on anal intercourse, 126-27; and media stereotypes, 96-97; mistreatment associated with homosexuality, 19, 28; Muslims seen as threat to, 23; and pathological homosexuality, 95; proportion of cases (1891-1907 Montreal), 86; proportion of cases (1937 Montreal), 92; protection of, 100-1, 107, 147; punishment for rape of, 38; rape of (1600s), 33-34; in redefining marriage (Canada), 134-36; in redefining marriage (France), 136; same- vs. opposite-sex acts, 56-57, 107-8, 109; sexual psychopath and, 86-87; silence of, 48; as society's cult object, 171; therapy for homoeroticism (1950s Montreal), 94; as victims in New France compared to France, 46-47; as victims in trials, 46-47
Children's Rights Committee (UN), 170
Chirac, Jacques, 149
Chisholm, John, 83
Christianity: and crimes against nature, 22-23; divided (Middle Ages), 21; early, 15-17; pre-Christian Rome, 13-14; Protestants and Catholics, 25. *See also* Catholicism; ecclesiastical and religious discourses
chronology of legal recognition of gays: in France, 160(f); in Quebec, 138-39(f)
citizenship, 8-9, 10, 151
Civil Code (France): Act 1382, 149; section 9, 149; section 81, 62; sections 6,

375, 900, 1133, 1172, and 1726 (good morals), 105. *See also* Penal Code (France)
Civil Code (Quebec): section 364 (marriage), 131
civil unions, 130-32, 132-37, 139; Bill C-38 (Canada), 134-37. *See also* marriage; Pacte civil de solidarité (Pacs) (France)
Clain, Olivier, 166
class and power: in analysis, 3; bourgeoisie vs. proletariat, 53-54; fear of homosexual epidemic, 103-4; in homoerotic lifestyles, 9-10; and legal penalties (Greece), 9, 14; in sodomy sentences (1600s), 32-33, 175nn12-13. *See also* hierarchy
classification of sexual practices: Blackstone's crimes against nature, 67-68; and crime classifications, 176n21; and documentation of, 61; in medicalization of homosexuality, 113-14; as mental illness, 147; and science, 58-60; US screening of, 90
Clément, Joseph, 85
clitoris as penis, 59
Club Bath Sauna (Montreal), 140
Code de la Sécurité sociale, 148-49
Code d'instruction criminelle: section 44, 62
Coke, Sir Edward, 66-67
Colas, Dominique, 69
Cold War years, 95
Comartin, Joe, 137
Commentaries on the Laws of England (Blackstone), 67
Commission des droits de la personne du Québec (1994), 142
Committee on Sexual Offences against Children and Youth, 125
common law, 130-32. *See also* marriage

communism, 90, 102

communitarianism, 153, 158

comparative sociology, 5-6

Comuzzi, Joe, 137

concupiscence. *See* desire and pleasure

consensual and consent (in law): 1791 France, 54; 1800s French Canada, 73; anal intercourse and, 126; in Bill C-150, 123-24; in cases of sodomy (1930-39 Quebec), 88; post-1942 France, 106; repression of, 56 (*see also* repression of homoerotic life-styles); in sentencing (1891-1907 Montreal), 87. *See also* age of consent/majority

contagion: blight of homosexuality, 23, 60-61, 109-10; child-focused society and, 169-70; of homosexuality (1960s France), 109-10; of homosexuality and venereal disease, 111; of inversion, 60-63; in medical discourses on homosexuality, 93; of pederasty (1850-70), 53-54; rise in fear of, 165; of sodomy, 38, 44, 47. *See also* teaching and promotion of homosexuality

contraception, 104, 108, 112

Contrat d'union sociale. *See* Pacte civil de solidarité (Pacs) (France)

conviction rates: compared among crimes (1930-32 Quebec), 88; compared Toronto and Quebec, 99-100; France (1968), 110; for homosexual vs. heterosexual assaults, 125-26; and socio-political changes, 89-90; for sodomy (1959-66 Quebec), 98-99; of sodomy cases (1946-59 Quebec), 97(t). *See also* statistics

Corbett, Judge, 127

Council of Trent (1546), 16

Cour de cassation, 57, 148, 149, 151, 160(f). *See also* Penal Code (France)

Court of the Sessions of the Peace (Montreal), 85

Crémazie, Jacques, 65

crime and homoeroticism: absent from English common law, 81; for the Ancients, 14; application of law not matching language, 75, 79; arrests in Paris 1700s, 32, 44, 45; assault with intent, 68, 71; and church divisions (Middle Ages), 21; of divine lèse-majesté, 23, 36-38, 40, 164, 176*n*21; early commentators of English statutes, 66-72; under European Parliament, 120-21; France (1972-82), 145; France removes from Criminal Code, 52-53, 54-55; judged as irrespon-sible, 114-15; medicine and, 112-13; in New France, 40-44; offence of at-tempting to commit sodomy, 72, 78; punish all sexual acts between men (1885), 71; in Quebec post–Second World War, 92; recriminalization (France), 83, 105-11; in Renaissance, 27-28; and repression, 79; Roman imperial law, 13; and science of sexu-ality (Middle Ages), 21-22; settled out of court (1600s), 32-33; unnameable crime, 24, 30-32, 36-38, 43, 44-46, 164. *See also* cases and trials; decriminal-ization; indecent assault; legal traditions; penalties for sodomy; police and policing

crime as created by the law, 6

Criminal Code (Canada): adoption of 1892, 77; bawdy houses, 139-40; creation of first, 70-71; definition of sexual psychopath (1961), 95; effect of revision (1890), 85-86; exceptions regime, 124, 184*n*18; French and English versions compared, 84; punish all sexual acts between men

(1885), 71; revised in 1954, 84, 98; sodomy replaced by sexual relations, 125; statute on sodomy (1841), 72; section 147 (sodomy), 83, 84, 181n8, 183n3; section 149 (gross indecency), 82, 83, 181n3; section 155 (sodomy), 123, 183n3; section 157 (gross indecency), 123; section 158a (indecent action), 98; section 159 (anal intercourse), 126-28; section 163.1 (pornography), 170; section 172 (Internet), 170; section 173, 126; section 174 (sodomy), 84; section 178 (gross indecency), 82; section 202, 181n8; section 206 (gross indecency), 181n3; section 260 (indecent assault), 83, 181n4; section 293, 148, and 156 (indecent assault), 83, 181n4; sections 318, 319, and 718.2 (on hate), 138(f), 142; section 359 (indecent assault), 83; section 661 (sexual psychopaths), 83, 95. *See also* Omnibus Bill (1969)
Criminal Code (France). *See* Penal Code (France)
Crusades, 21, 23

Dagenais, Daniel, 50, 76, 169
dancing, 108, 160(f)
Danet, Jean, 55-56, 79, 110, 145
d'Angerville, Mouffle, 51, 60, 178n4
data sources as scarce, 7-8
Davis, Lydia, 59
Day, Stockwell, 135
de Gaulle, Charles, 107, 108, 167
de Prüm, Reginon, 20
de Rosset, François, 38
de Schutter, Olivier, 121
de Vouglans, Muyart, 38
Deacon, Edward E., 71
death penalty. *See* capital punishment

Declaration of the Rights of Man and the Citizen, 52
decriminalization: Canada, 122-26; chronology of legal recognition of gays in France, 160(f); chronology of legal recognition of gays in Quebec, 138-39(f); of consensual sex (Canada), 99, 101; Europe (1100s), 21; European Parliament, 121; France (1980s), 146-47, 184n16; France and Quebec compared, 111, 159, 161-62; French 1791 Penal Code, 54-55; overview of (France and Quebec), 167; role of medical discourse in, 112-13, 123, 125, 127. *See also* crime and homoeroticism
Defferre, Gaston, 147
Delon, Michel, 32-33
Delumeau, Jean, 45
Demers, Robert, 70, 85-86, 88
demonstrations and protests: France, 143, 155; France and Quebec compared, 161-62; Montreal (1976-77), 140-41, 162; New York (1969), 118; Paris (2005), 161
Denmark, 184n15
denunciations, 31. *See also* mouches (snitches)
Des Déserts, Sophie, 152
Deschauffours, Benjamin, 35, 38, 46, 174n1
desire and pleasure: in ancient Greece, 11-13, 14; categorization of, 59; Christian asceticism and, 22; condemned by early Christians, 19-20; in ecclesiastical discourse, 89; marketing of homosexual, 97; and procreation, 17; sodomy vs. virile love, 26
Diagnostic and Statistical Manual of Mental Diseases: (DSM-II), 94; (DSM-III), 118
Dialogues, 144

Diot, Jean, 30, 176n17

discrimination, protection from: chronology of legal recognition of gays in France, 160(f); chronology of legal recognition of gays in Quebec, 138-39(f); in Denmark, 184n15; in France, 147-50, 185n31; France and Quebec compared, 159, 161-62; Haute autorité de lutte contre les discriminations et pour l'égalité, 153-54; by Quebec Charter, 128, 141

divorce, 77, 104, 111

dominant discourses and method of analysis, 6

Les Dossiers de l'écran, 155

Drapeau, Jean, 98

Du Rousseau de la Combe, 36

du Tremble, Isaac, and Claude Fabre, 34-35

Dubois, Jean Filio dit, 41-42, 44, 177n25

Duclos, Denis, 115, 170

Duplé, Nicole, 129

Duplessis, Maurice, 89, 90-92

Durkheim, Émile, 6, 29, 36-37

Eagle, Bernice, 93

ecclesiastical and religious discourses: in British law, 68; Christian sect hate publication (France), 153; continued in French Canada, 4, 164-65; gap between practice and discourse, 176n16; post–Second World War, 90-91; sin and sinners, 4, 17, 92, 177n28; transition into medical, 51-52. *See also* Catholicism

ecclesiastical power: after Union Act, 72; in decline (1800s France), 165; in decline (1960s Quebec), 100; evident in conviction rates (Quebec), 88; in France (1850s), 179n14; in French

Canada (1800s), 63, 74-75, 76-79; and institution of marriage, 20; in Middle Ages, 18, 21-22; in New France, 43, 45-46; over laws (French Canada), 81; post–Second World War (Quebec), 91-92; in Quebec (1960s), 121-22; right to refuse same-sex marriages (Canada), 134; sodomy as crime against, 36-38; transferred to medical experts, 51-52, 60, 62-63, 179n10, 185n33; urban vs. rural, 76

Edward II of England, 25

effeminate behaviour: in classification of sexual psychopath, 90; condemned by early Christians, 20; fear of contagion of pederasty (1850-70), 53; fear of Paris 1800s, 57; in literature, 179n8; mollitia, 13; political repression of, 25; in Renaissance, 26; replaced by masculinization, 86. *See also* masculine sexuality

electroshock therapy, 93, 115

Ellis, Havelock, 113

employment rights, 150, 152, 153, 160(f), 184n17; unemployed and vagabonds (1720), 31-32; unemployment, 89

England. *See* Britain

entrapment, provocateurs, and snitches, 31, 87, 98, 110, 175n5, 175nn7-9

eraste (a lover), 10-11

Éribon, Didier, 8

eromenos (a beloved), 10-11

Essay on Paederasty (Bentham), 69

European Convention on the Rights of Man: sections 8-1, 14, and 15, 120-21, 149

European Court, 119

experts: in human sciences, 150; in legal-medical discourse, 166; in Pacs debates, 183n10; physicians as legal, 62, 113; used by church, 185n33. *See also* medical and psychiatric discourses

Fabre, Claude, 34-35, 46
Falconnet, Georges, 89
family units: changing view of, 187*n*45; church influence in French Canada, 76-77; in control of homosexuality, 169; gay rights and (Europe), 120-21; inverts as menace to, 60; offences against (1972-82 France), 145-46; post–Second World War (Quebec), 91-92; in redefining marriage, 134-35, 136; science discourse to defend heterosexual, 149-50; and self-regulation, 47-48; sexuality of adolescents in, 86; silence to protect, 102; society's focus transferred to children, 171; statutes on (1939 France), 107; structure of immigrants, 180*n*25. *See also* marriage; reproductive sexuality
Farge, Arlette, 36-37
fascism, 103
Fassin, Éric, 150
Fasti de Praenesti, 9
Fecteau, Jean-Marie, 65
fellatio, 22, 82, 87, 184*n*12
feminism, 118
feminization: fear of contagion of pederasty (1850-70), 53; fear of Paris 1800s, 57. *See also* effeminate behaviour
Féré, Charles, 57
Fernet, Mr., 108
Fillieule, Olivier, 157
First World War (Canada), 81, 84-87, 90, 103, 167
Florence (Italy), 27
foreigners, 24, 25, 28, 105
For-l'Évêque, 35
fornication: in Middle Ages, 20-21; in New France, 40

Fortin, Andrée, 122
Foucault, Michel: ancient Greek customs, 12-13; exposing sexuality, 61; on medicalization, 116; political operators, 25; power to punish, 38; practice of leniency, 32; prevention, 166; "psychiatric species," 114; roles of eraste and eromenos, 10-13; sodomite to homosexual, 59, 80; surveillance as repression, 55
Fournier, Jacques, 98
Fournier, Marcel, 78
France-Dimanche, 94
Freemasons, 24-25, 26
Freitag, Michel, 166
French as sodomites (1200s), 25
French Revolution, 52, 101, 105, 112
Front homosexuel d'action révolutionnaire (FHAR), 143, 144, 155
Front national, 119
Fruit Machine project, 95, 182*n*18
Futur, 110

Gagné, Gilles, 77-78
Gagnon, Nicole, 78
Gai pied, 158
Gaie Presse, 144
Garapon, Antoine, 116, 165, 170
Garnot, Benoît, 47
Gauvard, Claude, 23, 24, 26, 37, 50
Gauvin, Yvon, 94
gay, use of term, 118, 183*n*2
gay liberation movements: birth of, 118-19; brief history of French, 155-59; in France, 186*n*42; France and Quebec compared, 159, 161-62; reforms predating, 123
Gay Pride Week, 118, 161
Gay Village (Montreal), 141-42
Genet, Jean, 155
Germany, 104

Gerson, Jean, 20, 23

Gigeroff, Alex K., 66, 99

Girard, Jacques, 109, 110, 117, 144, 146, 155, 162

Girard, René, 171

Goodich, Michael, 20-21

government publications (Quebec), 141

Grand Prix national de littérature, 155

Greece (ancient): Antiquity, 8-14; codification of homoerotic sexuality, 9-13, 172*n*3; homoeroticism as normal, 2

gross indecency: in Bill C-150, 124; charges in Montreal (1953-54), 98; charges in Toronto (1961), 99; contact not essential, 180*n*1; convictions for sodomy (1930-39 Quebec), 87(f), 87-88; fellatio as, 184*n*12; heterosexual vs. homosexual, 124; as indistinct in law from sodomy, 85; origins of law, 81-82; prosecuted under "indecent act," 126; repression of homoerotic behaviours, 85-86. *See also* indecent assault; indecent exposure

Guillaume, Pierre, 62

Guillebaud, Jean-Claude, 27, 60, 146, 163, 170

guilt: in silence of victims, 48

Guyot, M., 27

gynaecea (young man), 10

Hahn, Pierre, 59

Hamel, Emmanuel, 153

Hamelin, Jean, 78

Hanger, Art, 135

Harper, Stephen, 135, 136, 137

hate propaganda and hate speech, 142, 145-46, 153-54, 170-71

Haute autorité de lutte contre les discriminations et pour l'égalité, 153-54

Hendricks, Michael, 132

Henry III of France, 25, 173*n*12

heretics and infidels, 24-25

Hergemöller, Bernd-Ulrich, 19

Hernandez, Ludovico, 27, 174*n*1

heterosexuals: conviction rates vs. homosexual assaults, 125-26; family units as, 149-50; and homosexual categories, 8; included in gross indecency law, 82; legal definition of marriage as, 129; vs. homosexual gross indecency prosecution, 124; vs. homosexual indecent exposure prosecution, 108-9, 144; vs. homosexual sodomy prosecution, 70-71, 158

hierarchy: in 1810 Penal Code, 54-55, 165; of homoerotic lifestyles, 9-13; of sexes and gender (Renaissance), 26; of sins, 24, 173*n*11. *See also* class and power

Higgins, Ross, 96, 98, 100, 119, 139-40, 140-41

High Middle Ages, 18-19

Hirschfeld, Magnus, 113

hirsuteness in ancient Greece, 10

historical periods: explanation of divisions, 3, 4-5; as not homogeneous, 7

historical sources as unreliable, 8, 30, 172*n*2, 173*n*6, 174*n*3

Hocquenghem, Guy, 59, 109, 111, 143

homoerotic behaviours and lifestyles: categorization as regulation of, 59; criminalization of, 73-74 (*see also* crime and homoeroticism); distinct from homosexuality, 8; language used to describe, 78; not identity, 4 (*see also* identity); opinion polls on, 142-43 (*see also* statistics). *See also* anal penetration/sexual relations; effeminate behaviour; gay liberation movements; pederasts and pederasty;

repression of homoerotic lifestyles; sodomy
homoeroticism as aggravating factor, 55-58
homophobia: encounters with, 1-2; in Paris (1800s), 54; and population density, 142. *See also* discrimination, protection from; hate propaganda and hate speech
homosexual and homosexuality: as object of study, 113; as social labels, 183*n*3; the term, 5, 8, 59
Hôpital St-Jean de Dieu (Montreal), 93-94
Hubert, Eugène, 80
Huguet, René (Le Tambour), 41, 44
Human Rights Tribunal, 129
Hurteau, Pierre, 62-63, 65-67, 73-74, 82, 85-87, 91, 95, 123, 124
hypnosis, 114

identity: desexualization of homosexual, 158; emergence of gay, 5; homosexual as, 90; of homosexual recognized in law, 168; and human rights, 187*n*5; in law on anal intercourse, 127; in medical classification, 113-14; sex as basis for, 59; universalization of, 122
De l'illégalité à l'égalité (Commission des droits de la personne du Québec), 142
Immigration Act (Canada), 96
impudicitas (passivity), 10. *See also* passive vs. active
In, 144
in flagrante delicto (1750 France), 30-31
incest: compared to sodomy, 84; indifference to, 101, 146; in Middle Ages, 19, 20-21; in New France, 40
indecent action, 98, 125

indecent assault: abrogated (1983), 125; in British law (acts of indecency), 68-69; Canadian history of law, 82-84; France (1881), 104; France (1972-82), 145; improper use in courts of, 57; not in Bill C-150, 125; replaced by sexual assault, 125; use of charges of (1850-89 Montreal), 73; used against homosexuality (France), 101, 107-8, 182*n*25; whipping as penalty for, 180*n*2. *See also* crime and homoeroticism; gross indecency; indecent exposure
indecent exposure: in chronology of legal recognition of gays in France, 160(f); France (1881), 104; France (1972-82), 145; and homoerotic behaviours (France), 106; homosexual vs. heterosexual (France), 108-9, 144; improper use in courts of, 55, 57; used against homosexuality (France), 178*n*7, 182*n*25. *See also* indecent assault
infidels, 24-25
inheritance for same-sex couples, 151-52
Inquisition, 21
insane asylums, 58. *See also* Bicêtre Hospital; medical and psychiatric discourses
Institut national d'études démographiques (INED), 108
Institutes of the Laws of England (Coke), 66-67
Insurance Act (Quebec), 130
intermediary sex, 113
Internet crime, 170
inversion: fear of contagion of, 60-63; as medical classification of perversion, 113; as prominent perversion, 58
invert: use of term, 4
Italians, 25

Jablonski, Olivier, 110
Jarrell, Richard A., 77
Jenkins, Philip, 86, 90, 101, 118, 146, 169, 170
Jilly's (Montreal), 140
Journal of Social Hygiene, 93
judicial practice: as aggravating factor (France to 1942), 101-5; denial of rights through medicalization, 114-15; in heterosexual vs. homosexual assault, 125-26; post–Second World War (Quebec), 91; repression (France 1970s), 144-45; therapy for homo-eroticism (1950s Montreal), 94; up to First World War (Canada), 84-87; use of medical expertise in, 92, 113. *See also* legal traditions
jurisprudence: on attempted assaults, 73; on decriminalization, 121; on discrimination, 128; distinction between homosexual and heterosexual, 57; on exceptions regime, 124, 129; on gay saunas, 140; on legal definition of sodomy, 66-67; as limited, 65, 79; on marriage, 135, 148, 151; on minors, 144; on pederasty, 176*n*18; use of Sodom and Gomorrah, 36
Justinian, 15, 19, 173*n*7
Juventus, 110

Kallmann, Franz J., 93
Kinsey Report, 91, 94
Kinsman, Gary, 95
Klippert, Everett George, 95, 123
Krafft-Ebing, Richard, 113

La Contamine, Philippe Bouvet de, 33, 46
La Forest, Justice Gerard Vincent, 129
la Roze, Jean Forgeron dit, 41-42, 44, 177*n*25

Labouchère Amendment (1885), 71, 81
Labour Code (France), 148
Labour Standards Act (Quebec), 130
Labrèche, Diane, 124
Lachance, André, 40, 44
Lafaucheur, Nicole, 89
laicization of society: France and Canada compared, 77-78. *See also* ecclesiastical and religious discourses; ecclesiastical power; medical and psychiatric discourses
Lang, Jack, 155
language: application of law not matching, 75, 79; describing homo-erotic behaviours, 78; hate rhetoric updated, 154; of morality and AIDS, 157-58; of morality used in courts, 55-56; of public hygiene, 165-66; from sodomite to pederasts, 45; from sodomy to sexual relations, 84, 125; use of "gay," 118; use of "unnatural" in laws, 109. *See also* ecclesiastical and religious discourses; medical and psychiatric discourses; nature and natural (as concepts)
Laqueur, Thomas, 58-59
Lasch, Christopher, 122
Lascoumes, Pierre, 144-45, 146, 147
Latin, 22
Latran III Council, 22
Le Goff, Jacques, 17
Le Mystique (Montreal), 141
Lebel, Jean Baptiste, 46
LeBœuf, René, 132
Lebrun, François, 47
legal traditions: after French Revolution, 52-53, 54-55; British system instituted, 64; divergence between Quebec and France of, 3, 164-66, 178*n*3, 179*nn*16-17; French system restored, 64-65; of

New France, 39, 176n20. *See also* crime and homoeroticism

Léger Marketing poll, 142-43

legislation as protection: chronology of legal recognition of gays in France, 160(f); chronology of legal recognition of gays in Quebec, 138-39(f); emergence of, 5; France and Quebec compared, 159, 161-62. *See also* discrimination, protection from

Lemelin, Justice, 132

Lemieux, Lucien, 65

Lemieux, Raymond, 75, 122

Lenoir, Bruno, 30, 176n17

Lenoir, Lieutenant General, 31

Leroy-Forgeot, Flora, 16-17, 18, 121, 149, 151

lesbians: adoption by (France), 159; civil unions (Quebec), 132; as dangerous, 95; included in gross indecency law, 82; liberation movement, 118; parental rights of, 161; police harassment of, 140; same-sex marriages (Quebec), 137(t); as sodomists, 59; spousal recognition (France), 149

L'Estoile, Pierre de, 27

Letellier, Louise, 129

Lever, Maurice, 29, 31, 34, 44, 48, 174n1

Libération, 144

Linteau, Paul-André, 88-89, 91, 100

lobotomy, 93-94

Louis IX of France, 26, 174n13

Luxembourg, 55, 175n10

Magnan, Victor, 113

Malaurie, Philippe, 185n23

Malhi, Gurbax, 135

Manitoba, 184n11

Manitoba Court of Appeal, 82

Marais neighbourhood (Paris), 156

Marcellin, Raymond, 144

Marouër, Antoine, 46

marriage: abolish ban on same-sex (Europe), 119; anal intercourse and, 126; Bill C-38 (Canada), 134-37; civil unions (Quebec), 131(t), 131-32; common-law relationships, 162; France and Quebec compared, 161-62; legal definition as heterosexual, 129; between men banned (342 CE), 17; opinion poll on same-sex (Canada), 143; Parliament questions Court on same-sex (Canada), 133-34; as place for sexuality, 20; protected through criminal code, 77; public opinion on gay (France), 158-59; recent history of same-sex, 168; recognition of same-sex by province, 132-33, 133(f); same-sex (France), 148-49, 150-54; same-sex (Quebec), 137(t), 139; for same-sex couples, 130-32, 132-37, 139. *See also* family units; Pacte civil de solidarité (Pacs) (France)

Martel, Frédéric, 144, 146, 155, 157-58

masculine sexuality: Antonine law, 15; controlling through law, 81; and masculinization of gay culture, 86; in pre-Christian Rome, 13-14, 172n4; transformation of, 158. *See also* effeminate behaviour

Massachusetts Supreme Court, 168

Master List (1725), 31

masturbation: as gross indecency, 124; leading to homosexuality, 86, 181n10; linked to homosexuality, 94; in Middle Ages, 20, 22-23

Maylan, Michel, 153

McCarthy, Joe, 90-91, 96

Mécary, Caroline, 121, 151, 161-62

media: and AIDS, 119; coverage of bathhouse raids (Montreal), 140; government and public publications

(Quebec), 141; homosexual representations in, 104, 141-42, 144, 155, 185*n*26, 186*n*43; homosexuality as negative or taboo, 96; influence in Quebec, 121-22; pedophilia and, 187*n*6; repression of homosexual press, 110; support of demonstrations (Montreal), 141; support of repressive legislation (France), 110. *See also* censorship; public and private

medical and psychiatric discourses: to defend heterosexual family unit, 150; demedicalization of homosexuality, 118-19; denial of rights through, 114-15; determining perversion or insanity, 80; discovery of perversion, 58-60, 74; English and French Canada compared, 75; explanation of homosexuality, 181*n*13, 183*n*32; France and Canada compared, 77-78; France and Quebec compared, 161; homosexuality, treatments for, 92-94, 156; homosexuality as a mental illness, 93-94, 160(f); hostile scientific (France), 155; and impact of religious discourse, 122; influence on public attitudes, 112-16, 157; internalized by homosexuals, 108; and inversion contagion, 61-63; in legislation (France 1960s), 109-10; mental illness classification, 147; in Pacs debates, 183*n*10; post–Second World War (Quebec), 91-92; rise in, 4-5, 45, 92-98, 165-66; role in decriminalization, 123, 125, 127; sexual psychopath, 86; in social regulation, 123; transition from religious to, 51; urban vs. rural, 76; use of term "homosexual," 8; used by homosexuals (France pre-1942), 102. *See also* experts

Medical Aspects of Human Sexuality, 118

medical institutions as punishment, 30, 33. *See also* Bicêtre Hospital

Metrazol, 93

Meyer, Catherine-Anne, 120, 121

Michéa, C.F., 62, 179*n*13

Middle Ages: codification of homo-erotic sexuality, 15-26; reliability of historic records, 173*n*6; repression of minorities in, 21-22; urban vs. rural in, 17-19

middle class. *See* bourgeoisie

Migneault, Benoît, 96-97, 141

military: French Canada under, 63-65; service as penalty for sodomy, 33, 49, 176*n*15, 177*n*26, 177*n*35; sodomy in New France in, 49

minorities in Middle Ages, 21-22

Mirguet, Paul, 109

Mirguet Amendment, 160(f)

Mitterrand, François, 147

mockery of homoeroticism, 12

mollitia (effeminate lifestyles), 13

Le Monde, 161, 183*n*32

monogamy in early Christian marriage, 17

Montminy, Jean-Paul, 75, 122

morality: and AIDS crisis, 119, 157-58; and banning discrimination (France), 147-48; discourse used in courts, 55-56; dropping from laws, 165; fear of contagion of pederasty, 53-54; in law on anal intercourse, 127; legislature vs. courts, 127-28; and low birth rate, 103; New France regulation of, 39-43; offences (France 1972-82), 145-46; policing of (1700s), 31; psychiatrists policing, 115; and public hygiene, 58; recriminalizing homosexuality (France), 106; and sentencing of sodomy, 84; sodomy as crime against, 36-38, 68, 70-71; state and church in French Canada, 76; statutes on, 155; in strategy (Ancients), 14; as temperance, 12-13; virtue of modesty, 15

Moreuil, Léonard, 33

Morris, Polly, 69-70

mouches (snitches), 31, 98, 175n5, 175nn7-9. *See also* entrapment, provocateurs, and snitches

Mount Royal Park (Montreal), 98

Murray, General James, 63

Muslims, 23, 25

Mutuelle générale de l'Education nationale, 153

Muyart de Vouglans, 64

Le Mystique, 185n26

Napoleonic Code, 69

National Post, 135

national security and values, 101-3, 102, 105, 107; McCarthyism, 90-91, 96

nature and natural (as concepts): bestiality and sodomy in, 24; Blackstone's crimes against, 67-68; buggery as crime against, 66-67; challenge to concept of crimes against, 69; in language of law (France), 109; as procreative sex (Middle Ages), 19-20, 22-23; in redefining marriage, 136; sodomy as crime against, 36-38, 50, 164, 176n23; victims of rape as corrupted, 34

nefandum crimen (unnameable crimes), 24, 43, 45, 164. *See also* unnameable crime

Netherlands, 132, 136, 168

New France: children as victims, 46-47, 49-50; ecclesiastical power in, 43, 45-46; family structure of immigrants to, 180n25; regulation of morality in, 39-43; as rural, 47-49; use of term, 178n1. *See also* urban vs. rural

New Testament, 16. *See also* Bible and Scriptures

Nord Éclair, 154

Northwest Territories, 132, 133(t)

Le Nouvel Observateur, 119, 143, 155, 156

Nova Scotia Court of Appeal, 124

Nunavut, 132, 133(t)

nuns, 20

O'Brien, Pat, 134

Old Testament, 16. *See also* Bible and Scriptures

Olympic Games (Montreal), 140

Omnibus Bill (1969): chronology of legal recognition of gays in Quebec, 138-39(f); consensual sex decriminalized, 99; decriminalization, 122-26; on publications, 96-97; role of medical discourses in, 123

Ontario Court of Appeal, 127, 132-33

Ontario Supreme Court, 132

operant conditioning, 114

Ordinance No. 45-190, 160(f)

Ouellet, Monsignor, 137

Owensby, Dr. Newdigate, 93

Pacte civil de solidarité (Pacs) (France): in chronology of legal recognition of gays in France, 160(f); debates leading to, 148-50; debates over, 185n23; fewer guarantees than under marriage, 151-52, 186n36; France and Quebec compared, 136, 161-62; as marriage "lite," 150-54, 167; public opinion on, 159; statistics on same-sex vs. opposite sex couples, 152-53; taxes and employment under, 150-51

paganism, 19

Palais-Royal, 55, 175n10

Paris: arrests in 1700s, 32, 44, 45; capital of homosexuality (1950s and 1960s),

108; fear of pedophilia, 46-47; gay life goes public, 155-56; gay mayor elected, 159, 161; police surveillance, 182*n*24; population, 177*n*34; repression of pederasty (1850-70), 52-53; vice squad statistics (1850-70), 52-53. *See also* urban vs. rural

Parti québécois, 141, 143, 161

Partisans, 144

Paschal, Jean-François, 46, 52

Pasqua, Charles, 158

passive vs. active: active as masculine, 13; monitored by police (France pre-1942), 102-3; no distinction in courts, 67; Romans vs. Greeks, 14; sodomizing vs. being sodomized, 10-12

pederasts and pederasty: codes of behaviour (Greece), 10-13, 172*n*4, 173*n*5; Doric influence, 172*n*3; fear of (1700s), 44; involving children, 38; Paris police repress (1850-70), 52-53; questioned in 1720, 31-32; use of Penal Code (France) against, 56-58; use of term, 4, 45, 60, 125, 177*n*32. *See also* penalties for sodomy; sodomists and sodomites; sodomy

pedophilia: associated with homosexuality, 19, 96-97; child-focused society and, 169-70; France and Quebec compared, 161; and gay liberation movements, 118; hate directed toward, 145-46; indifference to, 101, 146; male homosexuality defined as, 62; new focus for hate, 170-71; repression rises with access (Internet, etc.), 100, 170, 187*n*6

Pell, George, 139

penal categories of therapy, 166-67. *See also* penalties for sodomy

Penal Code (France): adopted (1791), 54-55; in chronology of legal recog-nition of gays in France, 160(f); indecent assault, 104-5; medicalization of terminology, 62; role for medical experts, 62; used against homosexuals (1870-1918), 55-58; section 14 (writing), 105; section 28 (indecent assault), 144; section 42 (writing), 105; section 225-1 (discrimination), 147-48, 160(f), 185*n*31; sections 225-2 and 432-7, 154; sections 227-23 and 227-24 (pornography), 170; sections 263-90 (indecent assault), 105; section 330 (indecent exposure), 57, 106, 108-9; section 330-2 and 331-2 (homosexual relations), 146-47; section 331 (indecent unnatural acts), 57, 110, 144, 147; sections 331-33 (indecent assault), 107-8; section 332, 110; section 333, 110; section 334 (recriminalizing homosexuality), 56, 57, 106; section 334, clause 6 (public debauchery), 157. *See also* Civil Code (France); Criminal Code (Canada)

penalties for sodomy: in 1810 Penal Code (France), 54-55; for attempting to commit (Britain), 72; in Britain (1700-1835), 70; under British law, 66; confused with treatment, 115-16; as crime of divine lèse-majesté, 36-38, 164; early Christians, 15; effect of 1890 revision (1891-1907 Canada), 85-87; France 1600s, 32-35; judges' discretion (High Middle Ages), 26; life imprisonment, 84; Middle Ages, 20-21; not carried out in public, 26, 30-32, 44-46; of particular act, 87; in Renaissance, 27; shift from the act to choice of object, 81; as a social scourge (France), 110; when violent or involving children, 34-35, 36-38, 52;

whipping, 82-83, 85, 87, 180*n*2. *See also* burning at the stake; capital punishment; cases and trials; crime and homoeroticism; sodomy

Peniston, William A., 52-53

penitentials, 20, 23

Perreault, Isabelle, 93

perversion, defining of, 113-14. *See also* medical and psychiatric discourses

Pétain, Philippe, 106, 107, 167

Peyrefitte, Roger, 155

Philip the Fair, 24-25

Philip IV of France, 26

Philip V of France, 26

plagues, 15, 23

Plato, 7

pleasure. *See* desire and pleasure

Poirier, Guy, 20, 24, 26-27

police and policing: directed to stop discrimination (France), 147; documenting sexual practices, 61; entrapment, provocateurs, and snitches, 31, 87, 98, 110, 175*n*5, 175*nn*7-9; increased size of forces (Montreal), 100; in Montreal (1818), 65; in New France, 39; Paris vice squad (1850-70), 52-53; post–Second World War (Quebec), 91; pre-Olympic Games (Montreal), 140; as referee (1600s), 33; repression (1950s Montreal), 98; repression (1970s Montreal), 139-41; repression (France), 80; repression (to 1942 France), 101-5; repression around AIDS (France), 157; repression rises with density, 100. *See also* crime and homoeroticism; surveillance

political repression and sexual repression: constant in history, 19; with displays of violence, 35; in England (1533-1861), 70; France and Quebec compared, 161-62; legal torture as ritual of, 38; and medicalization, 116; in New France, 39-40; in Second World War, 103; sodomist as scapegoat in history, 23-26 (*see also* scapegoat). *See also* repression of homoerotic lifestyles; surveillance

Politique et Quotidien, 162

Poniatowski, Michel, 144

Pope Benedict XVI, 137, 163

Pope Gregory III, 20

pornography, 144, 145, 170

Pouliquen, Jean-Paul, 152

pre-Christian Rome: codification of homoerotic sexuality, 13-14. *See also* Romans

La Presse, 141

prevention, 166

Prince Edward Island, 132, 133(t)

prison instead of burning, 30, 33

privacy as defined in law, 124. *See also* public and private

Procès faits à divers sodomites jugés au Parlement de Paris, 174*n*1

Procopius of Caesarea, 19, 173*n*7

prostitutes and prostitution: in Antiquity, 8-9, 11; and bawdy house charges, 139-40; in Bill C-150, 125; children, 171; French Penal Code, 107; gross indecency law, 81; laws used against homosexuals, 178*n*7; in New France, 40; questioned in 1720, 31-32; repression around AIDS, 157; soliciting charges, 55, 57; toleration of male, 15, 17; Vagrancy Act (1898), 71

psychology, 123, 150

psychopathology, 90, 119, 123, 166, 179*n*13. *See also* medical and psychiatric discourses

psychotherapy, 93

puberty in ancient Greece, 10

public and private: and application of
the law, 79; Bentham's defence of
private acts, 69; in Bill C-150, 123-24;
censorship of homosexual representations, 104; controlling public sex
(France 1700s), 31; crimes kept from
public, 26, 30-32, 44-46, 52, 164; decriminalization of private acts (EU),
121; definition of privacy, 124; discrimination and, 129; distinction
institutionalized, 54; gay lifestyles,
155-56; as separate after French
Revolution, 101. *See also* contagion;
media; teaching and promotion of
homosexuality
public debauchery, 157
public education campaigns, 142
public hygiene: and control of deviance,
58; fear of syphilis, 110-11; France and
Canada compared, 77; post–Second
World War (Quebec), 91; public-
health doctrine, 61; rise in discourse
of, 165-66. *See also* medical and
psychiatric discourses
public urinals, 55

Quebec Act, 64
Quebec Charter of Human Rights and
Freedoms, 128-32, 184n14; Bill 88, 141;
chronology of legal recognition of
gays in Quebec, 138-39(f); France
and Quebec compared, 161
Quebec Court of Appeal, 124, 126-27,
132
Quebec Pension Plan, 130
Quiet Revolution (Quebec), 98-101, 111,
121, 182n20
Quignard, Pascal, 13

Raffarin, Jean-Pierre, 153
Ralite, Jack, 147

rape: as common, 36; compared to
sodomy, 67; crime against morality,
37-38; in hierarchy of crimes, 25; in
New France, 40; question of consent,
83-84; sentencing of (1600s), 33; sentencing of (1700s), 32, 52; treatment
of victims, 34, 42
Recherches "Trois milliards de pervers,"
144
recidivism, 115-16, 166, 183n30
rehabilitation, 114-15
Remiggi, Frank W., 141-42
Renaissance, 26-28; "sodomy-Other-
foreigner-heretic" association, 24
Rencontre, François Judicth dit, 42, 44
repression of homoerotic lifestyles:
contributes to fascination, 177n31;
entrapment by police (1930s
England), 87 (*see also* entrapment,
provocateurs, and snitches); in judicial practice (to First World War),
84-87; and medicalization of law,
112-16; moving to pedophilia, 171; by
police in Montreal (1970s), 139-41;
Quebec and France compared mid-
twentieth century, 111-12; and socio-
political changes, 89-92; through
penal therapy, 167; through surveillance, 178n5 (*see also* surveillance);
use of prostitution laws for, 178n7;
vs. of behaviour (1960s to 1982
France), 110-11. *See also* police and
policing; political repression and
sexual repression
reproductive sexuality: Christian targeting of all other relations, 19-21;
in definition of marriage, 132, 135;
and homophobic backlash, 118;
introduced in Middle Ages, 15; in
redefining marriage, 136; St. Augustine and, 16-17; and sex education,

89; in urban vs. rural, 17-19. *See also* birth rate and demographics; family units

Revenin, Régis, 55, 58, 102

Rey, Michel, 31, 32, 45, 46

Rituel du diocèse de Québec, 43

Robb, Graham, 113

Robinson, Svend, 138(f), 142

Rocher, Guy, 5-6

Röhm, Ernst Julius, 103

Roman Catholic Church. *See* Catholicism

Romans: codification of homoerotic sexuality, 10-13, 13-14, 172n4; imperial law, 13, 17

Roth Report (European Community), 119

Royal Canadian Mounted Police (RCMP), 95

Royal Commission on the Criminal Law Relating to Criminal Sexual Psychopaths (1958), 83, 94-95, 95-96

rural. *See* urban vs. rural

Russel, Lord John, 64

Russell, Stuart, 140

Saint-Lazare (religious establishment), 30, 35

Saint-Michel, Nicolas Daucy dit, 41-42, 44, 177n25

Saint-Vallier, Monsignor de, 43

Salas, Denis, 116, 165, 170

Sartre, Jean-Paul, 9, 144

Sartre, Maurice, 11

Saskatchewan, 184n11

Sauna Aquarius (Montreal), 139

Sauna Club (Montreal), 140

Sauna Cristal (Montreal), 140

Sauna Neptune (Montreal), 140

saunas, 139-40, 156, 157

Sawatsky, John, 95

scapegoat: birth rate and immorality, 103; during difficult periods, 88-89; sodomist as (Middle Ages), 23-26; sodomist as (Paris 1800s), 54; throughout history, 168

Schabas, William A., 127

Schmitt, Éric-Emmanuel, 51

Schwartzwald, Robert, 141

science. *See* medical and psychiatric discourses

science, clergy as teachers of, 77

Second World War, 81, 89, 103, 105, 112

Séguin, Robert-Lionel, 40, 42-43

sex education: ecclesiastical discourse in, 89, 92; to prevent homosexuality, 93

sexology, 123

sexual assault, 125. *See also* indecent assault

sexual liberation, 104. *See also* gay liberation movements

sexual psychopath, 83, 86-87, 90, 94-96, 181n5; in definition of dangerous criminal, 98

sexual revolution, 117. *See also* gay liberation movements

sexual roles, inversion of (Greece), 10

shared-life certificate (France), 148. *See also* Pacte civil de solidarité (Pacs) (France)

Sibalis, Michael D., 27, 31, 52, 70, 107, 108

Simon, Félix, 33

sin and sinners: Christian link between flesh and, 17; courts urged to be harsh with, 177n28; post–Second World War (Quebec), 92; sodomists as, 4. *See also* ecclesiastical and religious discourses

Sivry, Jean-Michel, 140

snitches. *See* mouches (snitches)

Socarides, Charles, 92

sociology, 5-6, 150

sociopathic personality disorder, 94.
See also medical and psychiatric
discourses

sodomists and sodomites: Freemasons
as, 25, 26; historic use of term, 2, 125;
lesbians as, 59; from punishment to
control of, 165-66; as sinners before
God, 4, 17

sodomizing vs. being sodomized
(Greece), 10-12

sodomy: in Bill C-150, 123-24; under
British law, 66-67, 68-70; as contagious, 38, 44, 47 (*see also* contagion);
conviction rates (1946-59 Quebec),
97(t); conviction rates (1959-66
Quebec), 98-99; convictions of
(1930-39 Quebec), 87(f); as a crime,
83, 84; crime of attempting to commit, 72-73; definitions of, 30, 174*n*2;
in New France, 40; offences under
(Middle Ages), 21; practised by
hetero- and homosexuals, 158; punishment for (early Christians), 15;
punishment for (Middle Ages), 20-
21; replaced by sexual relations, 84,
125; statistics compared for Toronto
and Quebec, 99-100; use of term,
176*n*18. *See also* crime and homoeroticism; pederasts and pederasty;
penalties for sodomy

Sofres poll, 119, 156, 159

Le Soleil, 170

Soman, Alfred, 27

Sot, Michel, 17

Sovereign Council (New France), 39,
40-43

Spain, 137, 168

Spencer, Colin, 107

St. Augustine, 16-17

St. Lawrence Valley, 178*n*1

St. Paul, 20

St. Thomas Aquinas, 22-23

Statistical Year Book of Canada (1901),
84-85

statistics: assaults against children
(1800s), 55; bawdy house charges
(Montreal), 185*n*26; churches, number of (1850s France), 179*n*14; civil
unions (Quebec), 131(t), 131-32; compared for Toronto and Quebec, 99-
100; court cases for moral crimes
(New France), 39-40; court records
(1891-1907 Montreal), 85-87; death
penalty in Britain (1700-1835), 70;
gross indecency charges (1953-54
Montreal), 98; gross indecency charges (1961 Toronto), 99; heterosexual
and homosexual sodomy, 158; homosexual vs. heterosexual assaults
convictions, 125-26; inaccuracy of
homoerotic acts, 84-85; in *Kinsey
Report,* 94; media representation of
homosexuality (1952-70), 96-97;
methodological problem for French,
182*n*22; Pacs unions, 152-53; Paris vice
squad (1860-70), 52-53; party voting
on Bill C-38 (Canada), 136-37; pederasts (1784 Paris), 178*n*4; penal (1972-
82 France), 145-46; prosecutions and
convictions (1945-55 England), 107;
public opinion on AIDS (France),
156; public opinion on homosexuality (France), 155, 156, 158-59; same-sex
couples and marriages, 132; same-sex
marriages (Quebec), 137(t); shared-
life certificates (France), 148; sodomy,
convictions (1930-39 Quebec), 87(f),
87-88; sodomy, convictions, (1946-59
Quebec), 97(t); sodomy, convictions

(1959-66 Quebec), 98-99; sodomy cases (1760-1840 Canada), 65; tolerance and acceptance (Canada vs. France), 142-43; trials (1850-89 Montreal), 73; unreliability of, 26; urban vs. rural population (Quebec), 180*n*27. *See also* cases and trials
Statute 25 Henry VIII 1533, 66
Stekel, Wilhelm, 93
Stephen, Sir James Fitzjames, 70-71
stereotypes: and AIDS, 119; and homophobic panic, 95; in media, 96; public education to combat, 142; supported by medical discourse, 92
stoicism, 15
Stonewall Inn (New York), 118, 141
Studio I (Montreal), 140-41
suicide, 15
Supplemental Pension Plan Act (Quebec), 130
Supreme Court of British Columbia, 128
Supreme Court of Canada, 123, 127, 128-29; chronology of legal recognition of gays in Quebec, 138-39(f); Parliament questions on same-sex marriage, 133-34
surveillance: detailed police (pre-1942 France), 102-3; documenting sexual practices, 61; high housing density and, 49; by middle class, 49; monitoring of children, 53; in Paris, 182*n*24; by police (1700s France), 32; by police (1960s Canada), 95; as repression, 55, 178*n*5; of sodomites (1700s), 31-32, 175*n*10, 175*nn*12-13; systematic (France 1940s), 108. *See also* police and policing
Sylvestre, Paul-François, 44
Symonds, John A., 12

syphilis, 53, 110-11. *See also* venereal disease

Tamagne, Florence, 25, 57, 71-72, 78, 89, 101-4
Tardieu, Dr. Ambroise, 51, 58, 61
Taxation Act (Quebec), 130
taxes and taxation, 130, 153, 161-62
teaching and promotion of homosexuality: and media censorship, 96; through public prosecution, 38, 44, 47. *See also* contagion
technoscience, 166, 187*n*3
temperance: in ancient Greece, 12-13; vs. abundance for Romans, 14
Test Act, 180*n*19
Tetre, René du, 34
Theodosius, 15
Théry, Irène, 117
Thuiller, Pierre, 118
Timarchus (364 BCE), 8-9
Toronto, 99
torture, 38, 42. *See also* burning at the stake
Tout! 144
Treaty of Amsterdam, section 13, 120
Treaty of Paris, 64
trials. *See* cases and trials
Trippodière, Lambert, 46
Trudeau, Pierre E., 123, 183*n*9
Trujillo, Alfonso Lopez, 137, 139
Trumbach, Randolf, 70
Truxx (Montreal), 141, 185*n*26
Tuileries, 175*n*10

Ulrichs, Heinrich, 113
Ultramontanism, 72, 78, 89
unemployment, 89; and vagabonds (1720), 31-32. *See also* employment rights

Union Act, 72

Union pour la démocratie française (UDF), 153

Union pour la majorité présidentielle, 154

United Kingdom. *See* Britain

United States: American Psychiatric Association, 94, 118; demonstrations and protests, 118, 141; gay marriage in, 168

unnameable crime, 8, 24, 30-32, 36-38, 43, 44-46, 164

uranist, 113

urban vs. rural: homoeroticism condemned in, 17-19; influence of Catholicism (Canada), 72; isolation vs. density, 48-49, 100, 170, 187n6; medical and ecclesiastical power in, 76; in medical authority, 63; and number of denunciations, 79; population of Quebec, 180n27; post–Second World War (Quebec), 91-92; public morality concept in, 165; in Quebec modernity, 122; self-regulation compared, 47-48. *See also* Paris

utilitarianism, 69

Vagrancy Act (1898), 71

Vanneste, Christian, 154

venereal disease: epidemic of, 109, 111; fear of contagion of pederasty (1850-70), 53; political use of, 107; syphilis, 110-11

Veyne, Paul, 13, 14, 15

Vichy regime, 105-11, 182n26

Vigarello, Georges, 32, 34, 36, 47, 55, 57-58, 146

Violain, Maurice, 33, 46

violence against homosexuals: in Paris (1800s), 54. *See also* homophobia

violence in sexuality: and 1810 Penal Code, 54-55; penalties for, 34-35, 36-38, 52, 164; unacceptable for the Ancients, 9, 14; and violence as common, 36-38, 67

Vive la Révolution movement, 144

Vivier, Jean-Loup, 151

La Voix du Nord, 154

Voltaire, 69, 187n1

Wake, Robert, 95

Wallace, Judge, 128

Walsh, Anthony, 125-26

Weeks, Jeffrey, 71

Weill, Claude, 151

Welfare Court, 94

whipping, 82-83, 85, 87, 180n2. *See also* penalties for sodomy

Wilde, Oscar, 102, 117

Wilson, Edward O., 93

Wilson, Justice, 127

Workers' Compensation Act (Quebec), 130

World Health Organization, 118, 147, 160(f)

Printed and bound in Canada by Friesens

Set in Univers Condensed and Minion by Artegraphica Design Co. Ltd.

Copy editor: Robert Lewis

Proofreader: Andrea Kwan

Indexer: Mary Newberry